T0271345

*Routledge Revivals*

# The Railway Clearing House

Originally published in 1968, and using official records, this book charts the history of the Railway Clearing House and shows the vital role it played in the development of British railways and the growth of the economy. The Clearing House established a common classification of goods; standardized signalling systems and telegraphic codes among the 120 railway companies which operated in Britain before the First World War. It was the nerve centre of the railway for nearly a century and at one time more than 2,500 clerks were employed in its huge offices near Euston Station in London.

# The Railway Clearing House

## In the British Economy 1842-1922

# Philip S. Bagwell

Routledge
Taylor & Francis Group

First published in 1968 by George Allen and Unwin Ltd.

This edition first published in 2023 by Routledge
4 Park Square, Milton Park, Abingdon, Oxon, OX14 4RN

and by Routledge
605 Third Avenue, New York, NY 10158

*Routledge is an imprint of the Taylor & Francis Group, an informa business*

© 1968 George Allen & Unwin Ltd.

The right of Philip S. Bagwell to be identified as the author of this work has been
asserted by him in accordance with sections 77 and 78 of the Copyright, Designs and
Patents Act 1988.

**Publisher's Note**
The publisher has gone to great lengths to ensure the quality of this reprint but points
out that some imperfections in the original copies may be apparent.

ISBN 13: 978-1-032-41073-9 (hbk)
ISBN 13: 978-1-003-35613-4 (ebk)
ISBN 13: 978-1-032-41074-6 (pbk)
Book DOI 10.4324/9781032410739

# THE RAILWAY CLEARING HOUSE
# IN THE BRITISH ECONOMY
## 1842–1922

BY

## PHILIP S. BAGWELL

LONDON
GEORGE ALLEN & UNWIN LTD
RUSKIN HOUSE, MUSEUM SRTEET

PRINTED IN GREAT BRITAIN
*in 11 on 12pt Plantin type*
BY ABERDEEN UNIVERSITY PRESS

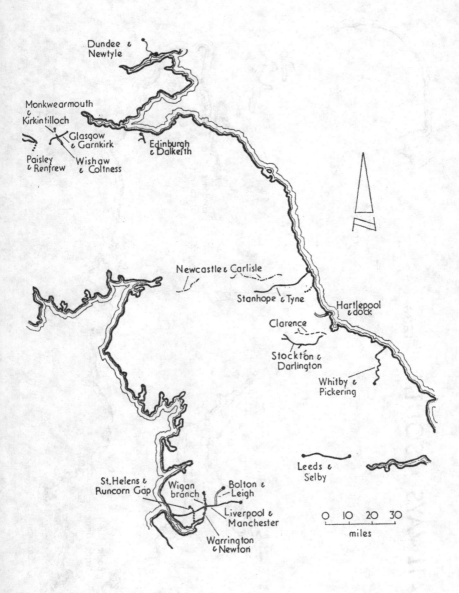

Dundee &
Newtyle

Monkwearmouth
&
Kirkintilloch

Glasgow
& Garnkirk

Edinburgh
& Dalkeith

Paisley
& Renfrew

Wishaw
& Coltness

Newcastle & Carlisle

Stanhope & Tyne

Hartlepool
& dock

Clarence

Stockton &
Darlington

Whitby &
Pickering

Leeds &
Selby

St. Helens &
Runcorn Gap

Wigan
branch

Bolton &
Leigh

Liverpool &
Manchester

Warrington
& Newton

0  10  20  30
miles

# RAILWAYS · NORTH     1836

G. Channon

j.w.l.f.

*Note the disconnected rail networks at this date*

# RAILWAYS · SOUTH

## 1836

Leicester & Swannington

London & Greenwich

Canterbury & Whitstable

Bodmin & Wadebridge

G. Channon.

0 10 20 30
miles.

j.w.t.f.

# RAILWAYS IN THE CLEARING HOUSE

## 1842

*The names of the nine original member companies of
the Railway Clearing House are printed in block capitals*

# PREFACE

My curiosity about the subject of this book was first aroused as a student when reading volume two of *The Economic History of Modern Britain* by the late Sir John Clapham who regretted that the early history of the Clearing House was 'obscure'. More recently Professor J. Simmons, in surveying the literature on British railway history in his book *The Railways of Britain*, commented that a history of the Clearing House was 'much needed'. With two such open invitations to the researcher it may seem surprising that no account of this remarkable institution has so far appeared. The explanation lies in the fact that only within the last five years has the opportunity been presented for filling this gap in our knowledge of British railway history. The transference of the records of the Clearing House to British Rail's Archives Department has made available to the student a wealth of material on the foundation and evolution of one of the most important business organisations of nineteenth-century Britain.

In this work I have endeavoured to place the progress of the Railway Clearing House in the wider setting of the transport services of the nation and the expansion of the British economy. Britain was exceptional among the countries of Europe in leaving the provision of railway services entirely to private enterprise. The existence of the Clearing House is seen as a major part of the explanation why this unusual state of affairs could have continued for so long. I have attempted an assessment of its importance in widening markets, overcoming regional variations in railway operation and establishing uniform standards in business and commercial practice. Since the Clearing House was also one of the largest employers of labour before the First World War it has been considered worth while to examine how the labour force was organised and disciplined and how the tendency for administrative costs to rise was countered.

The work of the Clearing House in the years after 1922 is dealt with more briefly than the earlier history of the organisation. The principal reason for this is that the official records for this period are not yet available to the student. This is not so serious a drawback as might at first appear to be the case as the four mainline railways which were created as an outcome of the Railways Act of

1921 assumed responsibilities formerly shouldered by the Clearing House.

I wish to express my thanks to Mr Atkinson and the staff of the Railway Archives Department of Paddington without whose help the preparation of this book would not have been possible. I am particularly grateful to Mr E. H. Fowkes who in 1964 first drew my attention to the minutes of the Clearing House Committee and has gone out of his way ever since to show me any records of relevance to the preparation of this book.

I wish to acknowledge the assistance given by the Governors of the Polytechnic, Regent Street, London, W.1, who agreed to the appointment of a research assistant to help me with this and other projects. Mr V. Pendred, Head of the School of Commerce has given me every encouragement and has allowed adjustments in my teaching programme to enable me to devote some time to research.

Since September 1966 Mr G. Channon has given valuable help as research assistant. He was responsible for compiling Appendices 1–3 and 6–9 inclusive, for making a rough draft of the two maps, and for providing information on the coal trade, the Gladstone Award of 1851, and the legality of railway pooling agreements. His services have always been willingly and efficiently given. I am looking forward to the time when his own study of the impact of coastal shipping competition on the Anglo-Scotch Traffic Agreement will be published.

I am grateful to my friend Mr J. W. L. Forge who has not only read through the entire typescript—in itself a sufficient imposition —but has also drawn the maps.

For assistance of various kinds my thanks are also due to: Mr S. W. Shelton, Archivist of Glyn Mills and Co. Bank, for reference to papers concerning George Carr Glyn; Mrs Ferrugia of the PO Archives Department, for information on the parcel post agreement in 1882–3; Mr Sidney Greene and the staff of the Secretarial Department of the NUR for reference to the policies of the ASRS: Mr R. F. Ayliffe of the Transport Salaried Staff Association, for showing me the records of the Railway Clerks Association; Mr P. Aldrich for a note about Post Office regulations concerning postmen; Dr J. Ranlett of Harvard, for references on railway difficulties in the early 1840s; Mr H. S. Cobb of the House of Lords Record Office, for making available the unpublished records of the House of Lords Committee on the Railway Clearing Bill in 1859; Mr G. L. Turnbull for letting me see his work on the early history of Pickfords; Mr George Ottley, for allowing me to consult his invaluable *Bibliography of British Railway History* before it was sent to the publishers; Mr O'Brien and the staff of British Rail for guidance on the recent history of the Clearing House; to Mr D. G. Allan, Librarian, Royal Society of Arts, for information on the work of the Postal Association, and Mrs J. Lawley, and Messrs J. Hurt and F. Moxley for reading parts of the typescript and making valuable comments.

I wish to thank the Illustrated Newspapers Group for permission to reproduce prints from *The Illustrated London News* of August 17 1847.

It would be misleading of me to suggest that over the past three and a half years my wife, Rosemary, has acquired an absorbing interest in mileage payments, demurrage or even the general classification of goods. My debt to her is therefore all the greater for having typed the entire manuscript, a labour as vital for the production of this book as was that of the Clearing House clerks for the smooth working of British railways.

## ABBREVIATIONS USED IN THE TEXT

BPP British Parliamentary Papers
BRB British Railways Board
BTHR British Transport Historical Records
The following are included in the BTHR classification:

BDJ Birmingham and Derby Junction Railway
GN Great Northern Railway
LBM London and Birmingham Railway
LY Lancashire and Yorkshire Railway
Mid. Midland Railway
ML Manchester and Leeds Railway
LNW London and North Western Railway
HL British Transport Historical Letters Series
PIC Pickfords
RCA Railway Companies Association

HLP House of Lords Papers
LECWS Locomotive Engineers and Carriage and Works
Superintendent. (A committee of the clearing
house)
RCH Railway Clearing House
REC Railway Executive Committee
LMS London Midland Scottish (Magazine)
GWR Great Western Railway (Magazine)
MR Midland Railway

The classification of railway clearing house records is explained in the Bibliography

# CONTENTS

# ILLUSTRATIONS

*after page 160*

# CHAPTER I

# THE TRANSPORT BOTTLENECKS
# BEFORE 1842

## I

In the earliest days of the steam locomotive in Britain, before any important railway had been opened to the public, a far-sighted pamphleteer, foreseeing the dangers of piecemeal construction, advanced 'a plan for a railway from London to Edinburgh, passing near to all the commercial towns of Leicester, Nottingham, Sheffield, Wakefield, Leeds, etc., with branch railways to Bristol, Manchester and Liverpool'. If this plan was followed, the writer claimed, 'it would be productive of incalculable advantage to the country at large.'[1]

Nineteen years later, when the Liverpool and Manchester Railway had already been opened seven years, another pamphleteer, in considering Parliamentary procedure in vetting railway bills, considered that

'the great mistake . . . consists in viewing these vast projects as *local* measures, and in referring them to local committees. No one can doubt that they are far too important in a national point of view to be so considered. It is in fact this very thing, which leads to the infusion of a local, consequently a restricted and not infrequently a selfish and exclusive, spirit into these undertakings.'[2]

With a similar public-spirited aim, Captain Richard Mudge in his *Observations on Railways*[3] urged the appointment of a competent

[1] Thomas Gray: *Observations on a General Iron Railway, Showing its Great Superiority Over all the Present Methods of Conveyance*, London, 1819.

[2] 'Cautus': *Some words on railway legislation in a letter addressed to Sir Robert Peel, Bart*, London, 1837.

[3] R. Z. Mudge: *Observations on Railways with Reference to Utility, Profit and the Obvious Necessity for a National System*, London, 1837, p. 79.

body of commissioners for establishing a system of railways in England and as a necessary corollary, for Scotland also'. The Board's task would be 'to examine every bill for railways and canals laid on the table of the House of Commons' with the chief object of determining 'the best main lines throughout the country'. Only by these means would it be possible for a 'train of carriages to pursue its quick and uninterrupted course from Edinburgh to Exeter or from Giants Causeway to Kerry'.

But the advice of these early writers on railway reform was brushed aside and soon forgotten. In the important formative years of railway building in Britain the influence of the economists on Parliament was increasing and relaxation of restraints on trade was the order of the day. In 1822–24 while the engineers and navvies were laying the track of the Stockton and Darlington Railway Huskisson at the Board of Trade was supervising a plan to liberalise the tariff. While mountains of earth were being moved to build a railway from London to Birmingham, Huskisson's successors in the Cabinet were sweeping away the excise duties which had for so long hamstrung many branches of the country's manufactures. Hence it is not surprising that when Parliament came to consider railways.

'No attempt was made to establish the new channels of communication in accordance with such general principles as would ultimately give them the character of a national system. On the contrary, each company was permitted to select the locality, to run its line in the direction, and select the gauge it thought best.'[1]

After an early phase when Parliamentary committees met proposals for new railways with 'determined rejection or dilatory acceptance', during the railway manias of 1835–36 and 1845–46 they tended to the opposite extreme of unlimited concession, as a consequence of which 'railways were projected in every possible and impossible direction, under rivers, over mountains, down precipices and across arms of the sea. Three routes between the metropolis and York were not thought too many.' In these years the frenzy of speculation affected

[1] *Railway Competition*: A letter to George Carr Glyn, Esq., MP, London, 1849.

'the courtly and exclusive occupant of the halls of the great as well as the homely inmate of the humble cottage. Duchesses were even known to soil their fingers with scrip, and old maids to enquire with trembling eagerness the price of stocks. Young ladies deserted the marriage list and the obituary for the share list and startled their lovers with questions respecting the operation of bulls and bears. The man of fashion was seen more frequently at his brokers than at his club. The man of trade left his business to look after his shares, and in return both his shares and his business left him.'[1]

After James Morrison, MP for Ipswich, had failed to persuade Parliament in May 1836 that it should exercise a more complete control over railway dividends and charges, there were increasing rumblings of discontent from traders at the railways' exercise of their near-monopoly power. Early in 1839 the House of Commons received a petition against the high rates charged by the most important railway in the kingdom—the London and Birmingham. There were rumours that the Government planned to take over the railways or at least subject them to a far more rigorous control.

George Carr Glyn, chairman of the London and Birmingham railway, took alarm. He was not opposed to Government interference to promote greater safety of travel and standardised operational procedures, but he wished to be master in his own house. Equally concerned were those solicitors who had made a profitable business of drafting railway bills during the first railway mania. On January 7, 1839, Messrs Burke and Venables, railway solicitors of 25 Parliament Street, Westminster, took the initiative. With the full backing of Glyn, they sent a letter to the secretaries of all the railway companies, seeking the support of the Boards of Directors for a railway association which it was proposed to form 'with a view to the protection of railway interests against any attack which may be contemplated upon them in the next session'. The companies were urged to 'act in concert in endeavouring to repel any improper interference with their vested rights'. It was considered prudent 'in order not to excite the jealousy of the public . . . to establish the society in the first instance, nominally on a scientific principle, as a society for the encouragement of public

[1] *Railway Competition*: A letter to George Carr Glyn, Esq., MP, London, 1849.

improvements'. Prudence also dictated that the new organisation should be established 'with as little publicity as possible'.[1]

The response to the appeal having been highly gratifying, the inaugural meeting of the Railway Society was held in Burke and Venable's office on March 9, 1839, when the representatives of numerous companies enrolled as members. By the time of the next meeting, on May 15, the appointment of a Parliamentary Select Committee on Communication by Railway—the first major public enquiry into the railways of the nation—had been announced in the House of Commons, and the society therefore decided to delegate to a small committee the task of 'watching over all matters affecting railway interests'. Five weeks later, on June 20th, the secretary of the society was pleased to report that the committee had kept a careful watch 'on all proceedings in Parliament at all likely to affect railway interests' and that 'the President of the Board of Trade had recognised the Society as the organ through which in future to seek for any information required on the subject of railways'.[2]

While it would be a mistake to exaggerate the importance of this first intervention of the organised railway interest in Parliament, nevertheless the fact remains that the recommendations contained in the reports of Lord Seymour's Select Committee coincided in many respects with the policies Railway Society members advocated as witnesses before the committee or in debate in the House of Commons.

Robert Stephenson, Carr Glyn and J. Baxendale (deputy chairman of the South Eastern Railway) all agreed that a superintending Board annexed to the Board of Trade would be useful to secure uniformity of bye laws and signalling arrangements and even to arbitrate in disputes concerning through fares.[3] The committee considered that railways should be subjected to 'some general superintendence and control through some department of the executive government' and that 'every bye law enacted under powers contained in the several railway acts should be

[1] BTHR, Gen. 31A: Railway Companies Association, formerly known as the Railway Society or the Railway Association.

[2] Ibid. and The Railway Times, June 22, 1839, p. 483.

[3] Select Committee on Railways, minutes of evidence BPP 1839, Vol. X, Qs 4739–42, 197, and 5730–1.

submitted to such department two months at least before it shall be obligatory'. There was to be no comprehensive control of the railway. There was to be no comprehensive

On the other hand the committee endorsed the opinion of the majority of the railway directors who appeared before it, that the interference of a government Board with the promotion and routing of railways would be undesirable: 'The Board . . . should not interfere with any proposed railway before the Act of incorporation has passed.'[1] In more general terms, there was not a great deal of difference between the view expressed by Mr Easthorpe, MP for Leicester and spokesman of the railway interest in the Commons, that 'the best plan was . . . to proceed without dangerous meddling,' and the words of the committee's report:

'Your committee in framing these resolutions have been guided by this consideration, that however improductively Parliament may in the first instance have granted to the railway companies such extensive powers, it is now advisable to interfere with them as little as possible, and to limit their recommendations to a plan which may ensure the effectual administration of the laws by which each railway company is incorporated. Your committee feel, moreover, that in adopting this course they are more likely to carry along with them the good feelings and support of the railway companies and their directors'.[2]

Lord Seymour's Railway Regulation Act of August 10, 1840, which was the outcome of the select committee's reports, was a pale shadow of the kind of measure that, at one time, many railway directors and solicitors had feared might be introduced. It gave the Board of Trade power to secure returns of railway accidents and to send its inspectors to ensure that adequate arrangements were being made for the safe operation of the traffic. The companies were required to send in information on traffic, rates and fares and to submit all bye laws for approval before putting them into effect.

[1] Third Report of the Select Committee on Railways, 1840, BPP 1840, Vol. XIII, p. 172. The Committee of 1839 was reappointed in 1840 with very little change in its composition.

[2] *Hansard*, 3rd Series, Vol. 55, July 23, 1840, cols 907–8. Third Report of the Select Committee on Railways, 1840.

It was evident that by this Act 'Parliament did little to control the railway'.[1] There was to be no comprehensive planning of routes and there were no provisions for encouraging through communication on existing or future lines. The railway directors were so reassured that they failed to maintain in 1840 the society they had so carefully created in the previous year.

II

While Lord Seymour and his committees were carefully listening to the witnesses from the companies and the trading community, the railway contractors and their armies of navvies had not been idle. When James Morrison moved his Commons resolution in May 1836 the railway map showed a scattering of short disconnected lines as far apart as the Dundee and Newtyle, the Bodmin and Wadebridge, the Liverpool and Manchester and the Canterbury and Whitstable; but there was as yet no semblance of a system of railways. By contrast, the map of December 1840 suggests, no doubt, to a misleading extent, the possibility of long distance through communication. In the three years from December 1837 to December 1840 the important railways in the industrial heartland of England, in a region which formed an inverted triangle with London as the apex and the Liverpool to Hull route as the base, were opened to traffic for the first time. In April 1838, when the London and Birmingham Railway had opened the line between Rugby and Birmingham, through communication, via the Grand Junction and Liverpool and Manchester railways, was in prospect with many of the important towns of Lancashire. Five months later, with the opening between Rugby and Tring, of the middle stretch of the London and Birmingham route, London was brought into rail connection with the North West. Between June and September 1839, through the agency of the Birmingham and Derby Junction and Midland Counties Railways, both Birmingham and Derby were linked with Nottingham. By midsummer 1840 the North Midland Railway had linked Derby and Leeds; the Midland Counties line from Derby via Leicester to Rugby had been opened and the Hull and Selby Railway had closed the remaining gap

[1] E. Cleveland-Stevens: *English Railways: Their Development and Their Relation to the State*, London, 1915, p. 79.

between the Humber and Leeds. In the North West through communication extended to Preston. By the end of 1840 the rails between Birmingham and Gloucester had been laid and the contractors had only two months more work to do before completing the main line between Manchester and Leeds.

### III

Physical contact between these important railways was one thing; businesslike conduct of through traffic was another. The legacy of the British Parliament's failure either to build the main lines as state enterprises as was done in Belgium after 1835, or at least to plan the main routes comprehensively as the French Government decided to do in 1842, was a medley of mostly short distance railways, whose managers had different systems of goods classification, an almost infinite variety of freight charges and an interesting but infuriating diversity of passenger accommodation and fare structures. As late as 1846 when important amalgamations such as those which brought into existence the Midland Railway in 1844 and the London and North Western Railway in 1846, had eliminated a number of the smaller companies, the average route mileage of the companies which were members of the Clearing House was only forty-one miles.[1] Hence the manufacturer or trader who wished to dispatch goods beyond a small radius from his factory or warehouse was in the majority of cases obliged to depend on the services of more than one railway, with the attendent risk of loss of his goods. The intrepid traveller, in attempting even a comparatively short journey, might well be cooling his heels on the platforms of three or four successive junctions along his route, as well as enduring—when lucky enough to be 'on the move'—that overdose of 'fresh air' which the open third class carriages of the day inevitably provided.

The minute books of the Boards of the principal railway companies for the years 1839–41 abound with complaints from passengers and traders about the numerous obstructions to through communication by railway. In some cases a company refused to allow the waggons of an adjoining company to pass over its lines,

[1] E. Cleveland-Stevens: *English Railways: Their Development and Their Relation to the State*, London, 1915, p. 178.

and goods had to be trans-shipped, with the inevitable delay and damage that resulted from such lack of co-operation. In October 1840 the Grand Junction Railway refused to allow the waggons of the London and Birmingham Railway to pass over its lines and goods had therefore to be trans-shipped at Birmingham. The Board of the London and Birmingham Company then retaliated by refusing permission for Grand Junction trucks to proceed southward beyond Birmingham. The difficulty had arisen because the Grand Junction Company was in the process of assuming full responsibility for goods carriage to the exclusion of the carriers, while the London and Birmingham merely provided the waggons, but left responsibility for goods carriage entirely to the carriers.[1] It is true that through traffic was resumed in a few weeks' time, but Pickfords were complaining early in 1841 that the Grand Junction were imposing the 'prohibitory' charge of 2s 6d per waggon per day for the use of its trucks on the 'foreign line'. The Grand Junction directors retorted that they were frequently called upon to supply for the traffic towards London double the number of waggons brought to them in exchange. From such squabbles it was the trader who suffered. *The Railway Times* reported that it was a 'subject of serious complaint' that on the two lines which formed the link between London and Lancashire there were not enough waggons available to carry the goods awaiting transit.[2]

In some instances, even though facilities for the through transit of goods were available, the charges made for the use of an adjoining company's lines were so extortionate that little traffic developed. The experience of the Birmingham and Derby Junction Railway after its opening in August 1839 is an interesting case in point. In its early years this company had a misleading name since it suffered from the serious disadvantage of having no station at Birmingham. Its customers were dependent upon the services of the London and Birmingham Railway for the short journey between Hampton and Birmingham. Although through traffic of passengers and goods was arranged, the London and Birmingham Company charged such heavy tolls for the use of its rails and terminal

[1] BTHR, LBM 1/22. *London and Birmingham Railway:* Report of the Goods Committee, November 27, 1840.

[2] *The Railway Times*, January 2, 1841, p. 8, January 16, 1841, p. 64, and March 6, 1841, p. 289.

facilities that the junior company was financially crippled. In June 1841, out of gross weekly receipts of £750 it was paying £160 in tolls to the neighbouring—but not very neighbourly—company, leaving it a revenue 'barely sufficient to cover working expenses'. Both because the route by rail to Hampton was longer and because the heavy tolls sent up freight rates, goods traffic between Birmingham and Derby remained largely in the hands of the road carriers. The obstacles which the Birmingham and Derby Junction Board had experienced in trying to increase goods traffic convinced it that it could be well worth while to incur the extra capital outlay in extending its own rails to Birmingham. The Bill authorising this extension received royal assent on June 4, 1840 and the new route was opened to traffic on February 9, 1842. Toll payments to the London and Birmingham line ceased in July of that year; but the experience of the previous three years had taught the Board a lesson. The company became a founder member of the Railway Clearing House in January 1842.[1]

From the beginning of 1841 through goods and passenger traffic from Gloucester to the Midlands and the North should have been possible, but it was not until the spring of the following year that discussions on an agreed scale of charges and division of receipts took place between the traffic managers of the Birmingham and Gloucester and the Birmingham and Derby Junction Railways. But no agreement could be reached because the Board of the Birmingham and Gloucester Company would not agree to a schedule of through charges, and in consequence much potential rail traffic was lost to the canals and roads.[2]

South of the Thames, the South Eastern Railway was having as much difficulty with the Croydon, London and Greenwich and London and Brighton Railways when it tried to arrange through traffic, as the Birmingham and Derby Junction Railway was experiencing further north. Mr J. Baxendale, the Deputy Chairman of the South Eastern Railway told the Select Committee

[1] C. R. Clinker: *The Birmingham and Derby Junction Railway, Dugdale Society Occasional Papers*, No. 11, 1956, pp. 13–16. BTHR, LBM 1/3, London and Birmingham Railway Board Minute 887, July 4, 1839. *The Railway Times*, March 7, 1840, p. 194.

[2] BTHR, BDJ 1/5: Birmingham and Derby Junction Railway Traffic Committee, June 15, 1842–October 21, 1842.

on Railways in 1841 that the company had encountered 'considerable difficulties' in making the necessary arrangements and that it was entirely dependent upon the goodwill of the Boards of Directors of the three railway companies concerned for its access to London.[1]

Undoubtedly there were companies that took the farsighted view that more was to be gained by amicable negotiations with neighbouring companies than by conflict. However, even when arrangements were made to encourage through traffic, unexpected difficulties arose. In February 1841 Captain Laws, general manager of the Manchester and Leeds railway, informed the Board that although they had a through traffic agreement with George Hudson's York and North Midland Railway, he had to write to Hudson complaining that the letters MLR on the waggons of the Manchester Company had been painted over and the waggons had been used for local traffic in York.[2] Because the difficulties over the exchange of waggons were of long standing, the Manchester and Leeds directors appointed Edward Gulliver to serve as a number taker at the junction of the two companies' lines in Leeds. It was an arrangement which offended the Board of the York and North Midland who instructed the secretary of the Company to write to Manchester protesting about Gulliver's activities.[3]

Mr Kenneth Morison, the first manager of the Railway Clearing House, was also aware of the difficulties of working an agreement for the exchange of waggons. He wrote that such arrangements were from the first 'very imperfectly fulfilled, and some of the companies came in the end to make an unacknowledged use of the carriages and waggons of others to an extent which amounted to a positive grievance'.[4]

The parochially minded outlook of the York and North Midland was, however, exceptional. Before 1842 a number of companies had

[1] Select Committee on Railways, 1841, BPP 1841, Vol. VIII Qs 1800–5.
[2] BTHR, LY 1/8: Manchester and Leeds Railway Board, February 22, 1841.   [3] *Ibid.*
[4] K. Morison: *The Origins and Results of the Clearing System Which is in Operation on the Narrow Gauge Railways with Tables of Through Traffic in the Year 1845*, London, 1846, p. 6.

learned to co-operate with each other honestly and trustfully. But given the greatest good will in the world there were still substantial difficulties to be overcome, the legacy of the method of piecemeal authorisation of railway construction and of varying business practices. In the spring of 1841 the Boards of the Manchester and Leeds, Leeds and Selby, and Hull and Selby Railways, reached agreement on a scheme to encourage through goods traffic, receipts being divided in proportion to the route mileage of each company. The difficulty in this case was how to settle up financially in view of the differing systems of accounts of the three companies.[1] Mr Baxendale, who was passenger and goods superintendent of the London and Birmingham line (as well as vice Chairman of the South Eastern), told the Select Committee on Railways in 1839 that he foresaw the time when—despite the existence of five different companies on the route from London to Edinburgh— 'they might find London and Birmingham carriages in Edinburgh or north of Edinburgh'. There was but one snag: 'keeping the accounts'.[2] Dionysius Lardner, recalling the days before the foundation of the Clearing House, considered that one of the greatest obstacles to through working of traffic was 'an intolerable chaos of cross accounts'.[3]

In view of the time-consuming work involved in negotiation between railways for the conduct of through goods traffic, a number of companies, including the influential London and Birmingham, transferred the entire business—apart from the provision of rolling stock—to the private carriers who collected the goods from the suppliers, loaded them on the railway waggons and unloaded them again at the nearest station to the point of final delivery. The companies which adopted this system hoped that it might simplify matters where transit over more than one company's lines was involved even though the arrangements might prove more costly to the consumer. If traffic superintendents and goods managers shared this optimistic hope it was not long before disillusionment set in. While it is true that in the circumstances of many companies at that time the arrangement had its advantages,

---

[1] BTHR, LY 1/8: Manchester and Leeds Railway Board, April 26, 1841. *The Railway Times*, August 15, 1840.
[2] Select Committee on Railways, 1839, BPP 1839, Vol. X, Qs 5720–1.
[3] D. Lardner: *Railway Economy*, London, 1850, p. 150.

it was certainly no complete answer to the needs of long distance goods traffic. Mr D. Stevenson, who worked as goods manager at Euston in the 1840s, recalled some of the frustrations of dealing with the carriers when he wrote:

'We discovered that the declarations of some of the carriers as to the description of goods loaded by them in the waggons were often systematically false, and we had to appoint a detective, who frequently found the real invoices of the waggons to differ entirely from the declarations given to the company. It also happened that when trade was brisk and waggons were in large demand, the carriers men would have a pitched battle for the vehicles; it was also found that loads made up at country stations where the weight could be checked, were overloaded to a dangerous extent'.[1]

In February 1841 Captain Laws was complaining to the Board of the North Midland Railway of the 'numerous frauds' committed by carriers at Leeds station.[2]

## IV

Goods waggons might be left neglected at a railway siding and their contents allowed to deteriorate without fear of an immediate rumpus; passengers unceremoniously turned out of a cosy compartment on to a freezing junction platform were a different proposition. Letters of complaint from aggrieved travellers written to the railway management and to the press eventually convinced the railway companies that they must allay the criticisms by making satisfactory arrangements for unbroken passenger travel.

In the early 1840s there was mounting evidence of the inconveniences suffered by the public. The inhabitants of Lancaster might be forgiven for jumping to the conclusion that since there was a continuous rail link with London it ought not to have been too difficult to complete such a journey in a day. Their disgust when learning that this was a luxury available only to those who

---

[1] D. Stevenson: *Fifty Years on the London and North Western Railway, and Other Memoranda in the Life of David Stevenson*, ed. Leopold Turner, London, 1891, p. 18.

[2] BTHR, LY 1/8: Manchester and Leeds Railway Board, February 22, 1841.

were prepared to buy a first-class ticket between Newton and Birmingham 'because the Grand Junction Railway made no provision for second or third class passengers between six o'clock in the morning and six o'clock at night', may well be imagined. A Parliamentary committee estimated that this class snobbishness resulted in at least 75,000 persons a year having to travel first class when they would have preferred to use cheaper second- or third-class accommodation.[1] The inhabitants of Preston were little better served. If they wished to travel to Birmingham they were not able to book through, even though there was a rail link between the two cities.

Even worse treated were passengers wishing to pass through Preston by train. Owing to a dispute between the different companies whose lines terminated in the town, passengers passing through were obliged to detrain and walk 200 yards in the open from the carriages of one company to those of another.

Because the South Eastern and the London and Brighton Railways were at loggerheads, the two companies built entirely separate stations at Dover. Those wishing to travel through from Dover to Brighton or vice versa had to trudge half a mile through the mud from one terminus to the other.

The directors of the Manchester and Leeds Railway in negotiations with the directors of Midland Counties and London and Birmingham Railways sought agreement to a proposal for cheap through passenger fares from Manchester to London. The attempt had to be abandoned because of the belief of the Midland Counties Board that they would gain a greater revenue from maintaining the old, higher level of fares. In consequence of this disagreement, booking clerks at Manchester were not able to book passengers beyond Derby and clerks at Derby were instructed not to issue tickets to stations beyond Rugby. The much abused passenger had to queue up at three booking offices instead of one; and the services of three clerks instead of one were required.[2] London passengers wishing to travel to York were similarly inconvenienced. By July

[1] Select Committee on Railways, 1841. Evidence of Mr J. Baxendale, BPP 1841, Vol. VIII Qs 1813-15. Select Committee on Railways, Fifth report, Appendix 2, 1844, XI, pp. 20-21.
[2] BTHR, LY 1/8: Manchester and Leeds Railway Board, June 14, 1841, minutes 2474 and 2476.

30, 1840, there was a complete rail link between these places, but for more than two months thereafter rebooking at Derby and Normanton was necessary.[1] The directors of the London and Birmingham Railway appeared to be in no great hurry to aid the travellers of the brewing firms. In March 1841 the Board of the adjacent Birmingham and Derby Junction Railway requested that passengers from London might be booked through to Burton, Tamworth, and other stations north of Hampton. The reply received from Mr Creed, secretary of the London and Birmingham Railway was 'that the arrangement may be carried out as soon as the Clearing System is established'.[2] This was nine months later.

Where a passenger had to travel beyond the limits of a single company's lines there was always the risk of being stranded at some bleak railway junction through having missed a connection with another train. An incensed victim of this kind of situation wrote indignantly to *The Times* in March 1840 that the booking clerk at Derby had informed him that if he took the 4 p.m. Birmingham and Derby Junction train to Hampton he would be able to change into an 'up' London and Birmingham train which would bring him to the capital that same night at 'about ten or eleven o'clock'. Engine trouble just before the train reached Hampton, however, had caused him to miss his connection. He was offered the alternative of cooling his heels for several hours on the comfortless Hampton Station until the next train for London arrived at 1.30 a.m., or of proceeding to Birmingham to await the next 'up' express. He chose the latter alternative and did not reach his destination at Euston until 6 a.m. On another occasion when the train from Derby was late in arriving at Hampton and missed the connection with the London train, passengers were 'forwarded to Coventry by chaise and gig'. The comments on their situation made by the inmates of the chaise were, no doubt, as unprintable as those of the constant reader of *The Times*, who arrived a good seven hours late at Euston.[3] No doubt these inconveniences were no worse than those experienced by stage coach passengers, but

[1] C. R. Clinker: *op. cit.* p. 17

[2] BTHR, BDJ 1/2: Birmingham and Derby Junction Railway Board, minute 2473, April 7, 1841.

[3] *The Times*, September 19, 1840. BTHR, BDJ: Birmingham and Derby Junction Railway Traffic Committee, August 12, 1842.

the travelling public were beginning to demand a better service from the railways.

When John Smith was a victim of railway mismanagement the directors lost little sleep over the mishap; it was a different case when titled persons were inconvenienced. On August 12, 1840, the Dowager Duchess of Richmond boarded a train at Euston intending to travel to Parkside Station. Because that particular train was not one for which it had been *agreed* to book passengers through and because the Duchess's name and destination had not been entered on the waybill, she was taken to Manchester by mistake. The secretary of the Grand Junction Company subsequently agreed with the London and Birmingham railway to meet the extra expenses which the Duchess had incurred, as a result of this mistake; but it may well be imagined that incidents of this kind helped to convince railway managers of the need for improved arrangements for through traffic of all kinds.

Railway companies were notoriously reluctant to accept responsibility for the transference of animals to another company's waggons at junction points. An indignant horse owner complained in a letter to *The Times* that although he wished to send his horse from Euston to Barnsley it could not be booked through beyond Derby where the North Midland Railway had its terminus. He was therefore obliged to send a servant to Derby simply to lead the horse from one train to another. Owing to the 'unaccommodating spirit' of the railway companies the expense of sending the horse was 'nearly doubled'.[1]

In the years before the railway companies had constructed branch lines to act as feeders to their original through routes, it was a common practice of well-to-do travellers to take their carriages and horses with them by train as far as possible along their route so that they would be available for the completion of the journey by road. On the long distance trains out of Euston it was not uncommon to see fifteen or twenty private carriages attached to the waggons of a single train. The owners often preferred the seclusion of a ride in their own coaches to the uncertainties of companionship in one of the railway company's compartments. As the horses were conveyed in separate waggons the hazards of

[1] *The Times*, September 19, 1840. BRB, HL 2/14 R323: Letter from E. J. Cleather to R. Creed, dated September 26, 1840.

this procedure, when change on to another company's lines was necessary, can be fully appreciated. A situation in which coach and horses were landed at different destinations was unlikely to generate much good will towards the railway companies. On July 23, 1839 the goods manager of the London and Birmingham Railway was questioned by a Parliamentary select committee about such mishaps:

'Have you not heard that there was quarrelling in certain portions of the line, in consequence of which coaches have been left without horses?'
'I think that there have been quarrels occasionally, and that coaches have been left without horses.'
'And of course to the very great inconvenience of passengers?'
'Of course.'[1]

The existence of almost as many kinds of railway tickets as there were different railway companies and the adoption of different rules for collecting tickets from passengers was bound to lead to misunderstandings. By 1840 the Newcastle and Carlisle, Manchester and Leeds, and Birmingham and Gloucester Companies had adopted the small stiff cardboard ticket familiar to railway travellers of the present day; but paper tickets of a great variety of shapes and sizes were being issued by other companies. On the Leeds and Selby line it was customary to collect tickets from passengers before the start of the journey. On the Great Western a similar procedure was followed, except that the compartment doors were locked as soon as tickets had been collected; on the London and Birmingham and London and Southampton lines tickets were collected at the last station but one on the route.[2] Such variations in procedure increased the opportunites for fraud and evasion.

The more frequently passengers had to change trains the more likelihood there was of luggage being lost and the easier it was for the companies to shift responsibility 'somewhere up the line' to other railways over which they had no control. For the recovery of possessions mislaid in travel and independent and

[1] Select Committee on Railways, 1839, BPP 1839, Vol. X, Q. 5724-5.
[2] Ibid. Q. 3968-72.

impartial lost luggage department was becoming more necessary each day.

By the early 1840s differences in waggon dimensions and braking, variations in locomotive performance and divergent rules for the operation of traffic were frustrating the efforts of those companies who sought co-operation with their neighbours in the promotion of through traffic. Thus the London and Birmingham Railway had in 1841 agreements with adjacent railways to forward each others through goods traffic but 'differences in the gauge of wheels in use on the lines in connection with the London and Birmingham' made it difficult to 'bring the trains up to London in the time ordinarily allowed'. Because of these difficulties, Mr Bury, the locomotive superintendent of the London and Birmingham line was instructed to meet the directors of the Liverpool and Manchester Railway and to request that the tyres and axles of waggons used by that company should be modified to make them more suitable to run on the main line to Euston.[1]

In the autumn of 1840 a spate of railway accidents reported in the newspapers helped to draw public attention to the grave deficiencies of the companies' traffic management. No doubt experimentation in signalling had its value; but locomotive men could be forgiven a sense of bewilderment at the variety of devices they encountered if ever they had the misfortune to traverse an unfamiliar line. Most companies used the 'time interval' method as one safety precaution against accidents. Under it the signalman was not allowed to give the all clear to an oncoming train until a given number of minutes—it might be as few as five or as many as twenty—had elapsed since the preceding train had passed. Sand glasses, known by signalmen as 'egg boilers' were provided to indicate the time interval to be enforced.[2] The riskiness of this method of accident prevention at a time when locomotive breakdowns were an everyday occurrence, and the time intervals varied from company to company, is all too apparent. A leading Yorkshire newspaper gave as 'the immediate cause of most recent collisions the starting of trains too nearly together'.[3]

[1] BTHR, LBM 1/22: London and Birmingham Railway, Report of Locomotive Committee, January 13, 1842.
[2] R. Blythe: *Danger Ahead: The Dramatic Story of Railway Signalling*, London, 1951, pp. 27–28.   [3] *Leeds Intelligence*, November 28, 1840.

V

The achievements of the railways in the 1830s had been impressive. Through the extension of the rail network many of the most important commercial centres of the nation had been drawn closer together than ever before. But if the pace of advance was to be maintained the introduction of less primitive technical and managerial aids to the organisation of through communications—overriding the artificial frontiers of the railway companies—was vitally necessary. As a contemporary observer saw it:

'The inconvenience to the public was so enormous and the clamour which it excited, both among the commercial classes, and those who travelled by the railways, was so irresistible, that it became manifest that some arrangement must be adopted by which the public would be accommodated, and the traffic both in goods and passengers expedited over the railways of different companies without being rebooked, repacked or transhipped.'[1]

[1] D. Lardner: *op. cit.* p. 150.

# CHAPTER II

# THE FOUNDATION OF THE RAILWAY CLEARING HOUSE

In 1892, on the occasion of the jubilee of the foundation of the Railway Clearing House, two well-known railway directors crossed swords through the correspondence columns of *The Times*. The eighty-one-year-old director of the Midland Railway, Sir James Allport, who had been general manager of the Birmingham and Derby Junction Railway in 1841 and had served as a delegate on the Railway Clearing House Committee as early as 1843, maintained that at a meeting of the Birmingham and Derby Junction Railway Board at which Robert Stephenson was also present, he had suggested that the railway companies 'should adopt a system similar to that which existed in London and known as the Bankers' Clearing House'. Sir Edward Watkin, seventy-three-year-old chairman of the South Eastern Railway, disagreed. He was sure that at the time the Railway Clearing House was established it was 'common knowledge' that the scheme owed its origin to George Carr Glyn (1797–1873), later Lord Wolverton, who was chairman of the London and Birmingham Railway and had employed Mr Kenneth Morison, chief accountant of the company, 'to work out the idea'.[1]

If Sir James Allport was right, the records of the Birmingham and Derby Junction Railway provide no confirmation of his claim. It would, however, be quite misleading to attribute the founding of the Railway Clearing House to any one person. Rather it was the product of the collective wisdom of the most influential leaders of the London and Birmingham Railway in the early 1840s.

Although he was not the author of the scheme, the company's chairman, George Carr Glyn, was its most influential sponsor. Without his enthusiastic backing it would not have seen the light

[1] *The Times*, January 30 and February 3 and 9, 1892.

of day. Although he had played a leading part in launching the Railway Society in 1839, Glyn was by no means a believer in unbridled competition. He called the London and Birmingham Railway 'this great national line' and saw it as linking the two greatest seaports of the country—London and Liverpool—with the most important industrial areas of England. In 1844, when the Government announced proposals for the eventual state purchase of railways, he was reported as saying: 'If a new start were being made I would be for a state system.'[1] More than most of his contemporaries, Glyn recognised the enormous wastefulness of competitive railway promotion. He believed that

'If instead of trying to destroy each other's interests railway companies can be brought to unite; if instead of encouraging competition, Parliament will impose an all railway companies a proper system of fares and charges, so as to secure the public welfare . . . the railways will continue to be a safe and sound investment.'[2]

In place of the damaging competition in railway building which Glyn so much deplored, the Clearing House seemed likely to prove an effective instrument for the co-operation of the companies. His acceptance of the chairmanship of the new venture was consistent with his ultimate objectives for the industry.

Robert Stephenson, the engineer of the London and Birmingham line, shared many of Glyn's views. He knew from first-hand experience the difficulties of dealing with a number of independent companies which, as often as not, were more concerned 'to overreach one another than to come to a simple understanding'. Three years before the Clearing House was set up he favoured the creation of a superintending board 'whose intervention would be useful whenever a difference arose between two companies as to a bye-law or a signal or even a price'.[3]

Before 1842 Richard Creed, the company's secretary, had his full mead of frustrations when trying to negotiate agreements for

[1] R. Fulford: *Glyns, 1753-1953*, London, 1953, pp. 123–6.
[2] Speech at a meeting of the London and North Western Railway February 18, 1848. Cited in Samuel Salt, *Railway Commercial Information*, London, 1850, p. 86.
[3] Select Committee on Railways, 1839, BPP 1839, Vol. X, Q. 4739–42.

the working of through traffic with neighbouring railways. He must have welcomed the instructions given him by the directors in April 1841 to invite the co-operation of the principal railway companies in establishing a Clearing House, whose secretary would (he hoped) take over many of the burdens he had carried over the past months.

The man who was most keenly aware of the compelling commercial reasons for a Clearing House, and played the greatest part in its establishment, was Kenneth Morison, who had been appointed head of the audit department in the autumn of 1839 when Glyn brought him in the company's service from his previous employment with the firm of Macaulay and Babington, East India Merchants.[1] As the railway network extended rapidly in the three years following his new appointment, Morison noted the contrast between the simplicity with which his former employer's accounts were settled through the Bankers' Clearing House (established as long ago as 1773) and the 'difficulty and confusion . . . long delays . . . and angry correspondence'[2] associated with the settlement of accounts between railway companies.

Morison must also have contrasted the existence at Golden Cross near Charing Cross of a Clearing House for the settlement of the accounts of the stage coach companies with the absence of such an arrangement for railways. A person wishing to travel from London to York by coach could buy a ticket valid for the whole journey, the various companies whose coaches he used dividing the fare between them in proportion to the mileage for which each company was responsible. But a person wishing to travel between the same two cities by train would have to book several times on the route.

In 1837 the proprietor of the 'Golden Cross', Benjamin W. Horne (1804–70), a wealthy coach owner, accepted an offer of partnership made by William Chaplin (1787–1859), head of the largest coaching business in England, a concern of sixty-eight coaches and 1,800 horses, bringing in a revenue of half a million pounds a year. Chaplin foresaw that with the rapid advance of the works on the London and Birmingham line, the time would soon come when the coaches on this important route would be driven out of business. In combination the two coaching firms would be

---

[1] BTHR, LBM 1: Board minute 589, October 19, 1838.
[2] K. Morison, *op. cit.* p. 6.

in a strong bargaining position with Glyn, chairman of the railway. On December 7, 1837, two years before Morison took up his new post as audit clerk, the bargain was struck. Chaplin and Horne were given a share in lucrative goods and parcels business on the railway and in the distribution of the merchandise from the rail head in return for their abandoning the coach business between the two cities. From 1839 onwards Morison had many financial dealings with Chaplin and Horne and, no doubt, gleaned from Horne a good deal of information about the working of the Clearing House at the Golden Cross.[1]

Morison knew that railway directors were becoming acutely aware of the need for a greater measure of co-operation if the companies were to achieve some uniformity in the rules for working the traffic. The alarm expressed in the newspapers at the growing number of accidents in the winter of 1840-1 persuaded the leading railway directors that it was necessary to forestall the growing criticisms of railway management. On June 19, 1841, therefore, directors and leading officers from nineteen companies—including seven out of the nine companies that joined the Clearing House the following year—met in Birmingham to draft a set of rules and regulations 'proposed to be observed by enginemen, guards, policemen, and others on all railways'. The meeting, which was chaired by Glyn, agreed unanimously to a resolution 'that there should be a uniform system of regulations and signals recognised as applicable to all railways'. The detailed rules agreed to include the requirement that all traffic should keep to the left-hand track; that extra precautions, including the frequent use of the engine whistle, should be observed in a 'fog or in thick weather'; that 'stopping', 'caution', and 'all clear' signals should be observed for both night and day working and that 'all engines travelling in the same direction should keep at least half a mile from each other!'[2] If the meetings of the Railway Society were the first indications of the directors organising for political purposes this Birmingham

[1] Stanley Harris: *The Coaching Age*, London, 1885, pp. 108, 111 and 188–212, and Charles G. Harper: *Stage Coach and Mail in Days of Yore*, London, 1903. Vol. 1 p. 322, Vol. 2 pp. 210–14. 222. *The Railway Official Gazette*, January 1892.

[2] BTHR, HRP 1/129: Resolutions etc., passed at a meeting of railway directors held at Birmingham, June 19, 1841.

meeting was important as the first occasion of their co-operation in matters of business.

Although he did not attract much of the limelight, Thomas Edmonson, a Lancaster Quaker, helped to lay the foundations between the years 1836 and 1842 of a system of through communications. After serving an apprenticeship as a cabinet-maker in his native town, Edmonson was engaged for a few months in a tea and grocery business. But finding that he was 'not fitted to commercial pursuits'[1] he took a job in 1836, at the age of forty-four, as station master at Milton (later renamed Brampton) on the Newcastle and Carlisle Railway. The station was a quiet one and Edmondson had time on his hands. At that time the system of 'booking' tickets characteristic of the coaching era was also used on the railways. The name, destination and fare of the passenger were all written on his paper ticket, the counterfoil being retained in the booking office. It was not an arrangement conducive either to honesty or efficiency and Edmondson set about devising improvements. First he replaced the flimsy paper tickets with more durable cardboard ones, measuring $2\frac{1}{4} \times 1\frac{1}{4}$ inches, of a kind so familiar to the present-day traveller. Then he constructed a small wooden block or hand stamp in which he inserted the necessary type, say 'Milton to Carlisle', with the class, fare, etc. When he had printed a substantial quantity of these tickets he numbered them consecutively by hand. The mechanical devices for the date stamping and numbering of 'runs' of tickets were improvements which followed after a few months' experimentation in 1837 and 1838. At about the same time he contrived the specialised containers or ticket racks which enabled the booking clerk without difficulty to remove the bottom ticket from the file.

As the directors of the Newcastle and Carlisle line were slow to appreciate the merits of his system, early in 1840 Edmondson

[1] John B. Edmondson: 'To Whom are we Indebted for the Railway Ticket System?', *English Mechanic and World of Science*, Vol. XXVII, August 2, 1878, p. 528. For further information on Thomas Edmondson (1792–1851) and his system, the following may be consulted: Lionel Wiener: *Passenger Tickets*, London, 1939, pp. 245–51, *L.M.S. Magazine*, Vol. VI (1929) p. 227; *G.W.R. Magazine*, 1933. BRB HL 2/8, London Midland and Scottish Railway Collection of Historical Documents R. 177; Select Committee on Railways, BPP 1840, Vol. XIII. Evidence of Captain Laws Qs 4340–1.

accepted the offer of Captain Laws, general manager of the Manchester and Leeds Railway, to transfer his services to that company at double his former salary. In his new appointment he was given every encouragement to introduce the new methods. Apart from the charge for equipment and installation of his new invention, Edmondson was paid a rent of ten shillings a year for each mile of line of the company's network. This was the method of payment made when other companies adopted the Edmondson plan.

The Birmingham and Gloucester Railway was the first to follow the example of the Manchester and Leeds, but they were quickly followed by the Birmingham and Derby Junction Railway at the beginning of August 1841. In May 1840 Kenneth Morison examined the arrangements in force on the Manchester and Leeds and reported favourably on them to the directors of the London and Birmingham who eventually agreed in August 1841 to adopt the new system.[1] The demand for the new machines was increasing at such a brisk pace that Edmondson handed in his resignation to the Manchester and Leeds directors in the summer of 1841 so that he might devote all his time to his invention. For a time after his resignation his former employers allowed him to use an office on Bolton station in which to demonstrate to booking clerks from other lines to use of the ticket machine and the method of sending in returns.[2]

Thus by the beginning of 1842 the widespread adoption of Edmonson's plan had paved the way to the introduction of through booking of passengers by those companies which were members of the Clearing House.

The exchange of traffic between companies was increasing in 1840 and 1841, despite the attendant difficulties. In September 1840, as an economy measure, the directors of the Manchester and Leeds Railway reached agreement with the North Midland Board to hire its locomotives for working the line from Hebden Bridge to Leeds.[3] In December that year the London and Birmingham Railway concluded an arrangement for the through booking of passengers to and from the stations on the Midland Counties and

---

[1] BRB, HL 2/8, R 177, LBM 1/95: London and Birmingham Railway Coaching and Police Committee. Resolution 1073 of August 18, 1841.
[2] BRB, ML: Resolution 2573 of the Board of Directors, August 23, 1841.    [3] *The Railway Times*, September 29, 1840, p. 802.

the Birmingham and Derby Junction lines.[1] The three companies which between them linked Manchester and Hull concluded an agreement for the through conveyance of goods traffic, receipts being divided on a mileage basis. It was this principle of division which was followed eight months later when the Clearing House was established.[2] As early as December 28, 1840, S. Dunn of the North Midland Railway had printed and circulated to the companies 'A Proposed Plan for ensuring a capital stock in merchandise waggons, to be furnished by each railway company whose lines and traffic are connected in exact proportion to the number of tons they severally convey, and also to apportion the cost of repairs in the same manner'. Dunn was seventy-six years ahead of his time. It was not until 1917, in the emergency of the First World War, that a scheme for a 'common user' pool of waggons, remarkably like the one he had proposed, was put into operation. No doubt it was verging on the utopian in 1840 to imagine that the 'whole stock of waggons' should be used 'by the united companies in common, but under the superintendence of one general inspector'. But the idea of a periodic balance of accounts between companies based on the ton mileage of goods transported on 'foreign' lines was essentially the same as one worked out by the Clearing House a few months later.[3]

The Post Office was another powerful influence in favour of a rational system of through communications. As early as September 24, 1838, the Postmaster General wrote to Richard Creed, Secretary of the London and Birmingham Railway:

Sir,

The Grand Junction Railway Company having acquiesced in a proposition made to them, that the railway travelling office shall run through from London to Warrington, provided the London and Birmingham Railway Company has no objections to the measure, I have to beg you will submit to the directors of the

[1] BTHR, LBM 1/22: Report on the Coaching and Police Committee, December 17, 1840.
[2] BTHR, ML: Resolution 2380 of Manchester and Leeds Railway, April 16, 1841.
[3] BTHR, HL 2/9, R 243: London Midland and Scottish Railway Collection of Historical Documents.

London and Birmingham Railway that it would be a great convenience to the public service if this course could be adopted.'[1]

The London and Birmingham directors agreed on the following day to make the necessary arrangements. But the GPO was not satisfied merely to achieve an uninterrupted journey for the mail trains irrespective of the time taken; they were to be sent through as quickly as possible. In writing to Richard Creed in this vein on January 25, 1839, W. Maberly of the GPO emphasised the need for 'acceleration of speed so loudly demanded by the public'.[2]

Thus there was no shortage of ideas on how to organise goods and passenger traffic more efficiently. What was lacking was a central and impartial body to give them a more universal application. It was Morison's unique contribution that he saw this need more clearly than anyone else and that he possessed the persuasive powers and the organising ability to make the dream a reality.

The plan for a Railway Clearing House was first discussed formally at a meeting of the Coaching and Police Committee of the London and Birmingham Railway on April 7, 1841, when Mr Glyn was in the chair. The minutes of the meeting record the unanimous decision reached:

'It appearing to the Committee that if the convenience of booking passengers through by the issue of a single ticket, to any first class station on the lines connected and working with this company, can be brought into use, without much additional expense or trouble, by adopting the system of clearance of tickets issued by all those empowered for the purpose, at one office in London or Birmingham, the convenience and comfort of the public would be so great as to make it desirable to recommend the same to the Board for adoption.'

'820 *Ordered*. That the Secretary and the Audit Clerk be instructed to prepare a report of the proposed plan and system for working an office of this description.'[3]

Messrs Creed and Morison were not slow in giving this proposition practical shape. Their report was available in manuscript

---

[1] BRB, HL/2 15, R 351, 9.    [2] BRB, HL/2 15, R 351, 13 and 17.
[3] BTHR, LBM 1/95, April 7, 1841.

form for the Committee to consider at its very next meeting a week later, and a printed version was in circulation before another week was up. It read: 'Proposals for facilitating the process of Booking Through on connected lines of railway by means of the Clearing House, 20th April, 1841'.[1] The Coaching and Police Committee, in a resolution to the Board, gave the scheme its enthusiastic backing. Its adoption was 'most earnestly' pressed, as the advantages it would confer would be 'so great not only as regards the companies themselves, but also to the public, by allowing each passenger to travel from London to any point on any of the lines connected with the London and Birmingham in the booking through plan, with one single ticket only, thus avoiding the great inconveniences which now arise'.[2]

The printed proposals, expressed in the confident and easy style of Kenneth Morison, were sent to the companies on April 27th. They were heavily weighted on the passenger traffic side. Apart from the one sentence. 'The principles of clearing as well as the details of it are understood to apply equally to passengers, parcels, carriages and horses, and where necessary to merchandize' —there was no indication of how through goods traffic would be organised. On the other hand precise details were given for the organisation of the passenger traffic. As soon as the member companies had decided on their 'booking through' stations, the Clearing House would supply the necessary tickets, books, and classified statements. Daily returns of the tickets issued, with their progressive numbers, the number of passengers booked, the fares paid, etc., were to be sent to the Clearing House from each 'booking through' station. Collected tickets were likewise to be forwarded to Euston—the proposed location for the Clearing House—each day. 'Clearing House Bags' were to be kept under lock and key at each station, one key being kept by the station clerk and one by the clerk at the Clearing House. Balances between companies were to be settled weekly. Morison was fully aware of the necessity of accurate information about the railway network and he therefore suggested that 'a skeleton map of all the northern lines, and the principal places with which they communicate' should be provided by the Clearing House for each 'booking

[1] BTHR, HL 2/9, R 242. For full version see Appendix.
[2] Ibid.

through' station. It was confidently claimed that the cost of running the new organisation would be more than offset by the saving which the adoption of through booking would effect in the clerical labour of the different companies.

There was no great rush to support the new project. It was not until after July 8th, when Morison was empowered to visit the secretaries and superintendents of the companies concerned and meet their hesitations and objections with his reassuring manner and his businesslike mastery of the facts, that quick headway was made.[1] As late as September 10th, George Hudson, chairman of the York and North Midland line, without whose co-operation through communication with the north would not have been possible, was still raising objections. On the other side of the country the Grand Junction and Liverpool and Manchester Railways were flatly declining to participate.

William Booth of the Liverpool and Manchester Railway informed Richard Creed that since his company had through booking arrangements with four companies with adjoining lines— the Preston and Wyre, Bolton and Leigh, St Helens and Runcorn Gap, and the Manchester and Bolton to Liverpool was 'in a small way the focus of a certain district' just as London was, and that, therefore, it 'did not require a Clearing House'. Moreover, the Grand Junction lines stood between the Liverpool system and the London and Birmingham with its feeder lines. So long as the Grand Junction had 'their own arrangements' the Liverpool and Manchester would remain 'only spectators' of the London Clearing House.[2]

The support of the Grand Junction Board was clearly of great moment for the success of the new venture; but because of a mere £300 a year it was not forthcoming. Early on in the discussions Captain Mark Huish, who negotiated on behalf of the Grand Junction Railway, wrote to Richard Creed that his Board had given its 'general approval' to the proposals. But when they came to consider the detailed arrangements, it became obvious that the Grand Junction Company would have to adopt Mr Edmondson's

[1] BTHR, LBM 1/95: London and Birmingham Railway Coaching and Police Committee, July 8, 1841, minute 1011.

[2] BTHR, R 242/5, HL 2/9: Letter from W. Booth to R. Creed, October 28, 1841.

system of consecutively numbered tickets if the through booking arrangements with other companies were to work smoothly. Though Captain Huish was convinced that Edmondson's system was 'absolutely the best', the cost of the new tickets would be 3s 6d per thousand—a penny a thousand tickets more than the company was then paying for its different system. The Board therefore came to the conclusion that 'it did not appear that any advantage to the public using the Grand Junction line would be secured which, in the present position of the company, would justify an additional cost of £300'.[1] It took the directors two and a half years to learn the lesson that the additional costs to the company incidental to membership of the Clearing House would be more than offset by the gains to revenue resulting from an increased volume of through traffic.

Despite these setbacks, Morison did not lose faith in his objective. Against the failure to recruit the two large companies in the North West he could set the success with Hudson, who was finally persuaded to support the plan, on behalf of the York and North Midland Railway, a few weeks before the office was opened in London. Moreover, seven other companies, apart from the sponsoring London and Birmingham, had pledged their support. Given good will and an energetic attention to the business in hand this was a sufficiently large and important group to ensure the success of the scheme. Morison believed that the nine pioneering companies would demonstrate the advantages of co-operation and would, before long, pull in the waverers.

III

The Railway Clearing House started business on January 2, 1842. Glyn had made available within a stone's throw of the Doric portico of Euston Station a small unpretentious house at 11 Drummond Street, a property which was destroyed by enemy action ninety-nine years later. The staffing was on as modest a scale as the accommodation. In addition to Kenneth Morison, the secretary employed until 1849 in a part-time capacity at £200 a year, there were six clerks including W. Dawson who was destined

---

[1] BTHR, HL 2/9, R 242/7A.

43

to succeed Morison as secretary in 1861. All owed their appointment directly to Glyn.[1]

Although there was no formal constitution to guide them, the staff were under the direction of the Clearing House Committee which comprised one representative from each member company. The railways that were represented at the first meeting of the committee, held on April 26, 1842, were all located north of the Thames and south of the Tyne and included the London and Birmingham, Midland Counties, Birmingham and Derby Junction, North Midland, Manchester and Leeds, Leeds and Selby, Hull and Selby, York and North Midland, and the Great North of England Companies.[2]

Whereas lines like the Newcastle and Carlisle or the Great Western were, in 1842, still largely self-sufficient in their goods and passenger traffic—the former because of geographical isolation and the latter through the artificial isolation created by the seven-foot gauge—the founder members of the Clearing House had the common characteristic of dependence on neighbouring lines for any substantial growth of their traffic. Thus the London and Birmingham needed the co-operation of the Midland Counties and the Birmingham and Derby Junction for access to Derby and the North; the Hull and Selby would have been isolated without access to Leeds and Selby and both the Great North of England and the North Midland needed an understanding with the lines to the south if their goods and passenger traffic were to reach London.

In view of the dominant position of the London and Birmingham railway in this complex of lines and the leading part which its chairman had played in establishing the Clearing House, it is not surprising that the committee chose Carr Glyn to chair its meetings. He was re-elected to this position each year until his death at the age of seventy-six in 1873. His enduring interest in the organisation and its staff, coupled with his tact and good humour, played a large part in ensuring its success.

In these early days the Clearing House had five main functions to fulfil. Wherever possible, passengers were to be booked through to stations on the lines of the member companies without change

[1] BTHR, RCH 1/13: K. Morison, report to the Railway Clearing House committee, April 26, 1842.        [2] *Ibid.*

44

of carriage. Each day tickets used for through travel, when collected, were to be sent to the Clearing House, and the companies involved were to be credited with their share of the fare, allotted in proportion to mileage. Horses and carriages were likewise to be sent through without change of conveyance. Goods, including minerals, were to be dispatched with similar facility. Companies were to pay a fixed rate per mile for such carriages and waggons, not their own property, as they had occasion to use, with an additional demurrage payment to be made for waggons detained beyond a prescribed length of time. Finally, all accounts for through traffic in passengers and goods were to be settled through the Clearing House and not through private arrangement by the companies concerned.[1]

The successful working of this plan required the exercise of considerable judgement and tact on the part of Morison and his staff. The companies' distrust of each other did not suddenly evaporate on January 2, 1842. There were misgivings lest the new organisation might become merely an offshoot of the London and Birmingham Railway, existing mainly to subserve its interests. The Clearing House had, as yet, no legal personality. The staff was therefore bound to depend on the good will of the companies for the honest observance of the rules laid down by the committee as there was no means of enforcing them. Thus, when Captain Huish drew attention to the inadequate supply of couplings for carriages and showed that it was causing delays, the committee could do no more than 'earnestly recommend' to the companies 'the desirability of having couplings permanently attached to the waggons and carriages.[2] Morison constantly stressed the voluntary nature of the association the companies had joined. In his reports to the committee he patiently explained the advantages of co-operation and pleaded for support for each new proposal—such as standardisation of method of accounting—which he advanced. He never attempted to coerce or bully companies into compliance with the wishes of the majority. Every company had the right of dissent. If its Board considered the decision of the Clearing House ill-advised it could inform Morison of its non-compliance and would

[1] K. Morison, *op. cit.* Major T. F. Dowden, R. E.: *The Railway Clearing House*, London.
[2] BTHR, RCH L/13, September 22, 1847.

suffer no penalty other than the injury it imposed upon itself through being 'out of step' with the majority of the companies.

The money to finance the work of the Clearing House was obtained in a characteristically simple and *ad hoc* fashion. At its first meeting the committee agreed that each company was to be charged £5 for each 'booking through' station on its line. As this would not bring in enough to cover expenses, the balance outstanding after deducting the flat-rate station contributions was to be met by levies on the companies proportional to their receipts from through traffic of passengers, horses, carriages, dogs and parcels.[1] By these means the modest sum of £895 3s 8d was raised to finance the first year's work of the Clearing House. During that year through goods and passenger traffic to the value of £193,246 8s 10½d had been organised. Appropriately enough the largest contribution to the common purse came from the London and Birmingham which paid £244 5s 8d. This sum can be regarded as a bagatelle compared with the company's gross receipts of £820,410, and net profit of £455,849 for the year 1842. It was undoubtedly an exceedingly small sum to pay for the benefits of increased through traffic and the important reduction in the Company's clerical expenses. Likewise the Hull and Selby's £15 contribution to the expenses of the Clearing House could scarcely have been begrudged considering the opportunities for increased traffic that the smooth functioning of the clearing system promised for the future. It was a figure that would scarcely be noticed out of a total revenue in excess of £60,000 annually.[2]

Morison was not given to exaggeration. The optimistic tone of his report of March 14, 1843 is therefore all the more worthy of attention:

'The experience of the last fifteen months', he wrote, 'has fully established the practical character of the Clearing House arrangements and (if the inference is warranted by the absence of complaints) that the system has worked to the satisfaction of all.'

The Clearing System might be extended to any limits without being rendered more complex or less efficient, and such an

[1] BTHR, RCH 1/13 R3, April 26, 1842.
[2] BTHR, RCH 1/13: Morison Report, March 15, 1843. *The Railway Times*, 1842, p. 897, 1843, p. 245.

extension would serve the twofold purpose of diminishing the share of the expense to be paid by the several companies and of more completely developing the object of the establishment by increasing to the utmost degree the accommodation of the public.'

Morison was mistaken in thinking that the work would not become more complex. But he was abundantly right in his vision of a Clearing House with a vastly extended range of responsibility.

# CHAPTER III

# THE PASSENGER TRAFFIC

## I

Many of the merchants, industrialists and speculators who planned the first British railways expected that the most important business of the new companies would be in the carriage of goods. Although this expectation was fulfilled on the Stockton and Darlington and a few other railways, in the majority of cases the experience of the early years of operation was that revenue earned from carrying passengers exceeded that from the carriage of goods. In the country as a whole it was not until 1852 that the revenue from goods traffic for the first time exceeded that from the passenger services.[1]

By the time that the Clearing House was established in 1842 its sponsors were under no illusions about which kind of traffic was the most profitable to the majority of the companies. Understandably they gave closest attention to encouraging long distance passenger travel. The detailed arrangements for this aspect of its work made by the Clearing House committee at its first meetings were in sharp contrast with the scanty and vague recommendations for the through haulage of goods. The minute book of the committee for the years 1842–48 contains many complaints of shortcomings in the arrangements made for goods traffic: there were comparatively few complaints about the organisation of the passenger traffic. As early as April 26, 1842, Kenneth Morison was able to claim, in his first report to the committee, that 'passengers were able to book through from every town of any importance within the limits embraced by the Clearing House.[2]

Unfortunately no detailed accounts were published by the Clearing House for the years before 1848. The first breakdown of receipts appeared in Morison's report for the six months ended December 31, 1848, in which receipts from through passenger

[1] See Appendix 4.
[2] RCH 1/2: Minutes of Railway Clearing House committee, April 26, 1842.

traffic at £281,241 10s 3d amounted to over half the £474,453 6s 5d derived from through goods traffic.[1] Ten years later, passenger receipts at £690,573 7s 1d constituted little more than one third of the receipts from goods valued at £1,935,087 17s 5d.[2] In view of the absence of a common goods classification until after the publication of the first one issued by the Clearing House in 1847, not to mention early difficulties over such matters as the return of borrowed waggons, it can be asserted that the proportion of Clearing House revenue coming from passengers in 1842 was considerably greater than was the case six years later.

The success of the arrangements made for through passenger traffic sprang from their essential simplicity. Each ticket purchased for travel over more than one company's lines was forwarded to the Clearing House after the completion of the journey. Each company concerned was then credited with a proportion of the value of the ticket corresponding to its proportion of the journey mileage.

Such a simple plan required, for its successful implementation, arrangements for the issue of tickets which were both easy to understand and reasonably proof against evasion and fraud. As we have seen, Thomas Edmondson provided the answer.

Morison clearly came to regard the adoption of the Edmondson plan as the *sine qua non* of membership of the Clearing House. Captain Mark Huish of the Grand Junction Railway at least gained this impression.[3] That those companies which joined the Clearing House after its inception were similarly persuaded is illustrated by the following letter from the secretary of the Lancaster and Preston Railway to Richard Creed, written on July 5, 1844:

*Dear Sir,*
    I beg to appraise you that on and after Monday last 1st inst. our business through the London and Birmingham Railway will be passed through the Clearing House. On that day we begin to use Edmondson's ticket system.

*Yours faithfully,*
B. P. Gregson.[4]

[1] RCH 1/2: Railway Clearing House committee, March 3, 1849.
[2] RCH 1/2: Railway Clearing House committee, March 9, 1859.
[3] HL 2/8 R177/6: London Midland and Scottish collection of historical letters.
[4] Letters from Mark Huish to Richard Creed, December 9, 1841. HL 2/8.

For the sake of efficiency Morison wanted Edmondson to be given a complete monopoly of ticket printing. In September 1845 he was complaining to the committee of 'the indistinct and almost illegible manner' in which the tickets were printed by many of the companies, increasing the opportunities for forgery. He urged the adoption of Edmondson's proposal to set up 'a large central printing establishment with two or three subsidiary ones judiciously placed' to print the tickets for the whole of England by his new patent steam presses.[1] The committee did not immediately follow Morison's advice, but eighteen months later the plan to establish a central office for printing passenger tickets for all companies in the Clearing House was again discussed and Morison was instructed to report to the companies the detailed arrangements proposed by Edmondson.[2] The individualism of the companies and the death of Edmondson in 1851, at the comparatively early age of fifty-nine, delayed the implementation of this eminently sensible plan.

With the growth of excursion traffic there were new threats to the principles of ticket issuance that Morison so vigorously upheld. At their conference in February 1858 the general managers of Clearing House companies instructed him to urge the companies 'to discontinue at once so irregular and dangerous a practice as the issue of paper tickets having the same series of consecutive numbers for a variety of fares'.[3] Such lapses notwithstanding, it was largely thanks to Edmondson that already by 1845 more than half a million passengers were 'booked through' with so little inconvenience to themselves and such small cost to the companies.

The success of the arrangements for the through passenger traffic also depended on the acceptance of a simple plan for the exchange of passenger coaches. From January 1842 a charge of a penny a mile—known thereafter as 'mileage'—was made for each coach travelling over 'foreign' lines. Although some companies were at first reluctant to pay for the use of borrowed coaches and some mileage payments due for the year 1842 were still not paid in October 1843,[4] Morison was pleased to report in March of the

[1] RCH 1/2: Morison's report to committee, September 23, 1845.
[2] RCH 1/2: Committee minute 62, February 19, 1847.
[3] RCH 1/71: General Managers Conference, minute 261, February 11, 1858.
[4] RCH 1/2: Morison's report to committee, October 16, 1843.

following year that the charges were now being met.[1] It was quite otherwise with demurrage claims on goods waggons which were still the subject of much dispute.

To simplify the settlement of accounts for through traffic it was essential that there should be no dispute concerning the distances travelled either by passengers or goods on the different companies' lines. As early as 1845 the average passenger 'travelling through' passed over the lines of at least three companies. But as late as 1851 the Midland and the York, Newcastle and Berwick Railways were in dispute about the correct distance by rail between two such important centres as York and Newcastle.[2]

At one of the earliest meetings of the goods managers of the railways in the Clearing House the Boards of Directors of the companies were asked to authorise Morison 'to get a full and perfect list of tables printed from the official sources'.[3] The directors were dilatory in following this advice. In the meantime in February 1849 Mr Bradshaw showed the goods managers 'a skeleton map of railways and railway stations' which was not regarded as wholly satisfactory since only the shortest distances between stations were shown and not the distances by alternative routes.[4] In November of the same year a 'highly satisfactory' map designed by Mr Zachary Macaulay, who had been employed as a Clearing House clerk since 1847, was submitted to the meeting but was not officially sponsored because orders for 500 copies would have been needed to justify printing.[5] Thus by October 1851 'a general feeling of inconvenience was expressed at the want of authentic and authorised distance tables[6] and the secretary was requested to have such tables prepared and printed as soon as possible. The replies of the companies to Morison's circular requesting information make interesting reading. The return of the Lancashire and Yorkshire Railway, presented in manuscript,

[1] RCH 1/2: Morison's report to committee, March 14, 1844.
[2] RCH 1/179: Goods Managers Conference, minute 341, June 23, 1851.
[3] RCH 1/179: Goods Managers Conference, minute 4, October 4, 1847.
[4] RCH 1/179: Goods Managers Conference, minute 193, February 22, 1849.
[5] RCH 1/179: Goods Managers Conference, minute 276, November 22, 1849.
[6] RCH 1/179: Goods Managers Conference, minute 397, August 2, 1851.

contained many crossings out in red ink. An even grubbier document was submitted by the Norfolk Railway. The Newcastle and Carlisle Railway quoted odd distances in decimal points of a mile: the other companies referred to miles, chains and links.[1] From such a hotch potch there emerged in September 1853 the first *Clearing House Book of Distance Tables*, an invaluable work of reference of two hundred pages.

In the meantime Mr Macaulay had made his own arrangements with Smith and Ebbs, London publishers, to print his railway map, the first edition of which appeared in 1851. Four other editions appeared before Macaulay's death in 1860. Two other employees of the Clearing House then took up the work of preparation of diagrams and maps. H. Oliver, who joined the service on February 18, 1842, and retired fifty-five years later as head of the mileage department, was fully aware of the necessity for accurate information of the kind earlier provided by Macaulay. He therefore gave every encouragement to John Airey, a clerk who had joined his department in June 1852, to draft and have privately published his railway diagrams and maps of the principal districts of the United Kingdom. His first comprehensive map of the railways of England and Wales was published by McCorquodale's in November 1876 but was poorly designed and printed. Its successor, appearing in 1881, was a greatly improved article. In 1895 the Clearing House purchased Airey's business and the first official Railway Clearing House map of England and Wales appeared the following year. Not only the railway companies but also British cartographers in general had reason to be grateful for the initiative of three of the best-known employees of the Clearing House in having published accurate and well engraved maps of the British railway network. Without their work disputes between the companies on the division of the traffic receipts would have been far more numerous.[2]

[1] RCH 6/1: Contains the companies' replies to Mr Morison's circular.
[2] For information on the work of Macaulay and Airey see the valuable article by D. Garnett: 'The Railway Maps of Zachary Macaulay and John Airey' in *The Journal of the Railway and Canal Historical Society*, Vol. V, nos 3, 5 and 6, 1959.

## II

Many thousands of absent-minded travellers first came to hear about the Railway Clearing House and appreciate its work through the services of the lost property office. Mr Morison may have got the idea of setting up this new department through knowledge of the procedure on the London and Birmingham railway where it was one of the duties of the superintendent of railway police to keep a register of lost property.[1] Whatever may have been the inspiration of his plan we know that in his report to the committee on September 23, 1845 he proposed 'a few simple and inexpensive arrangements for facilitating the recovery and restoration of lost luggage'.[2] He recommended that every item of lost property discovered should be reported to the Clearing House where a register would be kept and staff would be employed to speed the return of articles to their rightful owners.

It was not until February 1847 that the committee acted on these proposals and instructed Morison to seek the co-operation of the companies in their implementation.[3] By September of that year all the companies, with one or two exceptions, had agreed to participate and by January 1848 the lost luggage department was set up in the Clearing House building in London. Although at first the reports sent in by the companies were incomplete and too sketchy, there was a rapid improvement by the end of the year. With the increase in numbers of the travelling public the work of the lost luggage department steadily mounted. By 1875 when the number of inquiries exceeded 15,000, new and more detailed instructions were issued for the lost luggage returns. At the headquarters of the Clearing House, by now transferred to Seymour Street, separate sets of books were kept for some of the items most commonly lost, including portmanteaux, hat cases, carpet bags, etc. By 1899 the number of enquiries for lost property exceeded 40,000 a year.[4]

The work in the lost luggage department was infinitely more varied and interesting than that in the coaching department

[1] HL 2/21: File of letters of the London and North Western Railway.
[2] RCH 1/2.
[3] RCH 1/2: Resolution of committee, February 18, 1847.
[4] Major T. F. Dowden: *The Railway Clearing System, As Practised in the Railway Clearing House in 1876*, London, 1877, p. 39.

(concerned with the settlement of accounts for through passenger traffic). Although the cause of most luggage going astray was similar to that which brought about the downfall of Lady Audley in the early Victorian best-seller *Lady Audley's Secret*[1]—the failure to remove old labels—there were a host of other reasons for the passenger and his possessions not reaching the same destination. In the case of the young lady who was travelling from Cheshire to Persia to join her fiancé, the trunk which contained her wedding dress went astray because the bride to be, at the last moment, decided to travel to the continent via a different port from that named on the trunk. In consequence of her thoughtlessness several anxious weeks of waiting followed her arrival in the Turkish capital. Somewhat more fortunate was the emigrant from Ireland bound for Christchurch, New Zealand, who had to start the long journey from London docks without most of his possessions. Urgent and persistent enquiries by Clearing House staff resulted in his luggage being found at Christchurch, Hampshire, from which it was sent to Plymouth in time to catch the same emigrant ship outward bound from London.[2]

Clerks in the lost luggage department prided themselves on their ability to discover almost any item of lost property, however unusual its character and however great the obstacles to its recovery. When a passenger who had travelled from Liverpool to London reported losing his false teeth when looking out of the carriage window, the staff at Euston might well have been forgiven for declining to follow up his enquiry. Nevertheless, numerous letters and telegrams were sent and there was jubilation when a set of false teeth was eventually found. But disillusionment quickly followed. The find had been made on the Manchester and Birmingham line and the teeth would not fit the mouth of the embarrassed traveller.[3]

The Clearing House also contributed to the convenience of passenger travel by encouraging the standardisation of time

---

[1] M. E. Braddon: *Lady Audley's Secret*. 8th (Revised) edition. London, 1862, Vol. 2, p. 170.

[2] Anon: *The Railway Clearing House: Its Origin, Object, Work and Results*, revised edition, London, 1901, p. 33.

[3] Illustrated interview with Mr Harry Smart, secretary, railway clearing house, *The Railway Magazine*, November 1898, p. 13.

throughout the kingdom. It could not claim to be the first influence in this direction since the Post Office arranged for the mail coach guard on the London and Holyhead (Irish mail) route to carry a watch bearing Greenwich time so that clocks could be adjusted at all stopping places *en route*. When railways replaced coaches for the conveyance of mail on this route the old custom was maintained until the outbreak of war in 1939.[1] But the Clearing House helped to make more universal a practice which had hitherto been largely confined to one route. At its meeting in September 1847 the committee resolved 'that it be recommended to each company to adopt Greenwich time at all their stations'.[2] Although it was not until the early 1850s that companies like the Great Western, which was still not a member of the Clearing House, adopted Greenwich time for all its stations, there was a speedy adoption of the committee's resolution by member companies.

### III

In the provison of greater comfort and more ample accommodation for the majority of railway travellers the achievements of the Clearing House were disappointing in comparison with those of the Board of Trade under the Railways Act of 1844 and the companies themselves under the stimulus of competition from the early 1870s onwards. Under the Railways Act of 1844 the companies were under obligation not only to provide at least one train a day with third-class accommodation in each direction on their lines, but also to ensure that the third-class carriages were provided with seats and protected from the weather

The railway department of the Board of Trade enforced these new regulations with vigour after 1844, insisting that its standards of comfort and hygiene should be met.[3] Before that time not only third-class passengers but also many second-class passengers had been obliged to travel in open trucks sometimes carried in mixed trains of goods and passenger waggons.

[1] Michael Robbins: *The Railway Age*, Penguin edition, 1965, p. 47. V. Stewart Haram: *Centenary of the Irish Mail, 1848-1948*, London, 1948, p. 31.   [2] RCH 1/2: Minute of committee, September 22, 1847.
[3] Henry Parris: *Government and the Railways in Nineteenth-Century Britain*, London and Toronto, 1965, pp. 93–99.

The figures in Appendix 4 showing a rise in the number of 'Parliamentary' train passengers between 1846 and 1852 of over 700 per cent indicate that Parliament and the Board of Trade did far more to encourage the habit of railway travel among the poorer classes than did the Clearing House by its arrangements to simplify through booking. Once the provisions of the Railways Act of 1844 came into effect the proportion of third-class and 'Parliamentary' train passengers to the total number of passengers rose rapidly in the course of five years from just over a third to more than a half of the total of persons travelling.

By contrast, particularly before 1872, the influence of the Clearing House in respect of the provision of ordinary third-class accommodation was a conservative one. When the general managers met in conference they appeared to be more concerned to augment the revenue from first and second class passengers than to extend facilities to the 'lower orders'. In March 1867 they decided that for distances over seventy-five miles there should be not more than two third-class trains each way daily, including the stopping 'Parliamentary' train. Although the North Eastern, in a minority of one, objected, they further recommended that the practice of carrying third-class passengers by express train and of allowing third-class passengers to ride in second-class carriages should be discontinued.[1]

On the other hand, egged on by the commissioners for the Great Exhibition, the Clearing House was eventually persuaded to make ample and detailed arrangements for the conveyance of railway excursionists to London in the summer of 1851. A resolution of the Clearing House committee on March 3, 1851, 'that the Secretary be instructed to summon a meeting of General Managers for Saturday 22nd instant to consider the arrangements which may be necessary to adopt with reference to excursion trains during the time the exhibition is open', was the occasion for the first regular meetings of the general managers. Before long these came to exercise more influence over railway policy than did the Clearing House committee itself.[2] To start with the general managers showed no great enthusiasm for the task assigned them. At their first meeting, after a prolonged discussion, they came to

[1] RCH 1/79: Minutes 719 and 720, General Managers Conference, March 12, 1867.    [2] RCH 1/2: Minute 166, March 12, 1851.

the conclusion that there were difficulties which for the moment were 'insuperable', preventing the larger companies from reaching agreement on a code of regulations for the excursion traffic. It was thought wise to 'defer the consideration of the matter to a future period'.[1] Meeting again at the end of April they decided that no excursion trains to London should be provided until July 1st. This did not satisfy Mr Paxton, the designer of the Exhibition building and one of the most influential members of the sponsoring commission. He attended the next meeting of the general managers on May 22nd and persuaded them to advance the starting date for the excursion trains to June 2nd.[2] When it was learned that the Leith to London steamship companies were also proposing to convey visitors to the Great Exhibition at reduced rates it was decided to make rail excursion fares competitive.[3] It was also conceded that not only the members of working-class clubs but also their families should be carried at the cheap rates, with children under twelve years old being carried at half the excursion fare.[4] So great was the demand for tickets that special rolling stock could not be provided for all the excursionists and it became necessary to allow them to travel home by ordinary trains.[5]

Although Thomas Cook had pioneered the idea of excursions by train as early as 1841, it was the Clearing House meetings in 1851 which produced agreement between the companies for a vast extension of the services. At the end of the first week of June 1851 a leading railway journal reported that the entire country was 'alive with excursion trains'.[6] By the time the Great Exhibition closed in October no less than 6,200,000 separate visits had been made to it. For the most part the visitors travelled by train. The traffic receipts of the eight railway companies with termini in London for the twenty-two weeks of the exhibition were up by 27·6 % over the corresponding period of the previous year.[7]

Although passenger receipts on lines not serving the metropolis

[1] RCH 1/70: Minute 6, General Managers Conference, March 2, 1851.
[2] RCH 1/70: Minute 16, General Managers Conference, May 22, 1851.
[3] RCH 1/70: Minute 12, General Managers Conference, April 30, 1851.
[4] *Ibid*. minute 11.
[5] RCH 1/70: Minute 28, General Managers Conference, June 10, 1851.
[6] *The Railway Times*, June 7, 1851, p. 572.
[7] *The Railway Times*, October 18, 1851, p. 1057.

were depressed, it is nevertheless true that thousands of wage earners had their first experience of railway travel on an excursion train to the Great Exhibition. For subsequent exhibitions such as the International Exhibition held in London in 1862 it was left to the meetings of the superintendents of Clearing House companies to arrange the details of excursion traffic.[1]

The attempts of the Committee of the Clearing House to make travel by train in winter less of a test of personal stamina by providing some form of warmth in the compartments was largely unsuccessful. Each October from 1864 to 1870 the superintendents were happy to recommend that all companies should supply foot-warmers to first-class passengers and to leave lesser mortals to freeze in their second- and third-class compartments; but in August 1870 the general managers urged the extension of the service to the second class 'at such stations as the companies may select'.[2] Little can have been done to extend the service, for two years later the general managers considered the question again and at greater length. They then resolved that foot-warmers should be supplied to all three classes of passengers at selected stations and that a charge of 3d be made 'except where a cold foot-warmer is replaced by a hot one'. A sub-committee comprising the superintendents of the ten principal companies was formed to draft regulations. Unfortunately three months later Mr Dawson, the secretary of the Clearing House, was obliged to report a bewildering diversity of replies from the companies to a request for their views on the policy to be followed. Six minor railways gave unqualified approval to all the proposals; the Great Western and the North Staffordshire Railways agreed to comply only if competing lines also complied; the Manchester, Sheffield and Lincolnshire, the Caledonian and the North British Railways objected to making a charge, while the London and South Western and the Brighton Line wanted to charge 6d to the first-class passengers. Mr Neele, superintendent of the London and North Western Railway, pointed out that as the Midland intended to make no charge to first- and second-class passengers his company

---

[1] RCH 1/114: Meetings of Superintendents, December 13, 1861, and January 23, 1862.
[2] RCH 1/114: Minute 800, Superintendents Conference, October 27, 1864.

could not very well make a charge to those travelling third class. Inevitably the general managers came to the conclusion that nothing could be done collectively and it was therefore agreed 'that arrangements for the supply of foot-warmers be left to the companies themselves to settle and act upon as they may consider desirable'.[1]

The determination of the Midland Railway to secure a larger share of the traffic between London and the North was responsible for a greater number of improvements in travelling comfort than any sponsored by the Clearing House. It first upset the apple cart by announcing in 1872 that third-class accommodation would be provided on all its trains. Three years later it abolished the second class and reduced first-class fares to the old second-class level. The result, according to one of the ablest traffic superintendents of the day, was that 'third class had to be adopted by all trains in which the Midland Railway were in competition with the London and North Western.' There was also a greatly increased provision of third-class tourist tickets to places which had previously only seen first and second-class passengers. If the Clearing House could scarcely be held responsible for this revolution it had to deal with its consequences. Special meetings of the superintendents had to be held in Seymour Street to arrange alterations in train marshallings and to make provision for the greatly increased quantity of rolling stock required.[2]

The existence of an organisation increasingly national in scope and with conveniently situated offices in London provided the coaching superintendents with a valuable opportunity to dovetail the timetables of their passenger services. There were, it is true, some superintendents who apparently did not give a fig whether or not their timetables fitted in with those of adjacent companies. It was said of Mr Scott of the London and South Western Railway that when he received complaints from an aggrieved passenger who found that his train was not timed to connect with those of another company he advised him to get up earlier and make an earlier start on his journey. On one occasion when he received,

[1] RCH 1/115: Minute 1091, General Managers Conference, August 11, 1870.
[2] RCH 1/99: Minute 3 of Superintendents Conference, November 14, 1850.

through the post, a complaint that a train was overcrowded, he turned up one corner of the letter and wrote his reply:

'Take my advice and start your journey earlier and if you miss one train you will get the next. I cannot afford to wait till 9 o'clock in the morning, I start long before that on my work.'

Most of the superintendents, however, took a more tolerant view of the frailties of their fellow human beings and conceded that co-ordinated timetables were worth a good deal of time and thought to achieve. When the first Conference of Superintendents was held at Normanton, in November 1850, one of the first items on the agenda was the dovetailing of passenger services. The third resolution passed at the meeting read 'that the time tables of trains for the ensuing month be considered fixed unless notice of any alteration be received by the parties interested, by the following Monday's post'.[1] It was decided to hold the meetings as frequently as once a month largely for the reason that it was hoped to accommodate each company's services to those of the others as much as possible. These monthly meetings continued without a break until the railways were nationalised in 1948.

IV

By examining the figures given in Morison's booklet alongside others printed in the Parliamentary Papers in 1846 it is possible to assess the importance of the work of the Clearing House in the growth of the passenger traffic in the early 1840s. Appendix V shows the number of passengers 'booked through' and the total number of passengers carried by the companies in the Clearing House during the year 1845. At that time only 55% of the railway mileage was owned by companies which were members of the Clearing House. Thus although an average of 4% of the passengers carried by Clearing House companies were 'booked through' for the country as a whole less than 2% of railway passengers travelled over the lines of more than one company.

It might have seemed reasonable to expect that the smaller companies would have gained most from the establishment of a clearing system. But with the relatively unimportant exception of the Stockton and Hartlepool Railway it was the larger companies

[1] RCH 1/99 Superintendents Conference, November 14, 1850.

that gained most passenger traffic through joining the Clearing House. The importance of through booking to the London and Birmingham—the company which had most to do with the establishment of a clearing system, is clearly shown. More than a tenth of its passengers were booked to travel through on other company lines. Clearly this railway was acting as the main artery for passenger traffic between London, the Midlands and the North West.

Membership of the Clearing House did not give a railway any decisive financial advantage over non-member companies. The passenger receipts of the London and Birmingham and the North Midland Railways in 1842–44 inclusive were lower than they had been in 1841 while those of the Birmingham and Derby Junction and the Midland Counties Railways were only improved by a small margin over the same period of time. By comparison, three of the most important non-member companies, the Great Western, South Eastern and London and South Western experienced a 50% growth in passenger receipts over the same period of time largely because of the extension of their rail networks.

From the mid 1850s onwards the Clearing House showed separately in its half-yearly statements of through traffic, the receipts from passengers and from goods. By comparing these figures with the annual railway returns it is possible to discover what proportions of the total goods and passenger traffic were 'booked through'. During the entire period before the First World War the receipts from through goods traffic were never less than one-third and were sometimes nearly two-fifths of the total receipts from this type of traffic. Through passenger traffic brought in a much smaller percentage of total receipts from passenger services. Over many years it was remarkably consistent at between 13% and 14%. With the formation of great regional monopolies such as the North Eastern in 1854 and the Great Eastern in 1863, and the increasing rail networks of dominant companies like the Great Western and the London and North Western, with each year that passed it was possible for passengers to travel over ever longer distances within the network of a single company. The steady percentage which through passenger receipts bore to total passenger receipts disguised both an absolute increase in the number of persons booking through and an increase in the average length of rail journey.

# CHAPTER IV

# THE GOODS TRAFFIC

I

The unprecedented economic growth which the United Kingdom experienced in the nineteenth century would have been impossible without efficient arrangements for the long distance haulage of goods. It was the most important task of the Clearing House to organise this service. Nevertheless, despite the admitted importance of the task, it was not until more than eight years after the Clearing House was founded that it was possible for one of the leading goods managers of the railways to claim that some of the main problems of speeding the goods traffic had been solved.[1]

When the Clearing House started business it had been agreed that a mileage charge of $\frac{1}{4}$d a mile should be levied on waggons travelling on 'foreign' lines, the charge to apply only to the outward loaded journey and not to the return journey to base. In addition there was to be a charge of 6s a day demurrage for each day, other than the days of arrival and departure, that a waggon was detained by a company other than its owner.[2] These regulations were made to ensure that scarce waggons were not taken by unnecessarily long routes to their destination and were not unduly detained or put to improper use by the companies that did not own them.

It was many months before these simple principles for operating the goods traffic were generally accepted even by some founder members of the Clearing House. In his first report to the committee on April 26, 1842, Morison was forced to admit that the accounts for the exchange of goods waggons were 'not in so satisfactory a train' as were those for the passenger traffic. He

[1] See the statement of Mr Braithwaite Poole, p. 77 below.
[2] Reference to these regulations is made in RCH 1/2: minutes 19 and 20 of the committee, July 7, 1843.

believed that the remedy lay in 'the adoption of a uniform return' by the member companies. Nearly a year later he reported that no settlement of the balances due for the exchange of waggons had been made since the Clearing House started business. The returns sent in by the companies had been so inadequate that it had been found impracticable to keep an accurate account of demurrage charges.[1] Carr Glyn complained to the committee on March 15, 1843, of the 'serious inconvenience' to which the London and Birmingham Railway was subjected by the 'detention and unfair use' of their waggons by other companies. He warned that the inconvenience was so great that, unless there was an immediate improvement, his company would be obliged to restrict the use of its waggons to its own lines. The same meeting learned that the directors of the Manchester and Leeds Railway opposed all charges for the detention of waggons and were therefore not meeting the demurrage claims of other companies. By March of 1844 Morison had persuaded the companies to submit monthly accounts for mileage and demurrage on a standard form.[2] But at the end of February 1846 the balances for the mileage and demurrage accounts for the year 1842 were still outstanding. The Clearing House was keeping a large sum of money, undistributed, in the form of a 'suspense account' until the companies concerned agreed on the division of disputed parts of the receipts from the goods traffic.[3]

In an endeavour to prevent the improper detention and use of waggons the committee decided in July 1843 to appoint a waggon inspector at a salary of £120 and a free pass on the railways.[4] Three months later the decision to reduce the demurrage charge from 6s per waggon per day to 3s was a step of practical wisdom which helped to prevent the breakdown of the arrangements for the through transport of goods.[5]

The distrust and misunderstandings which emerged when the first attempts were made to organise the goods traffic were reflected in the small volume and low total value of transactions

[1] RCH 1/2: Morison's report to the committee, March 14, 1843.
[2] RCH 1/2: Morison's report to the committee, March 15, 1844.
[3] RCH 1/2: Morison's report to the committee, February 25, 1846.
[4] RCH 1/2: Committee minute 16, July 7, 1843.
[5] RCH 1/2: Committee minute 20, October 15, 1843.

made through the Clearing House. Five years after its foundation, by which time most of the railways north of the Thames were members, the value of through goods traffic supervised by the Clearing House was certainly less than half a million pounds. In the year ending June 30, 1847, the entire railway network of the country earned less than £3½ millions from the transport of goods. By comparison the twelve most important canals in the country were carrying nearly 14 million tons of goods in 1848 compared with just over 10½ million tons ten years earlier.[1]

In the country as a whole the railways receipts from goods traffic did not exceed those from passengers until 1852, the same year in which the value of through goods traffic cleared in Seymour Street for the first time exceeded a million pounds.

## II

What explanation can be given for the slow growth of the railways goods traffic?

One of the most important reasons was the inexperience of many railway managements in dealing with the goods side of their businesses. Particularly when goods had to be sent through, they preferred to shift responsibility for their safe delivery to private carriers who paid a toll for the use of the railway's rolling stock and other facilities; Edward Bury, the eminent locomotive superintendent of the London and Birmingham Railway, believed that there would be 'endless confusion' if railway companies had to negotiate with each other for the carriage of goods.[2] Richard Creed, the secretary of the same company and a man who helped to establish the Clearing House, was also opposed to railways being directly responsible for the carriage of goods. He believed that in cases where goods did not reach their destination the company receiving a complaint would maintain that the matter was the responsibility of 'the manager of the continuing line'. It was better, therefore, to make one carrier such as Pickfords, responsible for the goods from start to finish.[3]

[1] Return from all inland navigation and canal companies, 1869, BPP 1870, Vol. LVI, p. 679.
[2] Q. 2294: Minute of evidence, Select Committee on railways, 1840. BPP 1840, Vol. XIII. [3] *Ibid.* Q. 2582.

The Parliamentary committee before which both Bury and Creed had testified came to the same conclusion, following the tradition of Government policy for goods traffic on canals:

'Our own opinion . . . is decidedly against any inter-meddling on the part of the companies with their branch of the traffic, as we are convinced that the public can be better and more economically served by those whose sole study has been devoted to this species of enterprise. That a railway company might, under certain circumstances, carry goods throughout its own line at a cheaper rate than carriers who have to secure a profit for themselves, independent of the companies' charges, is probable enough: but when goods have to be transferred from one line to another (as they must be when consigned, for example, from London to Hull or York) the confusion and trouble which would arise would more than counterbalance any addition to the company's profits while . . . the public would have great difficulty in obtaining redress should damage occur at distant or disputable points on the route.[1]

Among the companies which in 1842 had delegated responsibility for at least a large part of their goods traffic to the carriers, were the London and Birmingham, Manchester and Leeds, North Union and the Bolton and Leigh. In the case of these companies the private carriers were, in effect, doing the work of the Clearing House in that they organised the through transport of goods over the lines of more than one railway. But the matter was complicated because there were other companies that retained to themselves all the goods business, and yet others, like the Grand Junction Railway, which *shared* the goods traffic with the carriers. By its Act of incorporation the Liverpool and Manchester Railway was required to undertake the carriage of any goods presented to it by any customer and it was the policy of the Board that the company should be the sole carrier of goods on its lines. Henry Booth, the company's treasurer, was convinced that this was a more economical method of doing the business as it cut out the middleman—the carriers. The managers of the Leeds and Selby and Newcastle and Carlisle Railways were similarly persuaded. If all the companies

[1] Fifth report, Select Committee on Railways, 1840.

had adopted one of the two main methods of organising their goods traffic it would have simplified matters, but there were frustrating difficulties in arranging the dispatch of goods when over a part of the route the railway company was the exclusive carrier while over the remainder the private carriers assumed the responsibility.

The long survival of the private carrier for long distance haulage was due to the fact that great concerns such as Pickfords or Chaplin and Horne had hundreds of offices and agencies throughout the country. Until the late 1840s their network of services was more complete than any that could be provided by railways even assuming the fullest co-operation between the railway companies. Among the facilities possessed by the carriers but not by the railways in the early 1840s were canal wharves and warehouses and fleets of canal barges. At the date of opening of the Clearing House there were around 4,500 miles of navigable inland waterways in the United Kingdom compared with less than 1,800 miles of railway. The private carriers were sometimes in a position to choose whether to send the goods committed to their charge by railway or by canal. If the customer was in no great hurry to have his goods delivered they were often dispatched by canal barge. Thus Pickfords sometimes opted to send goods to Birmingham by their own barges on the Grand Junction Canal, rather than to load them on to the waggons of the London and Birmingham Railway at Camden Town.

In 1847 Pickfords offered a carrying service to over 340 towns and cities in England and Scotland, covering a far wider area than that served by the recently formed London and North Western Railway. Indeed, the towns they served were more numerous than those within the territory of the railway companies in the Clearing House. By the mid 1840s Pickfords delivery service 'effectively covered most of England and parts of Scotland'.[1]

The substantial share gained by private carriers in the goods business of the railways was in some cases the result of farsighted bargaining on the part of the larger firms. As early as May 1837

[1] Statement made in a letter to the author from Mr G. L. Turnbull of the Department of Economic History, University of Glasgow. I am also much indebted to Mr Turnbull for drawing my attention to the Pickford's map and for the information concerning the number of towns they served.

Benjamin W. Horne was convinced that his coaching business would be 'annihilated' as the railway network spread.[1] The interesting case of the agreement between Horne and his partner Chaplin on the one hand, and the London and Birmingham Railway on the other, has already been cited. Under it Messrs Horne and Chaplin agreed to 'use their best exertions in forming efficient arrangements for the conveyance of parcels etc. to and from the railways to the various towns in its vicinity if so required by the railway company'.[2] At a time when the railway was still not completed, it is clear that the agreement had many advantages from the point of view of the London and Birmingham directors who were won over to the idea of private carrier haulage at an early stage in the history of the company. Their adherence to this plan was one of the principal hindrances to the success of the Railway Clearing House which they themselves had sponsored.

At an early date William Chaplin established a claim for a share of the goods traffic of the Great Western Railway, offering to 'fill in the gaps' in those parts of the provinces not yet reached by the railway and to undertake delivery of goods from Paddington and other termini to their local destinations. His policy to meet the growing challenge of the railways was revealed in a letter to Edward Mills, one of the officials of the Great Western Railway:

'I am inclined to think it good policy to encourage the carrier to co-operate with the railways by some temporary arrangement for his benefit, either by forwarding his load at the price it would cost him for horse power, or by some other mode of allowance on his passengers or goods, by which he would feel an interest in the railway, rather than linger on in competition in the hope of some legislative interference in the shape of reduced tolls, duty, etc., thereby depriving your revenue of the earliest supply.'[3]

It is important to record these understandings between the carriers and the railways since companies which had signed

[1] Select Committee on Taxation of Internal Communication, 1837. Q. 6 BPP 1837, Vol. XX, p. 297.

[2] BTHR, HL 2/6 R 34.

[3] BTHR, HLI/17: Letter from William Chaplin to Edward Mills, October 20, 1837.

important contracts with private carriers for through delivery of goods felt no great sense of urgency in co-operating with other railways in the Clearing House in formulating a workable plan for through goods traffic.

The carriers' role on the railways was a temporary one and gave place to Clearing House arrangements between the companies as exclusive carriers largely for three reasons. There were too many carriers for the efficient conduct of the business; some railway companies remained exclusive carriers on their own lines, making uniformity of arrangements with non-carrying railways difficult to achieve and sub-contracting the carriage of goods was more expensive than direct carriage by the railway companies.

In the early 1840s the London and Birmingham Railway had arrangements with no less than fifteen different private carriers for the goods trade between the two cities. The provision of separate loading bays, warehouses, etc., and the employment of a separate staff of porters by each of these concerns, was a wasteful method of conducting the business.[1] As each carrier hired separate waggons from the railway company and only exceptionally collected sufficient goods to fill them in time for the scheduled goods train, there was an uneconomic use of scarce rolling stock. The number of railway companies monopolising the goods traffic on their lines was increasing rather than declining. The Grand Junction Railway was involved in a prolonged legal dispute with Pickfords in 1841 when it decided to manage a larger part of the goods traffic itself.[2] In 1841 carriers paid the London and Birmingham Railway 30s a ton toll for the use of the company's waggons between the two terminals and charged traders a minimum of 60s a ton including porterage and delivery in London. As the expense of delivery could not have exceeded 15s, the carriers made a profit of at least 15s. for every ton traded.[3] With

---

[1] *The Railway Times*, February 27, 1841, p. 237: Letter from Henry Booth, Treasurer of the Liverpool and Manchester Railway. Also Mr Bury's evidence, Select Committee on Railways, 1840. Q. 2272, BPP 1840, Vol. XIII.

[2] In the Queens Bench Division Grand Junction Railway vs Messrs Pickford and Co. Reported in *The Railway Times*, March 6, 1841, p. 289. Discussed fully in Appendix of S. T. Jackman: *The Development of Transportation in Modern England*, revised edition, 1962.

[3] *Ibid.*

charges at this prohibitive level it is understandable that the volume of the railway's goods traffic increased but slowly and that a greater volume of goods was still transported by canal.

In 1844 Mr Braithwaite Poole, a goods manager for the Grand Junction Railway at Liverpool and one of the ablest goods managers of his day, who later became the first chairman of the Goods Managers Conference of the Clearing House, compiled a well informed memorandum on the disadvantages of sub-contracting the carriage of goods on the railways. He proved that where the railway companies took over the carriage of goods themselves the rates charged to the public were invariably lower than they had been when the carriers were in charge of the goods traffic.[1] He summarised the situation on twenty of the principal lines of the country as follows:

### 13 RAILWAY COMPANIES WHICH CARRIED GOODS THEMSELVES

| Company | Route miles | Average charge per ton | | |
|---|---|---|---|---|
| Great Western Railway[1] | 118 | £1 | 10s | 6d |
| London and South Western[1] | 77 | 1 | 3 | 9 |
| Grand Junction | 98 | 1 | 7 | 6 |
| Newcastle and Carlisle | 61 | | 17 | 6 |
| Bristol and Gloucester | 53 | | 18 | – |
| London and Brighton[1] | 52 | | 16 | 9 |
| Eastern Counties[1] | 51 | 1 | – | – |
| Edinburgh and Glasgow | 46 | | 11 | 3 |
| Birmingham and Derby | 42 | | 10 | 6 |
| Liverpool and Manchester | 31 | | 10 | 9 |
| Manchester and Birmingham | 31 | | 8 | 3 |
| Glasgow and Greenock | 22 | | 7 | – |
| Preston and Wyre | 20 | | 4 | 2 |
| TOTAL | 702 | £10 | 5s | 11d |

[1] Add 5s for cartage on these lines.

[1] Braithwaite Poole: *Twenty Short Reasons for the Railway Companies Being Themselves the Carriers of Goods Without any Intervening Parties Existing Between Them and the Public on the Same Principle as They are Carriers of Passengers.* Liverpool, 1844. BTHR, PIC 4/25.

7 RAILWAYS EMPLOYING OTHER CARRIERS

| Company | Route miles | Average charge per ton | | |
|---|---|---|---|---|
| London and Birmingham | 112 | £2 | 10s | –d |
| South Eastern Railway | 88 | 1 | 13 | 9 |
| North Midland | 72 | 1 | 17 | 6 |
| Manchester and Leeds | 60 | 1 | 10 | – |
| Great North of England | 45 | 1 | 2 | 6 |
| North Union | 22 | 1 | – | – |
| Lancaster and Preston | 20 | 1 | – | – |
| TOTAL | 419 | £10 | 13s | 9d |

That the possibilities for economy were substantial was demon-strated when the Grand Junction Railway took over from carriers the direct responsibility for the goods traffic between Lancashire and London. Reductions in charges of between 15s and 25s a ton, or upwards of 25% were effected.[1]

It was not until 1847 that the London and North Western Railway (the successor to the London and Birmingham) was finally convinced of the wastefulness of the system of toll carrying and started carrying directly for the public (although for many more years the service of the carriers was retained for deliveries from the railheads).[2] In the autumn of that year Morison reported to the committee of the Clearing House that:

'The Railway Companies north of London having on 1st September completed their arrangements for resuming the entire management of the goods traffic on their respective lines, the duty of analysing and apportioning the receipts of that traffic according to mileage devolved on the Clearing House.'

At last one of the major obstacles preventing easy working of through goods traffic on the railways had been removed.

In his report of September 1845 Morison pointed out another

[1] *The Railway Times*, August 15, 1840, p. 642. Grand Junction Railway Company, report to the general meeting.
[2] D. Stevenson: *Fifty Years on the L.N.W.R. and Other Memoranda in the Life of David Stevenson*, London, 1891, p. 21.

great stumbling block to the growth of the goods traffic of the railways:

'I would submit to the Committee the great confusion and dissatisfaction which will in time arise unless some steps are taken to introduce more uniformity than at present exists into the mode of keeping the accounts of the through traffic in goods and into the charges for the carriage of the same article on the various railways.'[1]

No thoroughgoing attempt to standardise the accounts of the railway companies was made until 1868 and then it was largely the work of a sub-committee of general managers of companies belonging to the recently formed Railway Companies Association. On the other hand the establishment of a reasonable degree of uniformity in charges for the conveyance of the same type of goods on different railways was largely the work of the Clearing House.

In January 1847, on the very first occasion when the goods managers of the Clearing House met separately, they agreed 'that an assimilated classification is indispensable.'[2] The thirteen men who met at Euston on that occasion must have been all too well aware that great diversity existed in the goods classification of the different companies and that variations in charges of up to 200% existed for the carriage of the same type of goods. The diversity arose from the very foundation of the companies when regulations concerning the carriage of goods were included in the Acts of Incorporation. The views of the promoters of railway bills and of the Parliamentary committees which vetted them on what constituted a suitable classification of goods varied from time to time and from one district of the country to another. A scale of charges which might appear reasonable to one Parliamentary committee in 1825 when steam locomotion was in its infancy, might appear excessive to another Parliamentary committee in 1832 when the speed and power of locomotives had been greatly enhanced.

Thus the Liverpool and Manchester Railway Act in 1827 authorised a charge not exceeding 8s a ton for the carriage of 'lime, dung, compost and manure' over the thirty-one miles between the two cities, or 3d a ton mile.[3] Six years later the Act of

[1] RCH 1/2: Morison's report to the committee, September 23, 1845.
[2] RCH 1/179: Goods Managers Conference, January 19, 1847.
[3] 7th George IV, Cap. XLIX, Clause 138.

Incorporation of the London and Birmingham Railway fixed a maximum charge of 1d a ton mile 'for all dung, compost and other types of manure and limestone, etc'.[1] The Whitby to Pickering Railway Act in 1833 placed lime in a different classification along with coal, pig iron, bricks, tiles, slates and potatoes—and allowed a charge of up to 3d per ton mile for its conveyance.[2] The Liverpool and Manchester Act placed all iron goods in the same category as sugar, corn, grain and flour, charging them at the rate of 3d per ton mile. The South Eastern Railway Act also put most metals in the same class as sugar, corn and flour—incidentally only charging 2d per ton mile—but excluded 'iron nails, anvils, vices and chains' which were put in the 1½d per ton mile category.[3] Manifestly, until this tangled skein of varying categories and charges was unravelled it would be a herculean task to make a correct division of receipts for the through merchandise traffic.

In addition to the above major obstacles to the growth of the through traffic in goods there were other problems which awaited solution. When goods travelled over the lines of more than one company should the terminal charges, i.e. the costs incidental to loading and unloading the goods, be included in the total receipts to be divided between the companies, or should they be deducted before the remainder of the receipts was divided? Should sheets and ropes covering goods waggons be 'sent through' and, if so, what should be the basis of compensation to the company that owned them? How could the different companies' ropes be identified? How should compensation be paid for goods damaged in transit? What arrangements should be made for payment for the repair of damaged waggons? While these problems remained unsettled the goods traffic would not flow as freely as it ought to have done.

### III

Between 1847 and July 1850 at their monthly meetings the goods managers got to grips with the formidable problems of the goods traffic and made a substantial contribution to their solution. Many of the principles then formulated for this all important part of the business of the railways proved to be so realistic and sound that

[1] 3rd William IV, Cap. XXXVI, Clause 172.
[2] 3rd William IV, Cap. XXXV, Clause 111.
[3] 6th William IV, Cap. IXXV, Clause 126.

they continued to be applied until the railways were nationalised in 1948.

The representatives from eight companies who attended the first meeting made impressive headway with the agenda. They agreed that railway companies should act as carriers; that the assimilated classification so indispensible to the growth of the traffic should be that of the London and North Western Railway; that the division of receipts should be on the basis of mileage; that terminal expenses should be deducted before any division of receipts was made; that any claims for losses or damage which could not be traced as having taken place on any particular line should be divided in proportion to the mileage run; that sheets and ropes should, for the time being, be provided by each company for use on its own lines, but that 'with a view to avoiding the impediments attending removals at each junction, an attempt should be made to find a simpler arrangement as soon as possible'; that returns of the value and weight of goods sent through should be sent to the Clearing House each week and that the companies should make monthly settlements of their accounts with each other.[1] A month later it was agreed that instead of being removed at junction points, sheets and ropes should be 'sent through' and that a mileage charge of one penny for every ten miles (with a minimum payment of sixpence a journey) and a demurrage charge of 2s per day should be levied on the sheets. For ropes the mileage charge was to be ½d for ten miles (with a minimum of 3d and demurrage at the rate of 3d per day.[2]

Before the foundation of the Clearing House some companies had employed men at junction points with other companies' lines to check the numbers and loading of waggons employed on the through traffic.[3] With the expansion of the long distance goods trade it was seen to be a more sensible arrangement to employ one man at each junction to act on behalf of the companies collectively as a Clearing House number taker than that each company should

[1] RCH 1/179: Goods Managers Conference, January 19, 1847, minute 5.
[2] RCH 1/179: Goods Managers Conference, minute 5, February 16, 1847, and minute 14, October 8, 1847.
[3] The London and Birmingham Railway employed a man in this way at Derby. London and Birmingham Railway Coaching and Police Committee, December 30, 1840. BTHR, LBM 1/95.

continue to employ its own staff for this work. At the Goods Managers Conference held in Derby in August 1847, therefore, it was agreed 'That the waggon tellers employed at the various junctions as Rugby, Northampton, etc., be placed under Mr Morison of the Clearing House'.[1] The committee of the Clearing House endorsed this decision a month later and in March of the following year decided that the cost of employing the number takers should be 'divided between the companies on the same principle as the other portions of the expenditure'.[2]

Undoubtedly the greatest achievement of the Goods Managers Conference in its first year of operation was the publication of the first official *Clearing House Classification* which member companies started to apply from September 1, 1847. By comparison with later nineteenth-century compilations, the classification of 1847 was remarkable for its simplicity. It was printed on one side of a sheet of cardboard measuring 9 × 7 inches.

There were five classes, class I including the lowest value goods such as chalk, bones, potatoes, timber and turnips and class V the goods of highest value including china, clocks, furs, plate glass, grand pianos and silks. All told 393 separate items were listed.[3] The classification was soon considered too crude and already by the autumn of 1849 the goods managers, at their monthly conferences, were discussing amendments. The *Second General Classification of Goods* was published in November 1851 and applied from January 1st, in the following year. Some of the items which it and its predecessor had included would leave modern railwaymen—not to mention the general public—completely bewildered. Thus in class I of the 1852 classification were included Canada plates, felloes and flummery; in class II besides cockles and mussels there were cutch, garancine and orchilla weeds; class III included Canada stoves, nux vomica and periwinkles; cornice poles, puncheons and teazles appeared in class IV and elephants' teeth figured prominently in class V. The principal innovation in 1852 was the introduction of a class for minerals only and a special class for full loads of not less than one ton. Although some of the more colourful items, such as flummery and nux vomica, had disappeared

[1] RCH 1/179: Goods Managers Conference, August 17, 1847.
[2] RCH 1/2: Committee, September 22, 1847, and March 9, 1848.
[3] RCH 7/38.

from the classification by the middle sixties, the grouping of goods made in 1852, in its essentials, was adhered to by the railways until 1928. By 1879 the *Railway Clearing House General Classification of Goods* filled a 129-page book.

When Parliament was debating the terms of the Railway and Canal Traffic Bill in 1888 it was considered axiomatic that the job of drafting a revised classification of goods for inclusion in the Bill should be given to the goods managers of the Clearing House.[1] They wisely seized the opportunity of inviting the Irish goods managers to confer with them in devising a classification which became applicable on both sides of the Irish Sea.[2]

Admittedly the Clearing House lacked the power to impose on the railway companies a uniform scale of freight charges. But the fact that it proved possible to achieve a common classification of goods undoubtedly simplified the task of standardising freight charges at a later date and certainly helped the settlement of accounts for through traffic.

While Braithwaite Poole presided over the meetings of the goods managers (which he did for a period of nearly ten years) he made strenuous efforts to obtain agreement on measures for the more economical working of the goods traffic. Although he had been obliged to bow to the majority opinion in October 1847, that one ton should constitute a minimum loading for a waggon, he always considered this rule as unnecessarily wasteful of rolling stock. In May 1852 he proposed 'that two tons weight in one waggon be run throughout as a minimum load', but he was unable to win the support of the other managers for this sensible proposition. In the five years that had elapsed since the rule was first drafted, many new railway goods depots had been opened up and it was felt that raising the minimum load to two tons 'would very seriously interfere with traffic at all small stations'.[3] In this way a practice became established on British railways of running goods trains at frequent intervals and with many of the goods waggons

---

[1] RCH 1/187: Goods Managers Conference, minute 394 of October 9, 1888.

[2] RCH 1/187: Goods Managers Conference, report dated October 26, 1888.

[3] RCH 6/179: Goods Managers Conference, minute 457 of March 20, 1852.

less than half filled, instead of providing a less frequent, but more economically loaded, service. Once the tradition had been established there was less incentive to build larger capacity trucks. Merchants and traders came to expect frequent and fast deliveries, and such competition as existed between the companies put a premium on the light loading of waggons and high speed and frequency of the goods trains. It is not surprising that goods transport on British railways was more expensive than it was in Belgium, France, Germany and the United States, where the organisation of the goods traffic was more economical.

At the beginning of the First World War freight charges on British railways for the conveyance of iron ore over a variety of distances were over 90% higher than on the railways of the USA, France and Germany. Average rates for the conveyance of timber in the United Kingdom were nearly three times those of the railways in France and the Netherlands, more than three times the level of rates in Belgium and Sweden and nearly double those of Italy. Freights for the carriage of grain were higher than those of the seven other principal grain-carrying railroad systems. Even in the carriage of textiles, charges on British railways were more than two-thirds higher than those in the United States.[1]

A complementary policy to the fuller loading of waggons on their outward journey was that of reducing to a minimum the number of occasions when they were returned empty to their owners. In October 1848 Braithwaite Poole secured agreement to the following resolution:

'That it is highly expedient to discountenance the practice of returning waggons empty because it involves an unprofitable use of locomotive power and opens a door to unfair dealing in those cases in which waggons may be returned in either of two ways, and that each member be requested to give the subject his attentive consideration with a view to providing such a rememdy as will prevent the present waste of locomotive power and ensure to the companies a fair remuneration for the use of their waggons.'[2]

[1] Bureau of Railway Economics, Washington, D.C. *Comparison of Railway Freight Rates*, *U.S.*, *the principal countries of Europe of South Australia and South Africa*, *1915*.

[2] RCH 1/179: Goods Managers Conference, minute 167 of August 31, 1848.

As empty waggons were not subject to a mileage charge there was a temptation on the part of companies that had borrowed them to return them by unnecessarily roundabout routes in order to keep direct, through routes clear for more profitable traffic. The recommendation 'that goods waggons should be returned by the shortest route'[1] was generally followed since the policy of frequent services and well below capacity loading intensified the demand for waggons. It was utopian to expect compliance with the earlier recommendation against returning waggons empty so long as the light loading of outward bound waggons continued.

The goods managers gave some small encouragement to agricultural improvement by their resolution of July 1848 which recommended that on the occasion of Royal Agricultural Society Shows cattle should be conveyed both to and from the nearest railway station free of charge and that no mileage should be levied on the cattle waggons employed in this task. Implements were to be charged normal rates to shows of the society but returned free if unsold.[2]

From September 1854 the recommendations of the goods managers had first to be approved by the Conference of General Managers before receiving their final vetting from the Clearing House committee.[3] It was a procedural change which did not benefit the farmers to whom the general managers were less inclined to make concessions.

## IV

Under the expert and far sighted leadership of Braithwaite Poole the goods managers during their first four years of co-operation had done a great deal to lift the goods traffic out of the doldrums of the years 1842–47. At the meeting held in July 1850 the chairman was in an expansive mood. He congratulated the twenty-five goods managers present on 'the businesslike manner in which their discussions had always been conducted' and considered that 'the

[1] RCH 1/179: Goods Managers Conference, minute 177 of September 22, 1848.

[2] RCH 1/179: Goods Managers Conference, minute 158 of July 21, 1848.

[3] RCH 1/3: Committee resolution September 13, 1854.

arrangements for conducting the through traffic had advanced so far towards maturity' that it would be sufficient thereafter to meet once in two months instead of monthly. No dissenting voice was heard.[1]

The statistics of the goods traffic, though incomplete, show that the meeting's optimism was not misplaced. Morison's reports reveal that the Clearing House receipts from goods traffic in the six months ending June 30, 1848 were more than 50% greater than the receipts from both goods and passenger traffic combined in the corresponding period of 1846, and yet the value of goods traffic cleared was more than doubled again by June 1851. In 1848 Clearing House receipts from goods traffic cannot have been more than one-sixth of total receipts from total railway goods traffic in Great Britain. By 1851 the Clearing House proportion had risen to one quarter and by 1857 to nearly a third of the national figure.

Contributing handsomely to this remarkable expansion in the value of transactions recorded in the Clearing House was the decision of those companies who were not already acting as goods carriers, to follow the recommendation of the first meeting of goods managers that 'companies should carry on their own account and in connection with each other'. Carr Glyn told the shareholders of the London and North Western Railway on February 18, 1848, that the 'new system' (of the company acting as carrier of goods) had 'fully answered expectations'. On the following day George Hudson told a meeting of the Midland Railway that although there had been many complaints when the company first undertook the carrying of goods, they had soon died down and the goods traffic had 'considerably increased'. Reports from other companies were in a similar vein.[2]

There was an impressive growth in the number of important companies represented at the conferences of goods managers: from eight in 1847 to seventeen in 1850 and twenty-three in 1852. Among the companies unrepresented at the first meeting but participating in 1850 were the Midland, the Great Northern, the Manchester, Sheffield and Lincolnshire, the Chester and Holyhead,

[1] RCH 1/179: Goods Managers Conference, minute 334 of July 18, 1850.
[2] Samuel Salt: *Railway and Commercial Information*, London, 1850, p. 105.

the Newcastle and Carlisle, and the North and South Stafford-shire. With all the important railways north of the Thames taking part—though the Southern companies were still conspicuous by their absence—it is not surprising that the value of goods exchanged should have increased so dramatically.

It can safely be asserted that it was largely through the agency of the Clearing House that by 1852 on the nation's railways the receipts from goods traffic exceeded those from the carriage of passengers.

### V

The influence of the Clearing House on the growth of railway goods traffic was substantial; its control over arrangements for the transport of coal was minimal. The slow growth of the coal traffic on the railways has often been the subject of surprised comment.[1]

It was unfortunate from the viewpoint of the growth of long-distance coal haulage by rail that just at the time the extension of the rail network was making such a development physically possible, competition from sea-borne coal was intensified. Coal deliveries to London by rail began in 1845. That same year there came to an end 'The Limitation of the Vend' by which, since 1603, the Tyneside coal vendors had carefully regulated the amount of coal sent coast-wise to London to prevent prices falling to un-remunerative levels. After 1845 the price of sea coal sold in London fell sharply. By March 1851 it was down to 14s a ton for the best quality and 12s a ton for 'seconds'. Coal factors pleaded with the coal owners on Tyneside to take steps to halt 'the reckless race to ruin', but more than twenty years later a House of Commons select committee reported that there was no reason to suppose that any system of restriction of coal output existed.[2] The extreme competitiveness of sea borne coal prices undoubtedly reduced the railway companies' incentive to engage in the traffic and increased the importance of satisfactory Clearing House arrangements for the economical long distance haulage of coal by rail.

In 1845 railways carried but 8,377 tons of the 3,472,000 tons of coal brought to London. It was not until 1867 that the quantity

[1] See B. R. Mitchell: 'The coming of the Railway and United Kingdom Economic Growth', *Journal of Economic History*, Vol. XXIV, 1964, p. 315.
[2] Raymond Smith: *Sea Coal for London*, London, 1961, pp. 276-84.

of coal carried to the London railheads exceeded that brought into the Pool of London by sea. By this time railway waggons were hauling over three million tons of coal to the capital. But it is clear that it had taken the railways the best part of thirty years to establish their ascendancy in this particular market. That the growth of the coal traffic was at a slower pace than the traffic in general merchandise was in part due to the failure of the Clearing House to establish an agreed set of regulations for this vitally important part of the railways' business.

While it is true that in the early years of Queen Victoria's reign domestic consumers had an irrational prejudice against 'inland coal' and much preferred the 'sea coal' to which they had grown accustomed, this prejudice would have been more quickly over-come had coal conveyed by rail been cheaper in price.[1] It is also true that because of the attractiveness of the passenger business the construction of goods waggons took second place to the build-ing of passenger coaches. In December 1844, in a letter to Carr Glyn, congratulating him on the decision of the London and Birmingham Board to branch out into the business of carrying coal, George Hudson observed that the coal owners were 'like us all short of waggons and blame the companies for what is their own fault'.[2] Nevertheless, had efficient arrangements been made for the through haulage of coal the profits to be earned from this traffic would have stimulated a rapid increase in the supply of waggons.

A more serious obstacle to the growth of the coal trade was the widespread variation between the railway companies' tonnage rates and tolls. In 1844 the Liverpool and Manchester Railway charged but $\frac{1}{2}$d per ton mile. At the other extreme the Edinburgh and Dalkeith levied a toll of 4d per ton mile. In 1846 prices ranged from the $\frac{1}{4}$d per ton mile charged by the Great North of England Railway through the $\frac{1}{2}$d per ton mile of the Hull and Selby line to the $1\frac{1}{2}$d per ton mile of the Leicester and Swannington. At a halfpenny per ton mile coal could have been carried from the South Yorkshire coalfield to London at a charge of 5s 5d a ton which would have been competitive with sea borne coal which

---

[1] Royal Commission on Railways, 1866. Evidence of general manager of the Great Northern Railway. BPP 1866, Vol.–Q. 1263981.

[2] BTC HL2/9, R 236 London Midland Scottish Collection of Historical Letters, Hudson to Carr Glyn, December 27, 1844.

cost 5s to 5s 8d per ton to bring down from Newcastle, plus lighterage and other charges in the Pool of London at 2s 7½d, making a total of 8s 4d.[1] But standardisation of such competitive charges under the aegis of the Clearing House proved unattainable for two principal reasons; the failure to secure agreement to impose demurrage on coal waggons and the independence of the private owner of the coal waggons.

The Clearing House Committee gave attention to the regulation of the coal trade at a comparatively early date. After disagreements between the companies had been aired in a long discussion at the meeting on September 22, 1847, it was resolved 'that no demurrage be charged for coal waggons'.[2] It was not a decision which satisfied the York, Newcastle and Berwick and other Northern companies which stood to profit most from an extension of the coal trade. They reopened the discussion at a meeting of the goods managers in September 1848 but failed to secure the complete reversal of the earlier decision of the Clearing House committee. The meeting came to the conclusion that it would not be feasible to charge demurrage for coal and coke waggons consigned to private parties but that demurrage at the rate of 3s per day should be allowed for all waggons consigned to railway companies.[3] The recommendation was passed on to the general managers who gave it somewhat leisurely consideration. However, by December 1851 they had agreed to a list of 'Proposed regulations for charging demurrage on coal and coke waggons'. They endorsed the goods managers' plan to charge demurrage on railway-owned coal waggons, but also proposed that if either coal or coke waggons were detained by private parties for more than three days, the company on whose sidings they had stood should be charged demurrage by the owners of the waggons.[4] Had these proposals been endorsed by the companies it is arguable that the country's coal trade would have benefited by a quicker turn round of rolling stock.

But when the general managers' plan was put before the Clearing

---

[1] Anon: *Ships and Railways*, London, 1846. (British Museum reference number 1396 h 30 10), pp. 11, 22, 30. BPP 1841, Vol. XXV, Appendix XVI, p. 508.    [2] RCH 1/2: Minute 69.

[3] RCH 1/179: Goods Managers Conference, September 22, November 17, and December 21, 1848.

[4] RCH 1/70: General Managers Committee, December 9, 1851.

House committee the following day the views of the companies' representatives proved to be 'very conflicting', and the managers were asked to revise their proposals in the light of the criticisms made.[1] Three months later the amended proposals, which exempted from demurrage waggons carrying coal or coke intended for shipment by sea, river or canal, were approved by the committee to take effect from April 1, 1852.[2] No sooner had the members of the committee congratulated themselves on solving a tricky problem than fresh difficulties emerged. At the meeting on June 9th Morison was obliged to confess that 'letters had been received from several companies declining to adopt the regulations for charging demurrage for coal and coke waggons'. In his report Morison gave a characteristically clear summary of the reasons why many companies were not co-operating:

'The regulations . . . are resisted by several companies and on different grounds. Some deny their liability for demurrage because they receive merely a toll for the carriage of the coals; others limit their liability to those cases in which they pay mileage for the waggons—which is virtually nullifying the regulations. For by the custom of the trade in England the coal owners pay the mileage. A third class refuse to be bound by regulations which are practically repudiated by those with whom they have interchange stock. Of the companies which have not openly objected to the regulations, few as yet have sent returns of the waggons they receive. This state of things will ultimately tell against the companies who, admitting their liability, neglect to send the necessary returns.'[3]

The general managers' way out of the difficulty was to suggest that the new regulations be applied only to those companies that agreed to them and that they should be inoperative on the lines of the dissenting companies.[4] The committee later agreed to this suggestion.[5]

Such an unrealistic compromise quickly proved to be useless. Three months after it was attempted, Morison conceded that the

[1] RCH 1/2: Committee Resolution 207 of December 10, 1851.
  See also British Railways Board: *The Reshaping of British Railways* (The Beeching Report), 1963, p. 30, indicating the survival of this problem into the 1960s.
[2] RCH 1/2: Committee resolution 220 of March 10, 1852.
[3] K. Morison's report to the Committee, June 9, 1852.
[4] RCH 1/70: General Managers Committee, July 13, 1852.
[5] RCH 1/2: Committee resolution 248 of September 8, 1852.

revised scheme had 'proved inoperative' since 'the greatest number of the companies had availed themselves of their traditional right of withdrawing their assent were in doubt as to the proper construction of the rules. Consequently the Clearing House had been unable to keep an account of any part of the stock used for the carriage of coal and coke. It was a complete breakdown. With his usual perceptiveness Morison had warned the committee, in September 1852,

'that where an option is given either to adopt or reject regulations involving pecuniary liabilities, companies will take advantage of this option whenever such step is dictated by their immediate interests. It would appear, therefore, that in cases of this kind your committee can pursue no middle course between making such regulations equally binding on all, or abandoning them altogether'.[1]

Bowing to the inevitable, the committee, at its December 1852 meeting, rescinded the Resolution 220 passed in March of that year and resolved that in future demurrage would not be charged on any coal waggons but would be charged on coke waggons consigned to railway companies.[2]

These setbacks might have been overcome later had it not been for a Court of Chancery ruling in the case E.S. and A.S. Prior vs The Great Northern Railway in 1858. This company had played a leading part in developing the rail transport of coal to the London area and until 1859 it directly marketed its rapidly growing consignments to householders and commercial and industrial customers. The colliery companies and coal merchants strongly resented this incursion into their business preserves and on March 24, 1857 the Coal Meters Committee of Newcastle voted a sum of £500 to be spent in combating the growth of railway coal merchanting. There is no evidence that the coal merchants E.S. and A.S. Prior were directly backed by the Coal Meters Committee, but there can be no doubt that the Court of Chancery ruling that the Great Northern Railway was not legally entitled to engage in the sale of coal must have pleased its members. From 1859 the railway company was obliged to confine itself to the levying of tolls on coal

[1] RCH 1/2: Morison's report to the committee, September 8, 1852.
[2] RCH 1/2: Committee resolution 255 of December 8, 1852.

carried for others.[1] Had the court ruling been in favour of the railway instead of the coal merchants, it is not unreasonable to assume that the Great Northern's coal merchanting business would have expanded and that this company's profitable example would have been followed by other railways. Had the marketing of coal become dominated by large concerns, it would have been easier for the goods managers of the Clearing House to agree on a standardised pattern of mileage and demurrage charges at low enough levels to encourage the more rapid expansion of the railway companies' coal traffic.

With the success of the coal merchants in 1858 and the rapid opening up of new collieries the number of privately owned waggons cluttering up the railways greatly increased. One of the most profitable outlets for a man with a couple of hundred pounds of spare capital was to invest in a coal waggon whose useful life might exceed twenty-five years. He, or the coal merchant to whom it was dispatched, could use it in a railway siding as storage space for coal awaiting sale to domestic consumers. Neither the wagon owner nor the merchant were prepared to recognise the authority of the Clearing House in the matter of demurrage charges though they were prepared to settle privately with the railway company for payment of siding rent.

The consequence of the absence of Clearing House control and the diversification of railway waggon ownership were the multiplication of coal traffic agreements negotiated on a company to company basis. With the inevitable variation of charges thus negotiated it proved more difficult to fix through freight rates for the carriage of coal which were competitive with the freights charged for coastwise transport. As early as the summer of 1849 Braithwaite Poole, in a farsighted report to the directors of the London and North Western Railway had recommended signing contracts with large colliery concerns such as the Clay Cross Company for 'full train loads' of coal. He urged upon the directors the abandonment of the 'inflexible rule of per ton per mile', as if coals were as valuable 'as silks and other goods'.

Although there were individual instances of such agreements

[1] BTHR, GN 1/24 and 1/25: Great Northern Railway Board meetings. Minutes 228 of March 30, 1858, 622 of August 3, 1858, and 528 of March 8, 1849. *Herapath's Railway Journal*, July 17, 1858, p. 589, August 27, 1859, Raymond Smith, *op. cit.* p. 284.

for trainload consignments of coal, as late as 1963 there were complaints about the uneconomic loads the railways were being called upon to transport.[1] The failure of the Clearing House to obtain agreement on a policy for the coal traffic meant that for at least a century this branch of the railways' business was conducted in an inefficient and expensive manner.

The rail haulage of coal grew despite the existence of the Clearing House, not because of it. The disadvantages of high freight charges and the slow turn round of waggons were partially offset by the rapid increase in the number of the coal depots. The general manager of the London and North Western Railway told the Royal Commission on Canals in 1908 that the railways had no less than 155 depots conveniently situated all over the Metropolitan area so that merchants could deliver coal to householders with the minimum amount of cartage.[2] Nevertheless these numerous depots were still being used a generation after the arrival of the motor lorry had made the continued functioning of the majority of them unjustifiable.

In the later part of the nineteenth century there were frequent complaints from traders that the terminal charges levied by the railways were excessive. It is important to examine how the terminal charges came into being and to what extent they were justifiable.

The majority of railway companies in the 1830s delegated the management of the goods traffic to the private carriers, merely charging a toll for the use of rolling stock and the station services. In these circumstances no question arose of a terminal charge by the railway company and no mention of such charges was made in any of the early railway acts. The first use of the word terminal came in the Lancaster and Carlisle Railway Act in 1844 and the only other use of it in a private railway Act was in the North Staffordshire Railway Act of 1880.[3]

In the course of 1847, however, when a large number of important companies decided to switch to a policy of direct management

---

[1] Braithwaite Poole: *A Report to the Road and Traffic Committee of the Northern Division of Directors of the London and North Western Railway on the Coal Traffic*, September 20, 1849. British Railways Board: *The Reshaping of British Railways: Report* (The Beeching Report), 1963, p. 31.

[2] Royal Commission on Canals, BPP 1908, Vol. IV, Qs 26607–9.

[3] W. R. Lawson: *British Railways: A Financial and Commercial Survey*, London, 1913, p. 140.

of the goods traffic, they had to decide whether or not to make a separate charge for the station services (i.e. maintenance of sidings, loading bays, warehousing, portering, etc.) at both ends of the journey, and for the costs of collection and delivery of the goods, or whether to make the freight charges inclusive of these terminal expenses. Since some companies already managed a part of the goods traffic on their own lines and already had a charge for station-to-station freight, it was decided to make the terminal charge quite distinct from the charge made for simply conveying the goods between two terminals.

The goods managers examined the question at their very first conference in January 1847. They established the principle that in the division of traffic receipts the terminal charges should be deducted before the remainder of the proceeds were split between the companies concerned on the basis of mileage. This decision immediately established the individual companies vested interests in the maintenance of these separate charges. At the same meeting it was decided that terminal expenses in London should be calculated at 8s 6d per ton on all goods carted to or from Camden Station (the London and North Western Railway goods terminal) but that the charge should be only 2s 3d when the goods were not carted to or from the station by the railway company. Terminal charges in the country were to be at the rate of 4s a ton on carted goods and 1s 6d on goods not carted.[1] These were decisions of the greatest importance since the precedent established with respect to Camden in 1847 was followed for other London termini at subsequent dates irrespective of variations in the cost of land, labour, cartage, etc. In November 1850 the Great Northern claimed the same charges at their London termini.[2] In 1852 the London and North Western Railway claim to make the same charges at Poplar and 'other Metropolitan stations' as were made at Camden, was granted by the goods managers.[3] Other companies with terminals in London followed suit. In 1867 the Great

[1] RCH 1/179: Minutes 24 and 25 of Goods Managers Conference, January 19, 1847.

[2] RCH 1/179: Minute 366 of Goods Managers Conference, January 23, 1851.

[3] RCH 1/179: Minute 449 of Goods Managers Conference, March 19, 1852.

Eastern was authorised to make what had now become the standard London charges at Devonshire Street, London Docks,
Victoria Docks and Blackwall.[1] For goods not subject to special
terminal charges, the rates remained substantially unaltered until
the First World War, and yet, commenting upon them twenty
years after he had had a hand in first imposing them, Captain Mark
Huish, one time general manager of the London and North
Western Railway, declared that the particular figures chosen were
'jumped at very much in the first instance'.[2]

A number of conscience-stricken goods managers, convinced
that terminal charges were excessive, from time to time endeavoured to persuade their opposite numbers meeting in conference
to alter the decisions made in January 1847. Their efforts were
fruitless. In November 1849 the goods managers of the Chester
and Birkenhead and Scottish Central Railways proposed:

'1. That the allowance to be made by the Clearing House under
the head of terminal expenses on goods shall be restricted to the
payment of such charges as fairly fall under the denomination of
terminal expenses, viz: cartage, loading and unloading of goods,
proportion of rent and maintenance of goods station, fire insurance,
collective and guarantee of accounts, in the terms of the Clearing
House regulations.

'2. That the traffic returns sent to the Clearing House shall at
all times distinctly specify whether the goods have been carted or
not carted at the expense of the terminal party, and they shall be
signed by the goods agent and allowance made accordingly.

'3. That the terminal rates be reduced by one third of their
present amount.'

Mr Roberts of the Chester and Birkenhead Railway argued, in
support of these proposals, that it was important that the principle
on which the terminal was based should be 'strictly just'. Many
of the companies, he claimed, made a profit by the existing rates
especially in those cases in which the customer paid for cartage
which the railway did not perform. It was important that 'rates

[1] RCH 1/182: Minute 2694 of Goods Managers Conference, January
24, 1867.
[2] Royal Commission on Railways 1867, BPP 1867, XXXVIII, Q. 16,003.

87

allowed for terminal expenses should not exceed the expenditure incurred'. Both Captain Laws of the Lancashire and Yorkshire Railway and Captain Mark Huish of the London and North Western Railway opposed the new proposals. They claimed that the rates were not too high and that to reduce them would lead to a reduction in tolls generally and that it was therefore 'inexpedient to make any alterations'. Mr Roberts resolution was defeated by twenty-eight votes to two.[1] A similar attempt by Mr Braithwaite Poole made a year earlier was equally unsuccessful.[2]

A more rational defence of the regulations for terminal charges was made by Mr J. Allport, general manager of the Midland Railway, when he gave evidence before the Royal Commission on Railways in May 1866. He claimed that the reason why the goods managers had reached their decision in January 1847 was to avoid injustice to individual companies when dividing the traffic receipts. The charges were made with an eye to the achievement of rough justice between the companies: not as between traders and the railways. To illustrate his point he cited the example of the North Staffordshire Railway's carriage of ale to Liverpool. Some consignments used the tracks of the Midland Railway for the first three quarters of a mile of the journey. If the division of traffic receipts had been made solely on the basis of mileage, the share of the Midland Railway would have been 'some 2d or 2½'. With such a meagre return it would have been 'utterly impossible' for the company to conduct such business at a profit. The clerical labour involved if the Clearing House had attempted to arrive at a just terminal charge for each particular case would have been prohibitively high. The general regulation of the Clearing House was, no doubt, arbitrary and unjust in particular cases, but it was based on a general principle of a just balance being struck between the claims of the companies.[3]

Nevertheless, the maintenance for more than half a century of the fixed charges for terminals meant that there was no competition

[1] RCH 1/179: Minute 266 of Goods Managers Conference, November 22, 1849.
[2] RCH 1/179: Minute 150 of Goods Managers Conference, June 30, 1848.
[3] Royal Commission on Railways 1867, BPP 1867, XXXVIII, Q. 16,930.

between the companies in respect of prices charged. Instead the companies competed with each other in respect of the frequency, range and promptitude of deliveries, in generosity in making good losses or damage, etc. They did this until the cost of these extravagantly provided services began to approximate to the terminal charge made. What was happening was that part of the costs of business organisation and management were being shifted from the trader to the railways. A railway goods manager from the potteries told the members of the Royal Commission 1866 how it worked out in practice:

'Do you think the public have gained in facilities, although they have gained nothing in competition as regards the rates? They have gained enormously in facilities. In our own district of the Potteries it has been so. We used to call on the producers as it suited our convenience; but we now have to call upon them four, five or six times a day, and as fast as a manufacturer has packed a crate he has a team and cart waiting for it; so that it relieves him of the expense of finding warehouse room. He used formerly to have to find warehouse room for his goods, and to keep them on hand until he could complete his order. Now as fast as he packs his crate we take it from him and store it, thus saving him the expense of warehouse room. It is really quite as much competition of facilities as of rates.'[1]

It is clear that a decision of the Goods Managers Conference in the Clearing House had had a profound effect on the costs of distribution of British merchandise. Collection and delivery services were unnecessarily duplicated. It is very doubtful whether the saving in warehousing costs was sufficient to offset expensive terminal charges which were at a higher level than they need have been given rational planning of the services of distribution.

[1] Royal Commission on Railways 1867, evidence of P. Morris. Q. 14,284.

# CHAPTER V

# THE PARCELS TRAFFIC: THE CLEARING
# HOUSE AND THE GPO

I

Within six years of the establishment of the Penny Post in Britain
an early writer on railway management showed remarkable
prescience when he wrote about one aspect of the railways' goods
business:

'Viewing the question of the delivery of parcels as respects
regularity and economy, it is probable that the Post Office authorities by having the distributory apparatus ready at their hands, and
already adapted for this special service, could accommodate the
public at rates lower than separate companies, all requiring to
incur the expense of separate management. It behoves the companies, therefore, if they wish to retain this source of traffic under
their own control without any intermediate agency, to make the
charges so low that there shall arise no public or general desire
that it should be confided to the Post Office'.[1]

It was the failure of the companies to recognise the soundness of
this advice which delayed the introduction of a comprehensive and
cheap parcels service for at least twenty years.

In January 1842, when the Clearing House started business,
three different systems for the carriage of letters and parcels were
in operation on the railways of Britain. At the time of the introduction of the Penny Post on January 10, 1840, those companies,
such as the Grand Junction and the London and Birmingham,
which had contracts with the GPO, were paid on the basis of the

[1] J. Butler Williams, F.S.S., F.G.S.: 'On the Principles of Railway
Management'. Paper read before the Statistical Society of London, March
16, 1846.

weight of the mail irrespective of the distance it was carried. The carriage of other packets and parcels was the responsibility either of the carriers who paid toll to the railway companies for the use of their waggons, or of the railway companies themselves acting as carriers. In both these cases the charge was made proportional to the distance as well as to the weight. After 1847, when most railway companies had decided to become exclusive carriers of goods on their lines, the practice of charging on the basis of both weight and distance was continued. But great variations in policy remained. Some companies exercised their statutory right to charge all parcels of less than 5 cwt. the full rate for a quarter of a ton. Others lowered charges in the expectation of attracting more custom. The policy of the Great Western Railway and many other large companies was to vary charges not only according to distance but also according to the time of train by which the parcels were dispatched—an arrangement unpopular with businessmen since it was an irksome thing to have to remember the proper time for sending parcels at the lower rates.

Because of the high charges made for parcel conveyance on the railways and the variations in practice of the different companies, it became increasingly common for traders to split up their parcels into smaller packets and send them through the post. But not all consignments were capable of such division and, before 1847, the Post Office would not accept packets weighing more than 1 lb. Furthermore charges were prohibitively high, the postage on a packet weighing 1 lb. being 2s 8d.

In the same year in which the Clearing House was founded Rowland Hill advocated the introduction of a parcel post on the same basic principles as his penny post scheme recently adopted— a uniform national charge based on the weight of the package and irrespective of the distance it was to be carried. His dismissal from the Treasury later in 1842 prevented him from giving the idea practical application, but in July 1843 he elaborated his plan before the Select Committee on Postage.[1]

In 1846 the directors of two railway companies were more alive to the possibilities of extending the parcels traffic of the

---

[1] Sir Rowland Hill and George Birkbeck Hill: *The Life of Sir Rowland Hill and the History of the Penny Postage*, London, 1880, Vol. 2, p. 336. Select Committee on Postage, minutes of evidence, Q. 82, BPP. 1843. Vol. VIII.

railways than were most of their contemporaries on other railway Boards. On March 14th the Board of the London and North Western Railway gave its general manager, Captain Mark Huish, authority to introduce, for an experimental period, for all places between London and Preston, a uniform rate of charge on parcels irrespective of distance, the scale being: under 3 lb., 1s; 3 lb. to 6 lb., 1s 6d, 6 lb. to 12 lb., 2s. The plan was also approved by the Board of the Leeds and Manchester Railway for stations on its line.[1] However, the Boards of other railway companies were in no hurry at all to follow this example and it was many decades before such proposals were generally followed.

In the meantime Rowland Hill made a further attempt to improve the postal services from his new vantage point as secretary to the Postmaster General. Once more he toyed with the idea of a parcels post, but finding that the proposal 'would raise more opposition in the railway companies' than he thought it 'prudent to encounter',[2] he was content to settle, in 1853, for a book post by which open-ended parcels of books would be sent through the post for a charge of 6d per pound weight. While this was a concession particularly welcomed by scholars and lending libraries it by no means satisfied the commercial community.

The innovation was particularly resented by the railway companies which considered that the new scale of post office charges had led to a reduction of their receipts from parcels traffic. Thus Mr Badham, general superintendent of the Bristol and Exeter Railway, complained to the Select Committee on the Conveyance of Mails by Railway in 1854, that he knew of cases in which the ordinary charge for parcels would have been 2s 9d, but by putting them in the letter bag with ends open they were conveyed for 6d. At the same time Captain Huish bemoaned 'the steady decrease in parcels' conveyed directly by his railway following the introduction of the book post.[3]

[1] BTHR, LNW 1/20: Minute 33 of Board of Directors, 1843, Vol. VIII, London and North Western Railway. *The Morning Chronicle*, March 11, 1846. Before the Select Committee on Railways in 1844. Captain Laws had advocated a uniform rate of 1s for all parcels under 28 lb. in weight. BPP 1844, Vol. XI, Q. 6227.

[2] Hill: *op. cit.* Vol. 2, p. 22.

[3] BPP 1854, Vol. XI: Select Committee on Conveyance of Mails by Railway, minutes of evidence, Qs 3467, 2581.

## II

Although the railway companies that had mail contracts could look forward to a share of the increased revenue brought in by the book post, it was becoming more urgent to make the railway parcels service more competitive. Nevertheless the charge for parcels was not appreciably reduced after the introduction of the book post.

In one respect indeed the railway parcels deteriorated rather than improved in the early 1850s. Until 1852 a number of the railway companies had carried pattern and sample parcels free of charge, but the general opinion of the goods managers expressed at their meeting on January 16th of that year, was that this concession to businessmen 'should be discontinued with as little delay as possible'.[1]

The high cost of dispatching parcels—whether by carrier or by railway—and the failure of the Post Office to extend its services more rapidly, was a matter of concern of those members of the Society of Arts (later the Royal Society of Arts) who had sponsored the great Exhibition of 1851. No sooner had the work in connection with the exhibition been largely completed than they set about forming a postal association to agitate for a parcel post and improved postal communications with overseas territories. Information and support was quickly gathered from seventy of the largest towns in the kingdom.[2] In 1858, at a big public meeting held in the metropolis, a report on the need for better postal services, drafted by Edwin Chadwick, was enthusiastically adopted. Nevertheless, in the opinion of Rowland Hill, 'the ill judged opposition of the railway companies remained a constant obstacle'[3] to any improvements which required Parliamentary sanction.

The failure of both the railways and the GPO to extend the principles of the penny post to the parcels traffic encouraged the carriers in their efforts to circumvent the high charges of the railway companies for the conveyance of 'smalls'. In the knowledge

[1] RCH 1/179: Minute 432, Goods Managers Conference.
[2] *Journal of the Society of Arts*, November 4, 1870, Vol. XVIII, no. 937. I am grateful to Mr D. G. Allan of the Royal Society of Arts for this information.　　　　　　　　[3] Hill: *op. cit.* Vol. 2, p. 336.

that the cost of sending large consignments of goods was less than
that of a corresponding weight split up into a large number of
small parcels, they purchased huge hampers, stuffed them with a
large quantity of small parcels for different addresses in the same
large town or city, and consigned the hamper to themselves at the
railway terminal. The contents of the hamper were then distributed
to local addresses by the carrier or his agent. Instead of bending
all their energies to make the railway parcels service more competitive by means of a low scale of charges made irrespective of
distance, the railway companies sought by every means, including
frequent, but largely futile, resort to law[1] to prevent the carriers
employing the packed parcels 'escape hatch'.

Apart from individual railway companies' resort to law, many
attempts were made by the goods managers in conference to reach
agreement on a method of deterring carriers from making up large
packages or hampers of small parcels. In July 1848 they recommended the following scale of charges for packed parcels:

| | |
|---|---|
| For distances up to 100 miles | 1d  per lb. |
| For distances up to 101–200 miles | 1½d per lb. |
| For distances up to 201–300 miles | 2d  per lb. |
| For distances up to 301–400 miles | 2½d per lb. |

An extra charge of ½d was made for every additional 100 miles.[2]
In June 1849 it was agreed to recommend that packages of packed
parcels be not received unless fully prepaid locally and that no
company should book them over another company's line.[3] A month
later, however, the subject was again discussed at great length in
view of the reluctance of a number of companies to limit their
parcels traffic to their own rail networks, and it was agreed to delay
implementing the decision of the previous meeting.[4] Nothing
further was done along these lines because of the continuing
disagreement among the companies. In the mid 1860s there was

[1] E.g. from Pickford vs Grand Junction, *Herapath's Railway Journal*,
November 12, 1845, to Baxendale vs London and South Western Railway.
*Railway Times*, February 3, 1866, p. 123.

[2] RCH 1/179: Minute 1571, Goods Managers Conference, July 21,
1848.

[3] RCH 1/179: Minute 226, Goods Managers Conference, June 21,
1849.

[4] RCH 1/179: Minute 233, Goods Managers Conference, July 20, 1849.

renewed concern at the success of the carriers and in April 1866 the goods managers unanimously recommended that

'a special rate, say double the ordinary small rate or double the 5th class rate, be charged on all consignments of small packages (whether loose or packed together) the whole of which, although consigned to one individual, are not intended for his own use; and that notice be given to the public that packages containing parcels for various persons, but consigned to one person, and packages sent loose and intended for various persons, although consigned to one person, will be charged the higher rate, as before quoted'.[1]

If the goods managers thought that by the passing of this resolution they had dealt a mortal blow to the business of the carriers they were quickly disappointed. One after another of the legal advisers of the big railway companies warned that the railways lacked the necessary statutory powers to carry out the policy recommended. Not a single company was prepared to take the bold action the Goods Managers Conference had recommended.[2]

Largely because of the opposition of the London and North Western and the Eastern Counties Railways to a policy of high charges for packed parcels, agreement on a scale of charges for this type of traffic was not reached until 1877. In April of that year the following, more moderate, scale of charges was agreed for application from October 1, 1877:[3]

(a) Packages containing only one description of goods (such as drapery, silk, stationery, drugs, etc) the contents of which are specifically declared, are to be charged at the ordinary rates for such articles.

(b) Packages the specific contents of which are not declared, and miscellaneous lots of small parcels containing different descriptions of goods, and intended for distribution to separate persons, be classified as under:

[1] RCH 1/182: Minute 2555, Goods Managers Conference, April 26, 1866.

[2] RCH 1/182: Minute 2583, Goods Managers Conference, July 26, 1866.

[3] RCH 1/185: Minute 5041 and 5111 of Goods Managers Conferences of April 26, 1877, and August 7, 1877.

(i) Packages under 500 lb., enclosed in hampers, cases or wrappers, sent by one consignor to one consignee, containing small packages for delivery to separate persons.      5th Class

(ii) Lots of small packages, under 500 lb. sent loose from one consignor to one consignee.      5th Class +25%

(iii) Parcels in lots of 500 lb. and upwards packed or loose      5th Class +25%[1]

The carriers meanwhile had found other means of circumventing the high charges of the railway companies. To the bigger business firms with large and regular consignments of goods, they offered yearly contracts at much reduced rates. Thus Sutton and Co. agreed with individual firms to carry parcels under 12 lb. in weight, between London and Nottingham, for between £6 and £12 per annum, depending on the ascertained volume of the traffic.

The goods managers spent so much time in devising means to counter the packed parcels threat to their own 'smalls' business that they made slow progress with the more constructive task of drafting an agreed scale of charges for through traffic in parcels. It was not until April 1857 that the general managers on the recommendation of the Goods Managers Conference, gave approval to the following scale:

### RATES FOR PARCELS FOR THROUGH TRAFFIC

| All distances | Not exceeding 3 lb. | Above 3 lb. but under 14 lb. | Above 14 lb. for each additional lb. |
|---|---|---|---|
| over 300 miles | 1s 6d | 2s 6d | 2d |
| 250–300 ,, | 1s 6d | 2s 3d | 1¾d |
| 200–250 ,, | 1s 6d | 2s 0d | 1½d |
| 150–200 ,, | 1s 3d | 1s 9d | 1¼d |
| 100–150 ,, | 1s 0d | 1s 6d | 1d |
| 50–100 ,, | 8d | 1s 0d | ¾d |
| 30– 50 ,, | 6d | 9d | ½d |
| 1– 30 ,, | 6d | 6d | ¼d[2] |

[1] RCH 1/71: Report of a sub-committee of the General Managers Conference, November 4, 1861.

[2] RCH 1/71: Minute 211 of General Managers Conference, April 7, 1857. G. P. Neele: *Railway Reminiscences*, London, 1904, p. 59.

The companies showed no enthusiasm to standardise their charges on the above lines. Nearly a year after the general managers had approved the new rates only a minority of the member companies had replied to Mr Morison's enquiry as to whether or not they were applying them. Of those companies which did condescend to reply but four reported unconditional acceptance of the plan. In the circumstances the general managers decided to rescind their previous recommendation.[1] Contrariwise, the companies appeared to develop greater enthusiasm for the 1857 scale of charges once the general managers had withdrawn their support for it. By the summer of 1859 twenty-four companies (including a majority of those north of the Thames) were still standing out.[2] Towards the end of 1859, however, the traffic superintendents noted that 'all or nearly all' of the great companies had adopted the scale with satisfactory results both to the companies and to the public.[3]

## III

Because there was a greater approach towards standardisation of charges for 'smalls' by the early 1860s, it must not be imagined that the trading community were satisfied with the services provided either by the railways or by the Post Office. Between September 1862 and November 1863 the Postmaster-General was bombarded with memorials from the Chambers of Commerce of Bristol, Leeds, Bradford, Huddersfield, Manchester, Halifax, Edinburgh and the City of London demanding improved postal services for small parcels. The Annual General Meeting of the Associated Chambers of Commerce, meeting in Westminster on February 24, 1853, pointed out in a further memorial that

'in France (including Algeria), Belgium, Prussia, and other countries, the Post Office carries with dispatch, and at surprisingly

[1] RCH 1/71: Minute 258 of General Managers Conference, February 11, 1858.
[2] RCH 1/114: Minute 508 of Superintendents Conference, July 21, 1859.
[3] RCH 1/114: Minute 523 of Superintendents Conference, November 17, 1859.

low rates, parcels of all kinds under a certain weight; thus conferring a great advantage on merchants and traders, of which they largely avail themselves.'

In Britain on the other hand, a businessman wishing to send through the post a packet of samples or patterns weighing 1 lb. would be faced with the almost prohibitory charge of 2s 8d, though if the same packet were sent to France or Algeria it would only be charged 1s. Logically enough the memorialists demanded of the Postmaster-General the extension of the same privilege which had been granted to France and Algeria, to Great Britain and Ireland, the colonies and the continent of Europe.[1]

The result of this barrage was the introduction of the sample post later in 1863. Bona fide samples and patterns, having no intrinsic value, might be sent through the post to any part of the kingdom at the following rates:

Under 4 oz.   3d
4– 8 oz.   6d
8–16 oz.   1s
16–24 oz.   1s 6d

In the autumn of 1864 the rates were reduced by one third and in 1866 the rates were again altered to a uniform 2d for 4 oz. with a maximum of 24 oz. Merchants, shopkeepers and the general public quickly made use of the new service and the number of 'sample' packets sent through the post rose from half a million in 1864 to four million in 1870.[2]

While the introduction of the Sample Post was still under discussion, Rowland Hill, the secretary of the Post Office, urged on his chief the immediate introduction of a fully fledged parcel post service. He believed that in the course of time the impracticability of limiting the post to actual patterns and samples would be 'more and more manifest'. As they would, in any case, be subjected to new demands from the railway companies it would be wiser to be bold. But Lord Stanley, the Postmaster-General took the path of caution. He did not wish to encounter the strong opposition

[1] Post Office Records 3764/64.
[2] HMSO: *The Post Office: An Historical Summary*, June 1911, p. 15.

which he knew the railways would put up to any proposals for a parcel post.[1]

Rowland Hill's predictions were wholly justified. In February 1871 one of Lord Stanley's successors received a memorandum which reported that 'fully half' the packets sent the sample post were not samples. In the country

'grocers, linen drapers, hosiers, fishing tackle makers, and tobacco dealers often extended their trade beyond the immediate neighbourhood and carried on a good business by sending packets of goods through the post at sample rate. Indeed ... some industries were actually created on the strength of the facilities assumed to be offered by the sample post.'

It had also become a widespread habit to send presents of all kinds through the same medium, examples of such gifts including bonnets and shawls, sweetmeats, anti-macassars, bouquets of flowers, skates, purses and even a brace of snipe.[2]

With the prospect of their 'smalls' traffic being transferred by the Post Office sample post, the traffic superintendents saw the necessity of bringing down the scale of charges for the conveyance of parcels by passenger train. In February 1864 they adopted a new scale of charges under which the charge by rail was as cheap as or cheaper than the postage rates for distances up to 300 miles. For greater distances the Post Office charges were the cheaper.[3]

[1] Post Office Records, 3764/64: Memo from the secretary of the Post Office, the Postmaster General, July 1, 1863. Rowland Hill, *op. cit.* Vol. 2, p. 373.      [2] Post Office Records, 7535/1871, file.

[3] The new scale was:

| Up to | 1 lb. d | 1–3 lb. s | 1–3 lb. d | 3–7 lb. s | 3–7 lb. d | 7–10 lb. s | 7–10 lb. d | 10–16 lb. s | 10–16 lb. d | 16–24 lb. d | Above 24 lb. |
|---|---|---|---|---|---|---|---|---|---|---|---|
| 1–30 miles | 6 | | 6 | | 6 | | 6 | | 6 | | ½d per lb. |
| 31–50 miles | 6 | | 6 | | 8 | | 8 | | 8 | Above 16 lb. | |
| 51–100 miles | 6 | | 6 | | 8 | | 10 | 1 | | Above 16 | ¾d per lb. |
| 101–150 miles | 6 | | 8 | | 10 | 1 | | 1 | 4 | Above 16 | 1d per lb. |
| 151–200 miles | 6 | | 9 | 1 | | 1 | 4 | 1 | 8 | Above 16 | 1¼d per lb. |
| 201–250 miles | 6 | | 10 | 1 | 2 | 1 | 6 | 2 | | Above 16 | 1½d per lb. |
| 251–300 miles | 6 | 1 | | 1 | 4 | 1 | 9 | 2 | | Above 16 | 1¾d per lb. |
| 301–400 miles | 8 | 1 | 2 | 1 | 6 | 2 | | 2 | 8 | Above 16 | 2d per lb. |
| 401–550 miles | 9 | 1 | 4 | 1 | 9 | 2 | 3 | 3 | | Above 16 | 2d per lb. |
| Over 550 miles | 9 | 1 | 4 | 1 | 9 | 2 | 3 | 3 | | Above 16 | 2¼d per lb. |

RCH 1/114: Minute 745 of Superintendents Conference of February 19, 1864.

Within the next two months however Mr Currey, the traffic superintendent of the Great Northern Railway, did some sums. He concluded that the parcels receipts of his company at the revised rates would be lower than they were under the old rates and that in consequence he was not prepared to apply the new scale of charges. Because at the meeting on April 28, 1864 the representative of the North Eastern Railway also expressed dissent from the decision taken two months earlier, it was decided to withdraw altogether the new scale of charges pending their re-examination by a special meeting.[1]

In April 1865 therefore a revised scale raising the charges for the conveyance of parcels a distance of over 300 miles was unanimously adopted.[2]

The result of the adoption of this new scale was that railways smalls rates were cheaper than sample post rates for parcels weighing between 8 oz. and 1 lb. over distances up to 150 miles only, and for some parcels less than 2 lb. in weight for distances of up to 100 miles only. Thus the railways came to concentrate on smalls traffic for the shorter distances—a job which would have been better left to the Post Office—and did much less to develop the long distance haulage of larger parcels which they were better suited to undertake.

Of the two systems—the sample post system of a low charge based on weight alone and irrespective of distance, and the railways' system of charges proportional to both weight and distance —the former was much simpler to understand and clearly beneficial to the firm consigning goods over the longer distances. It is not surprising, therefore, that between 1864 and 1870, while the railway parcels receipts coming through the Clearing House rose by less than 100%, the number of parcels sent by sample post rose by 800%.

By 1870 the Postmaster-General was under pressure from two different directions. The railway companies were demanding that the sample post regulations should be tightened up so that only genuine samples or patterns of no intrinsic value should pass

[1] RCH 1/114: Minute 745 of Superintendents Conference, April 28, 1864.
[2] RCH 1/115: Minute 816 of Superintendents Conference, January 26, 1865, amended by minute 860 of April 27, 1865.

through the post at the cheap rates. The Chambers of Commerce, on the other hand, wanted the establishment of a parcel post at rates as cheap as those charged for the posting of books.[1] Edwin Chadwick again added his influence to the campaign for more satisfactory postal arrangements. In a letter to Frank Scuddamore written on August 14, 1868, he wrote:

'Let us have a parcel post, at two pence a pound, and a halfpenny for every quarter of a pound or fraction of a quarter of a pound and let us have halfpenny stamps for the purpose, since these rates will pay, as shown by continental postal examples.'[2]

But the Postmaster-General was in no mood for such a radical innovation. Early in 1871 he announced the abolition of the sample post, a decision which was put into effect on October 5th of that year. An attempt was made to soften the blow by a simultaneous reduction in letter postage rates for lightweight packets, but this by no means stifled the opposition to the change. More than three hundred letters or memoranda, protesting about the abolition of the sample post, were received at St Martins le Grand. They included resolutions passed by the Association of Chambers of Commerce and the Manchester Home Trade Association. But the the vast majority were

'from ladies, many complaining of the hindrance thrown in the way of their earning a livelihood by means of needlework, small parcels of which formerly passed at the sample rate; others residing in the country at some distance from a town, complaining of the inconvenience caused by not being able to send and receive at a cheap rate small parcels of gloves, lace, etc.'[3]

Having been moved by reading these protests the secretary of the Post Office, Sir John Tilley, KCB, wrote to his chief on October 28, 1870, urging that there should be 'an open parcel post, the only restriction being that the contents of a parcel should not be in the nature of a letter'.[4]

One of the Assistant Secretaries, Mr F. Hill, however, hit the

[1] Association of Chambers of Commerce, Annual General Meeting, February 23–25, 1869. Report p. 31.
[2] Post Office Records 1551/1883, file I.
[3] Post Office Records 7535/1871, file IV.
[4] Post Office Records 1153/1871.

nail on the head when he wrote that 'the delay in the adoption of such a post is not attributable to any doubt of the great public benefit which it would confer, but to difficulties of attainment—the chief of which have reference to the conveyance of parcels by the railways'.[1]

In the absence of a parcel post one alternative would have been for the railways to have organised their own prepaid parcel stamp scheme through the Clearing House. It was a plan which had a devoted and able advocate in the person of Mr G. P. Neele, for many years coaching superintendant of the London and North Western Railway. At least as early as 1855 the North Eastern, Midland, Manchester Sheffield and Lincolnshire, East Lancashire, and Lancashire and Yorkshire Railways used parcel stamps for the dispatch of newspapers by rail.

In May 1859 the General Managers Conference decided to appoint a sub-committee 'to report on the working of the system of parcels labels as hitherto in use on various lines: and on the question of how far, if at all, that system should be extended to parcels traffic generally and specially to those parcels which contain samples of articles for sale.' But the six members of the committee could not agree on a satisfactory scheme, and in November of the same year the General Managers Conference decided to bring the discussions to an end without positive result.[2]

In December 1864 Neele tried to persuade a meeting of the superintendants at the Clearing House to recommend the general adoption of this method for all types of parcels, but he met with a cautious and unenthusiastic response.[3] Less than two years later the Royal Commission on Railways revealed that it had been favourably impressed by Neele's plan when it reported:

'Looking at the extent to which the railway system has now reached, we consider that the time has arrived when railway companies should combine to devise some rapid and efficient system for the delivery of parcels. We do not feel called upon to

[1] Post Office Records 7585/1871. Observations of Mr F. Hill, assistant secretary to the Postmaster-General on Parcel Post, March 18, 1868.

[2] RCH 1/79: Minutes 348 and 351 of the General Managers Conference, May–November 1859.

[3] RCH 1/71: General Managers Conference, December, 12, 1855. RCH 1/114: Special Meeting of Superintendents, December 1, 1864.

suggest the precise manner in which this may be carried into effect, but the employment of a uniform system of adhesive labels for parcels, somewhat similar to that now in use on some of the northern lines for the conveyance of newspapers, is one of the most obvious methods for facilitating payment and accounting.'[1]

On the occasion of the abolition of the sample post in 1871 Neele again raised the question of prepaid parcel stamps at a meeting of the superintendents in the Clearing House. The sub-committee appointed to re-examine the question did not consider the scheme would be feasible unless there was a 'material reduction in rates' for the carriage of parcels on the railways. Such a reduction would not be desirable unless the companies could be relieved of all liability for loss, damage or delay as they were in the case of newspapers. In the course of the sub-committee's discussion a member suggested communicating with the Post Office authorities with a view to joining them in adopting some form of special freight label for packages not exceeding 2 lb. in weight, the Post Office undertaking the collection and delivery of the parcels and the railways merely conveying them from station to station. The general managers considered this a worthwhile proposal. They appointed their own sub-committee to meet the postal authorities and told the superintendents to defer further consideration of the question until the outcome of their talks was known.[2]

Unfortunately no record survives of what transpired at these important discussions between the general managers and the Post Office, other than a brief statement from Mr Ashley, the convenor of the general managers' sub-committee, that 'the interview did not result in any arrangement being come to'.[3] The consequence of the failure was that the country had to wait more than ten years longer for a nationwide and reasonably cheap parcels service.

The reduction of postage rates announced on October 5, 1871, provided the more cautious of the superintendents with a good excuse to postpone a decision on Neele's plan. It was decided at

[1] Royal Commission on Railways: Report, 1867, BPP 1867, Vol. XXXVIII, Part 2.
[2] RCH 1/104: Minute 1702 and 1782 of Superintendents Conference, January 25, 1871, and April 20, 1871.
[3] RCH 1/79: Minute 1169 of General Managers Conference, August 10, 1871.

the September meeting to watch for a period of three months the effects of the new Post Office rates on the railways' parcel traffic. But when this time had elapsed no further action was taken.

It was nearly seven years before the railway parcel stamp plan was again seriously considered in the Clearing House, although another sub-committee had been asked to report on the matter in 1874. Meeting at Plymouth in July 1878, the superintendents were treated to a detailed exposition by Neele of the proposed arrangements and the advantages that they would bring alike to the public and the railway companies. The outstanding reason for accepting the scheme, he claimed, was 'to cope with the arrangements of the packed parcels companies and to induce senders to adopt the railways as the direct means of transmitting such parcels, in preference to supporting the numerous packed parcel agencies, which are being established and extended throughout the kingdom'. The Clearing House would issue to the railway companies sheets of sixty fourpenny gummed labels, a discount of two per cent being allowed for such bulk purchases. The labels were to be honoured by all the railway companies in England, Wales and Scotland and the receipts from their sale were to go into a common fund. Twice a year the Clearing House would divide the receipts between the companies in proportion to the amount of their parcels traffic shown from time to time in their half-yearly returns. The fourpenny labels would be valid for parcels up to 2 lb. in weight carried any distance. Two fourpenny labels would be used for parcels weighing between 2 and 4 lb.[1]

On this occasion, after some minor modifications had been accepted by Neele, the superintendents gave their approval of the scheme and recommended its adoption by all the companies from January 1, 1879.[2] But once more the absence of compulsory powers by the Clearing House prevented the implementation of a policy which had been endorsed by those best able to judge of its value. Although the superintendents had at last been persuaded that the arrangements for the parcel traffic were due for a complete overhaul and simplification, the directors of a number of important companies thought otherwise.

[1] RCH 1/117: Meeting of superintendents, July 24, 1878.
[2] RCH 1/117: Minute 3499 of Superintendents Conference, October 22, 1878.

The members of the Board of the North British Railways refused to co-operate because they believed that it would offer to those clerks who were tempted to dishonesty the opportunity of pocketing the difference between the label rates and the ordinary parcel rates. Their contemporaries of the Lancashire and Yorkshire Railway were afraid that the proposed flat rate charges would bring the company reduced revenue from the long distance traffic. Only one portion of the freight was to be dealt with under the scheme—the paid parcels weighing under 4 lb. On a 'to pay' parcel, weighing up to 4 lb. and sent from London to Glasgow, the consignee would have to pay 2s, whereas if the parcel was prepaid the charge would be but fourpence. The Highland, London and South Western, South Eastern, and London Brighton and South Coast lines also refused to follow the superintendents' recommendation.[1] The principal reason for opposition to the scheme was that for distances between 100 and 400 miles the charge for parcels would be anything between a half and two-thirds of existing rates. The opposition was shortsighted. It did not take into account sufficiently the great augmentation of traffic that might come with lower charges and it failed to appreciate that a parcel post might come in any case, but that it would come all the more quickly if the railways failed to provide an acceptable alternative.

In the absence of agreement for a scheme for adhesive labels which would have greatly simplified Clearing House accounting, the railway companies were obliged to send in returns from each station accepting parcels for through delivery to stations on other companies' lines. The number of stations involved grew very rapidly with the spread of the rail network and the increase in the number of companies which were members of the Clearing House. In times of trade boom the number of parcels dispatched rose dramatically but the administrative expenses mounted more rapidly than did receipts. Thus in the twelve months ending December 31, 1864, the number of quarterly settlements for parcels traffic rose by nearly 39% and the number of stations 'booking through' by 27%: but the rise in receipts was only just over 5% compared with a nearly 15% rise in Clearing House expenses involved in the administration of the through parcels

[1] RCH 1/117: Minutes 3500, 3536 and 3537 of Superintendents Conference, October 30, 1878.

traffic.[1] Over the longer period from 1853 to 1873 the number of pairs of stations booking parcels traffic each month rose from 55,776 to 669,854.[2] This inefficiently organised but rapidly growing parcels traffic was the principal reason for the administrative expenses of the Clearing House rising at a faster rate than traffic receipts. Costs of administration as a percentage of traffic receipts cleared rose from 0·86% between 1860–64 inclusive to 1·32% between 1880–84 inclusive. The Clearing House committee in June 1865, as an economy measure, recommended companies to restrict, as far as possible, the booking of parcels from their own system to the *principal* and *terminal* stations of other companies only. It was also proposed that instead of parcels receipts being divided on the basis of mileage, as in the past, the gross receipts, less terminal charges, should be divided on a company to company basis on a percentage based on a traffic survey. Only in the case of the larger stations' traffic was division of receipts on the basis of mileage recommended.[3] In so far as companies adopted this recommendation, Clearing House expenses did not rise as rapidly as they would otherwise have done: but the small parcels traffic remained by far the most costly of the Clearing House services to administer. Thus in September 1872 The Superintending Committee (a body set up in 1862 to organise the management of the Clearing House) drew attention 'to the increased number of through settlements of very small amounts and the necessary increase in Clearing House expenses'. They recommended the delegates 'to instruct the secretary to draw attention to the companies concerned to the matter, with a view to those companies considering whether it is desirable to continue through bookings through the clearing system where traffic is of so exceedingly light a character—some of the settlements made by the Clearing House being, as your Committee is informed by the Secretary, of no more than one shilling in amount, such settlements at the same time costing in the clearing as much as settlements of £50 or £60'.[4]

[1] RCH 1/114: Report of superintending committee to Railway Clearing House committee, March 1865.
[2] RCH 1/28: Minute 830 of the committee, June 14, 1865. Statistical summary presented to Railway Clearing House committee, April 1874.
[3] RCH/14: Minute 830 of the committee, June 14, 1865.
[4] RCH 1/27: Report of superintending committee to the Quarterly Meeting of Delegates, September 11, 1872.

It is scarcely surprising that the companies' accountants, reporting to the Clearing House earlier the same year, urged the adoption of the prepaid label scheme since 'saving in account keeping would result'.[1]

## IV

Various committees of the Clearing House continued to play cat and mouse with Neele's plan throughout 1879. In an endeavour to meet previous criticisms, a revised scheme, increasing parcel charges for the longer distances, was submitted to the superintendents at their January meeting. At first it looked as if the compromise had effectively stifled the opposition, as it was agreed to recommend the plan to put into operation from June 2nd for one year as an experiment.[2] However, at a joint meeting of accountants and superintendents held in April, renewed opposition was voiced by the companies south of the Thames and by the North Staffordshire Railway, and at the General Managers Meeting in May a letter from Mr Tennant, the general manager of the North Eastern Railway, was read, which complained that the question had 'hardly received full and sufficient consideration'—though in some shape or form it had been under discussion for at least fifteen years! In view of these doubts and of others voiced by the general manager of the London and South Western Railway there was nothing for it but to refer back the whole subject to the superintendents.[3] Companies that had hitherto backed the scheme began to lose confidence in it when they learned that some of the major companies were not prepared to co-operate, and in June a sub-committee of the superintendents rejected by ten votes to four a motion to bring the label scheme into operation on August 1st.[4] The following month the general managers decided that the

[1] RCH 1/79: Report of companies' accountants on the question of light settlements, February 9, 1871.
[2] RCH 1/117: Minute 5389 of Superintendents Conference, January 21, 1879.
[3] RCH 1/75: Minute 1670 of General Managers Conference, May 8, 1879.
[4] RCH 1/117: Minute 3772 of Superintendents Conference, June 26, 1879.

whole question of parcel rates, whether with adhesive labels or without, should be referred to a committee of general managers and superintendents.

By the time this body met, plans for an international parcel post convention had reached an advanced stage. The Postal Congress in Paris in 1878 heard the director of the International Postal Union at Berne report that the governments of the principal European countries had already agreed to attend a conference in Paris in 1880 with the object of establishing an international parcel post.[1] The Postmaster-General was under strong pressure from the governments of other European countries to co-operate in this new venture. But this was scarcely possible so long as Britain was without a parcel post. The Association of Chambers of Commerce was again on the warpath demanding that the British Post Office should provide at least as good a service as that provided in Germany where parcels of up to 140 lb. in weight were accepted for delivery by the Post Offices and where the railways were under legal obligation to carry parcels of under 20 lb. weight free of charge.[2]

The first approach to an agreement with the railways was made by Mr A. Benthall, assistant secretary of the Post Office, who wrote to the general managers of the Great Eastern and London and North Western Railways on July 4, 1879, suggesting a meeting. After the views of some of the leading general managers had been ascertained, Philip Dawson, secretary of the Clearing House, responded by inviting Mr Benthall to a conference at Seymour Street building on November 14th.[3] The original plan of the Post Office was that parcels under 2 lb. in weight should be charged 6d. and parcels between 2 and 4 lb., 1s, receipts from the sale of the stamps being equally divided between the Post Office and the Clearing House (for the companies). Government parcels were to be carried free and the work of transferring bags and boxes of parcels at junctions was to be performed by the railway companies'

[1] RCH 1/75: Minute 1726 of General Managers Conference, May 6, 1880.

[2] Post Office Records 1551 of 1883, file VII, memo E 8397/80, and file XXXVIII, March 1882. Extracts from Mr Findlay's notes on a visit to the continent. Mr Findlay was general manager of the London and North Western Railway.

[3] Post Office Records 1551/1883, file VI.

porters. The Postmaster-General was to be as unfettered in the management of the parcel post as he was with the letter post.[1] Such proposals were very wide of the mark of the railways claims, as expressed by Mr Grierson for the General Managers Conference. In the first place they wished to establish the agreement in perpetuity, as they asserted that they were at the moment enjoying the virtual monopoly of parcels traffic and would be surrendering that monopoly if an agreement was signed with the Post Office. In return for this major concession, therefore, they wanted a guarantee that their position as carriers would be unimpaired in the future. Because of the increased volume of work which would result for the railways from the introduction of a parcel post they considered that they were entitled to receive at least 60% of the receipts. Instead of the Post Office scale of two charges of 6d and 1s they proposed the following alternative:

| 1 lb. | 2 lb. | 3 lb. | 4 lb. | 5 lb. |
|-------|-------|-------|-------|-------|
| 4d    | 6d    | 8d    | 10d   | 1s    |

Above all the companies could not accept the view of the Treasury that the Postmaster-General should be as unfettered in regard to the parcel post as he was in the conduct of other Post Office business.[2] Rather they desired an equal partnership between the railways and the Post Office.

The Postmaster-General felt quite unable to accept the counter proposals of the general managers. The suggestion that the management of the new service should be in any way shared with the railway companies was rejected, because 'it would confer on the companies the right to interfere with the mode in which the Postmaster General carries on the parcel post, while at the same time they would be free to carry on as they like their own competing business'.[3] As it was 'impossible to forecast accurately the results of the establishment of a parcel post' it was out of the question that the Government would sanction an agreement in

[1] Post Office Records 7840/78, file III.

[2] RCH 1/80: 'Report of the Committee Appointed by Minute 1787 of the General Managers Conference to Further Negotiate With the Post Office With Respect to the proposed Parcel Post', November 17, 1881.

[3] Letter from F. Cavendish on behalf of the Treasury to the Postmaster-General, July 4, 1881, RCH 1/80.

perpetuity, for the public would not tolerate being denied the opportunity of benefiting from any improved form of transport and communications that might arise in the future.

There were a number of reasons for the very protracted negotiations which followed. The change of government, as a result of a general election in April 1880, led to a shelving of previous proposals and a pause in the discussions while the new Postmaster-General, Henry Fawcett, found his feet. Furthermore an international parcel post convention was signed in Paris on November 3, 1880. As a result of the agreement, charges for dispatching a parcel weighing 3 kilograms (or 6 lb. 9 oz.) were as low as 8½d in France, 5d in Belgium and 4d or 6d in Switzerland.[1] In the new situation brought by this postal revolution on the continent Mr Benthall could see that the British public were 'not likely to be satisfied that a service which was becoming general almost throughout Europe, should be withheld from this country.'[2] He felt obliged to lower the proposed postage rates and extend the service to parcels of up to 7 lb. weight to make the projected service more comparable with those already operative on the continent. The scale he submitted to the general managers by letter on March 25, 1882, was as follows:

Not exceeding 1 lb.   3d
Not exceeding 1 lb.   6d
Not exceeding 5 lb.   9d
Not exceeding 7 lb.   1s

Henry Fawcett was aware that railway companies with an extensive route mileage in sparsely peopled areas would have strong objections to the charges being as low as 3d on a parcel of up to 1 lb. in weight. As a concession, therefore, to make the revised proposals more acceptable to the companies, he waived the demand that government parcels should be carried free of charge. However, the Treasury was not prepared to allow this concession unless payment should be made to the railways only in respect of parcels conveyed

[1] Post Office Records 1551/83, file XXXVII, minute no. 2098 from Mr Benthall to the Treasury, February 27, 1882.

[2] RCH 1/80: Letter from A. Benthall to J. Grierson, November 10, 1881.

by them. Before the division of parcel post receipts the Post Office would deduct the receipts from parcels conveyed by road or sea.[1]

The general managers considered the new proposals 'so great a departure' from the original ones made by the Post Office that they demanded further concessions. The Government sensed that it was in a weak bargaining position. As Benthall admitted to Grierson, the question of establishing a parcel post was 'becoming more pressing every day'.[2] He could not concede a higher scale of charges to placate the companies which were doubtful of supporting the scheme, for the revised scales were, in his view, 'the very highest that the public would accept as fair and reasonable'.[3] If the railways were granted a greater proportion of the receipts than 50% there were doubts whether the Post Office would cover its costs. Benthall had already warned the general managers that the Post Office was reaching the limit of concessions. Employing a most unusual metaphor, he told the general managers that 'the Post Office does not keep more cats than can catch mice, and as its work increases its expenses would increase in nearly the same proportion, especially in dealing with articles of so much greater bulk than letters'. Henry Fawcett was of the opinion that the equal division of parcel post receipts on rail carried parcels would be 'not only fair but liberal' to the companies. The one way out seemed to be to increase the duration of the agreement. It was therefore suggested that the ten years originally proposed should be extended to twenty-one.[4]

The general managers were by no means won over by this concession. Grierson's reply to assistant secretary Blackwood, extending over seven pages of foolscap, underlined all the disadvantages the companies would suffer under the proposed schemes. They would be involved in a 'very great outlay' of

[1] RCH 1/80: Letter from S. A. Blackwood, assistant secretary, Post Office, to J. Grierson, March 25, 1882. Post Office Records 1551/83, file XXXVIII.

[2] Post Office Records 1551/83, file XXXI, Benthall to Grierson, January 6, 1882.

[3] Post Office Records 1551/83, file XXXVII, minute no. 2098, Benthall to Her Majesty's Treasury.

[4] Post Office records 1551/83, file XXXVIII. Benthall's statement to the general managers' meeting, August 18, 1880, in file X.

capital, whereas for the Post Office comparatively little new outlay would be incurred. The companies would have to make drastic reductions in their own charges for parcels, resulting in a loss of revenue. There 'were good grounds for the view that the companies' proportion of the receipts should be more than 60 per cent', but they were prepared to settle for that amount in the interests of getting the agreement signed. The letter ended with the stern warning that, 'if no general agreement was made, the Post Office would have to settle with each company separately, and most probably have to do so from time to time by very tedious and expensive arbitrations'.[1]

In a final effort to avoid having to pay more to the railways, Blackwood proposed a reconsideration of the apportionment of the receipts three years after the date of introduction of the parcel post. He promised that if the railways could then prove to the Postmaster-General or the railway commissioners that they *should* have been receiving 60%, the Post Office would be prepared to make such a division retrospective from the inception of the service. The railways' reply was that they would settle for 55% from the start. On June 26, 1882, assistant secretary Baines talked the situation over with Grierson in the Clearing House building. He was there convinced that any attempt to press for new concessions would upset the negotiations. Reporting the same day to his chief he warned:

'There appears to have been great difficulty in procuring an approach to identity of opinions amongst the managers so far. It is more than likely that two or more of the great railway companies are, for reasons special to themselves, strongly averse to the Parcel Post scheme and would gladly seize the opportunity of reopening discussions which would be fatal to any present conclusion of the matter.'[2]

Thus was Henry Fawcett driven to accept a proposal to give to the railway companies a much larger proportion—eleven-twentieths—of the receipts from parcels than was warranted by the service

[1] Post Office Records 1551/83, file XXXVIII, Grierson to Blackwood, May 8, 1882.
[2] Post Office Records 1551/83, file XXXVIII, Blackwood to Grierson, May 11, 1882. Memorandum from F. S. Barnes, June 26, 1882.

they rendered. He knew that on the continent no higher a ratio than two-fifths was allocated to the railways for a similar service, despite lower postage rates. He believed three-sevenths would be a fair proportion to pass on to the British railways. But the public were demanding the new service and he was convinced that the 'cordial co-operation' of the railways was essential for its success.[1]

This co-operation the railway companies were happy enough to give once their final offer had been accepted. On July 5, 1882, Philip Dawson wrote to S. A. Blackwood at the Post Office that the special meeting of the general managers held that morning had voted unanimously for acceptance. Thereafter it was plain sailing. The Post Office (Parcels) Act received royal assent on August 18, 1882, and the new service began on August 1st in the following year.

## V

When the new arrangements were under discussion in the Spring of 1882 Grierson pointed out in a letter to Blackwood that the charge for carrying an 8 lb. parcel on the railways a distance of 200 miles was 2s whereas by parcel post a 7 lb. parcel would be delivered to any part of the kingdom for 1s. It would be 'manifestly impossible', he claimed, 'to charge for eight pounds double the rate for the seven pounds parcel.'[2] The sense of urgency felt by the general managers at their conference, held soon after the Bill had passed through all its stages in the Commons, is not difficult to understand. The lower charges which Neele had repeatedly urged, but which had hitherto been rejected by the companies because they feared decreased receipts on the long distance traffic, were now adopted under the duress of the Parcel Post. The new Clearing House scale of charges was lower than the projected postal charges on the shorter distances, but higher for the longer distances (see p. 114).

[1] Post Office records 1551/83, file XXXVIII, memorandum from Henry Fawcett to the Lords Commissioners of the Treasury. February 27, 1882, Leslie Stephen: *Henry Fawcett*, London, 1886, p. 417.
[2] Post Office Records 1551/83, file XXXVIII. Grierson to Blackwood, May 8, 1882.

CLEARING HOUSE SCALE FOR CONVEYANCE OF PARCELS BY PASSENGER TRAIN

| Miles | Weight not exceeding | | | | | | | | | | | | | Over 24 lb |
|---|---|---|---|---|---|---|---|---|---|---|---|---|---|---|
| | 1 | 2 | 3 | 4 | 5 | 6 | 7 | 10 | 14 | 15 | 16 | 18 | 24 | per lb. extra |
| 1–30 | 4d | 6d | 6d | 6d | 6d | 6d | 6d | 6d | 6d | 6d | 6d | 6d | 6d | ½d |
| 31–50 | 4d | 6d | 6d | 6d | 6d | 6d | 8d | 8d | 8d | 8d | 8d | — | — | ½d |
| 51–100 | 6d | 6d | 8d | 9d | 9d | 10d | 10d | 1s | 1s | 1s | 1s | — | — | ¾d |
| 101–200 | 6d | 6d | 8d | 9d | 10d | 1s | 1s | 1s 3d | 1s 6d | 1s 6d | 1s 6d | 1s 6d | — | 1d |
| 201–300 | 6d | 6d | 8d | 9d | 10d | 1s | 1s 3d | 1s 6d | 1s 9d | — | — | — | — | 1¼d |
| 301–400 | 6d | 6d | 8d | 9d | 10d | 1s | 1s 3d | 1s 6d | 2s | 2s | 2s | — | — | 1½d |
| Over 400 | 6d | 6d | 8d | 9d | 10d | 1s | 1s 6d | 2s | 2s 6d | 2s 6d | — | — | —[1] | 2d |

[1] RCH 1/80: Minute 1921 of General Managers Conference, July 20, 1882.

After their new charges were introduced on September 1, 1882, the railways had eleven months' head start over the Post Office. Within six months Dawson was able to report that the Clearing House parcels accounts had 'increased immensely' immediately following the introduction of the lower charges. The number of parcel settlements in October 1882 was up by more than 15% compared with the number in the corresponding month in the previous year'.[1] Railway parcel receipts, far from being depressed by the lower charges, increased at a faster rate after September 1882 than before that date. The arguments of the reformers that a reduction in parcel rates would benefit the companies financially had been fully vindicated.

In the year following the introduction of the parcel post the monthly total of parcels booked through on the railways fell slightly but receipts from parcel clearing rose by five per cent exclusive of the extra quarter of a million pounds the companies received from the post office under the provisions of the Post Office (Parcels) Act.[2]

For the Postmaster-General the results, at first, were less gratifying. The loss on the first year's working of the parcel post was at least £86,000 and it was not until the financial year 1886–87 that the deficit incurred during the three previous years was wiped out.[3] It was the rural letter carriers (known after August 1883 as postmen) who, by carrying heavier loads, helped to get the Post Office out of the red on the parcels service. In view of the financial position, it is not surprising to read the ruling made in 1883 that there was 'no extra pay to be granted to rural letter carriers on account of Parcel Post Work'.[4] Where the turn of duty was prolonged or the load exceeded a maximum of 35 lb. it had for many years been the rule that increased wages or additional help were to be provided. But parcels could be up to 3 feet 6 inches in length, or 6 feet in length and girth combined. As one historian of the Post Office has observed: 'the postman setting out with a load of

[1] RCH 1/118: Report of Superintendents Conference to the Railway Clearing House committee, December 13, 1882.

[2] RCH 1/16: Philip Dawson's quarterly report to the committee, September 10, 1884.

[3] Post Office Records 3856/86, minute 3586. Report to the Chancellor of the Exchequer, March 26, 1886.

[4] Post Office Records 12885/85, file V, minute E 2661/83.

parcels of this sort must have literally staggered under the burden'.[5] After August 1, 1883, the postman was carrying the maximum permissible load far more frequently than had been the case previously.

After the maximum weight of inland parcels had been raised to 11 lb. in 1886 and the number of inland parcels in the post had risen to over 26 million annually, the Postmaster-General, in an attempt partially to offset the poor bargain made with the railways five years earlier, revived the use of horsedrawn coaches to carry a part of the mail. From June 1, 1887, a regular coach service for the carriage of parcels was introduced between London and Brighton. It proved so successful that similar coaches were put into service on other routes to the provinces.[1]

The railway companies had to lower their own charges once more before the end of the century. In June 1897 as part of the Diamond Jubilee reforms, the postage rates on parcels had been reduced as follows:

| | |
|---|---|
| Not exceeding 1 lb. | 3d |
| Exceeding 1 lb. but under 2 lb. | 4d |
| Exceeding 2 lb. but under 3 lb. | 5d |
| Exceeding 3 lb. but under 4 lb. | 6d |
| Exceeding 4 lb. but under 5 lb. | 7d |
| Exceeding 5 lb. but not exceeding 6 lb. | 8d |
| Exceeding 6 lb. but not exceeding 7 lb. | 9d |
| Exceeding 7 lb. but not exceeding 8 lb. | 10d |
| Exceeding 8 lb. but not exceeding 9 lb. | 11d |
| Exceeding 9 lb. but not exceeding 11 lb. | 1s |

The superintendents' meeting in the Clearing House on August 18th that year, minuted that 'the recent reduction of the parcel post charges had affected more or less the receipts of all companies', and it was unanimously agreed that the scale of charges for the carriage of parcels by passenger train would have to be revised

[1] F. George Kay, *Royal Mail*, London, 1951, p. 119.
[2] *The Post Office: An Historical Summary*, HMSO 1911, pp. 18–19.

downwards.[1] Just over two months later agreement was reached on a new scale to be brought into force on February 1, 1898.

Although the spectacular increases in parcels receipts which had been characteristic of earlier years were not sustained in the twenty years immediately preceding the First World War the railways income from this source remained remarkably buoyant in the face of lower parcel post charges. The irrational feature of the country parcel services, however, remained, that the railway rates were the more attractive for the shorter distances and less attractive for the greater distances. The exceptionally large proportion of the railways parcel receipts which sprang from the short distance carriage helped to delay by many decades the substitution of the motor car for the railway train in this part of the service.

The railways' parcels charges introduced in 1898 had come nearer the principle of a rate determined by weight alone. Neele's plan, which more fully embodied this principle, was given its final airing and final rejection at the Conference of Superintendents held in November 1897.[2] Only in respect of the carriage of newspapers did Neele's policy gain partial acceptance. As early as 1866 for the traffic between Scotland and England the prepaid label plan was adopted though the amount payable was dependent on

| [1] Distance | Weight not exceeding — lb. | | | | | | | | | | | | |
|---|---|---|---|---|---|---|---|---|---|---|---|---|---|
| | 1 | 2 | 3 | 4 | 5 | 6 | 7 | 8 | 9 | 10 | 11 | 12 | 13 |
| Not exceeding 30 m. | 4d | 4d | 5d | 6d | 6d | 6d | 6d | 6d | 6d | 6d | 6d | 6d | 6d |
| Exc. 30 but not exc. 50 m. | 4d | 4d | 5d | 6d | 6d | 6d | 6d | 8d | 8d | 8d | 8d | 8d | 9d |
| Exc. 50 but not exc. 100 m. | 4d | 4d | 5d | 6d | 7d | 8d | 9d | 10d | 11d | 1s | 1s | 1s | 1s 1d |
| Over 100 | 4d | 4d | 5d | 6d | 7d | 8d | 9d | 10d | 11d | 1s | 1s | 1s 1d | 1s 2d |

| Distance | Weight not exceeding — lb. | | | | | | | | | | | Over 24 per lb. |
|---|---|---|---|---|---|---|---|---|---|---|---|---|
| | 14 | 15 | 16 | 17 | 18 | 19 | 20 | 21 | 22 | 23 | 24 | |
| Not exceeding 30 m. | 6d | 6d | 6d | 6d | 6d | 6d | 6d | 6d | 6d | 6d | 6d | ½d |
| Exc. 30 but not exc. 50 m. | 9d | 9d | 10d | 10d | 10d | 11d | 11d | 11d | 1s | 1s | 1s | ½d |
| Exc. 50 but not exc. 100 m. | 1s 1d | 1s 2d | 1s 2d | 1s 3d | 1s 3d | 1s 4d | 1s 4d | 1s 5d | 1s 5d | 1s 6d | 1s 6d | ½d |
| Over 100 | 1s 3d | 1s 4d | 1s 5d | 1s 6d | 1s 7d | 1s 8d | 1s 9d | 1s 10d | 1s 11d | 2s | 2s | 1d |

[1] RCH 1/129: Minute 5777 of Superintendents Conference August 18, 1897.

[2] RCH 1/129: Minute 6522 of Superintendents Conference, November 11, 1897.

distances as well as weight. By 1874 the scope of the service was extended to most of the railways of the kingdom. But because of the regularity, certainty and economy of packing, newspapers represented 'the commodity par excellence' for the railway companies and it proved far less difficult for them to agree on a scale of charges roughly half the ordinary parcels scale, especially as the trade was conducted at 'owners' risk'.[1]

## VI

There are sound reasons for claiming that had it not been for the existence of the Railway Clearing House the British public would have been provided with a satisfactory and inexpensive parcels delivery service some twenty or thirty years earlier than was in fact the case.

The tradition that no majority decision of any Clearing House committee would be enforced on a company reluctant to adopt it, gave a single large concern the effective power of veto on any reform however meritorious and however widely it was accepted by the majority of the railways. A few companies whose Boards of Directors failed to appreciate the enormous increase in business that would result from lower charges, were able to block the adoption of both a low scale of rates based on weight and distance and a prepaid label system of charges based on weight alone. Ultimately the companies were obliged to lower their charges under the stimulus of Post Office competition, but when this happened the railways had to *share* the revenue on the Parcel Post, a situation which Neele had prophesied would come about if the companies persisted in maintaining high rates.[2]

Speaking in the second reading debate on the Railways Bill in 1844 Gladstone declared:

'There is no likelihood that the great experiment of the greatest possible cheapness will be tried under the present system. . . . The Boards of Directors of those companies are bound to produce the largest possible dividend to their shareholders—they have no

---

[1] RCH 1/115: Minute 914 of Superintendents Conference, January 25, 1866. Minute 2457 of Superintendents Conference, July 22, 1874. R. Bezzant: *Newspaper Carriage and Parcels Traffic on British Railways*, London, 1949.　　　　　[2] Neele: *op. cit.* p. 202.

national object to promote, and therefore if you come to deal with nine or ten railway companies in this matter, nine out of the ten may be disposed to try the experiment, but then it will be found that the tenth is able to so order matters as to baffle the experiment.'

The same fundamental obstacle which Gladstone said had delayed the introduction of adequate third-class passenger services also held back the introduction of an adequate parcels service.

If the Clearing House was weak in its inability to command uniformity of practice by the companies, it was powerful when it came to external negotiations. The chairman of the General Managers Conference or the secretary of the Clearing House could speak for *all* member companies when it came to a question of demanding more generous terms for co-operating in a parcel post scheme. The Postmaster-General therefore regarded the support of the Clearing House as essential for the success of any negotiations. In the background also was the Railway Companies' Association, able to marshall the support of a large proportion of the more than one hundred railway director MPs whenever the interests of the companies were threatened. Respect for the influence of the railway interest, whether exercised through the Clearing House or the Railway Companies' Association, meant that the country was fobbed off with a book post instead of a parcel post in 1853 and a sample post instead of a parcel post in 1863. When the parcel post finally came in 1883 it was on terms over-generous to the railways.

Had no Clearing House existed, the Government would have had a better excuse to introduce legislation to compel the carriage of postal parcels on the railways if negotiations on a company basis proved unfruitful. As an alternative, the parcel post service might have been extended region by region as the companies discovered the wisdom and profitability of co-operation. Before 1842 such an extension of service in co-operation with individual railways had taken place with the penny post. Had the situation developed in either of these ways Britain would then have been strongly placed to maintain her leadership in the postal service, so magnificently achieved in 1840. In the event, it was not until nearly the end of the nineteenth century that the lost ground of the previous fifty years was made good.

# CHAPTER VI

# THE ORGANISATION OF THE CLEARING HOUSE

## I

The directors of the nine companies which were founder members of the Clearing House were well aware that they had entered into a purely voluntary agreement. They had associated together for the limited purposes of dividing receipts on through traffic and tracing out the movement of rolling stock which passed from the lines of one railway company to those of another. They considered that the enlightened self interest of the companies would ensure the smooth working of the system and that there was no necessity for resorting to greater formalities or for making their agreement legally binding. In so far as thirty-four other companies joined them by the spring of 1848 it seemed that this assumption was well justified.[1]

The collapse of the railway mania and the aftermath of the financial panic of 1847 brought to an abrupt end this brief period of confident informality. In the course of 1848 some member companies failed to meet their obligations to the Clearing House and to their fellow members. As early as March 9, 1848, Kenneth Morison was reporting that many of the companies were very backward in the payment of sums due from them but that the Eastern Union and East Anglian Railway Companies were the worst offenders. When this report was considered by the committee of the Clearing House, Carr Glyn proposed that legal proceedings should be taken against the defaulters and that, to make this possible, a Deed of Association should be drafted and signed by the members.[2] This recommendation was adopted and a lengthy

[1] RCH 3/1: 'Draft Deed Respecting the Railway Clearing System'; drawn up in 1848, lists forty-three member companies.
[2] RCH 1/13: Minutes of committee, March 9, 1848.

document was prepared by Messrs Parker, Hayes and Co. and dispatched to the Boards of member companies for their comments. Although the main purpose of the deed was to facilitate the payment of debts, there were clauses providing for the settlement of disputes by arbitration, and the giving of three months' notice of any intention to resign from the Clearing House. The deed was never signed. The concensus of opinion among the railway companies lawyers being that statutory powers were needed to enforce the payments of debts, it was agreed, in December 1849, to ask Messrs Egerton and Dodson to draft a Bill for consideration by the Clearing House committee in April 1850.

In its original form the Bill would have given the Clearing House authority to make regulations for the better administration of the railways as well as conferring powers for the recovery of debts. But the majority of the committee favoured a Bill of more limited scope, and after a long discussion it was agreed to erase clauses 5, 6 and 19 which would have increased the responsibilities of the Clearing House beyond the mere settlement of accounts for through traffic. The truncated Bill had an easy passage through Parliament and on June 25, 1850, became law as the Railway Clearing Act.[1]

After the Queen had signed the new law the Clearing House was more restricted in its powers than it had been during the first eight years of its existence. Hitherto its authority was as wide as the member companies chose to make it, but from midsummer 1850 the only important powers retained were those associated with the collection of the debts owed by the companies. These were included in sections 12–14 of the Act and were, within their limited range, completely effective. In June 1851 the committee gave Morison authority to direct legal proceedings against both the Eastern Union and the East Anglian Companies. Three months later he reported that not only had these two offenders paid up, but that 'the companies generally had paid more punctually than heretofore'. No doubt the transformation was, in part, due to the buoyant effect of the economic recovery on railway revenues. But this was not the only explanation. According to one

[1] RCH 1/2: Minutes of committee, April 10. House of Commons Journals, 13–14 Victoriae, Vol. CV, various references from March 20–June 25, 1850.

account an official of one of the recalcitrant companies was given short shrift in the court by Vice Chancellor Kindersley.

' "What," said the indignant judge, "not obey the order of this court! What's his name? Officer of the court, take that man and"— this of course was sotto voce—"cast him into outer darkness." A shriek of wild despair went up from the terrified official, representing the company, seated on one of the back benches of the court. He was not, however, consigned to the durance which his contempt of court had merited, but his personal liberty was only retained on the condition that the amount claimed should be immediately forthcoming.'[1]

These were not the only legal proceedings taken by the Clearing House for the recovery of debt. In December 1854 the secretary was authorised to proceed against both the Oxford, Worcester and Wolverhampton, and the St Helens Companies. No less than seven companies were sued early in 1867 and another three in the summer of 1879.[2]

As railway services rapidly extended in the course of the 1850s the limitations imposed by the Act of 1850 were more and more keenly felt. The railway companies were establishing more links with steamboat services in the English Channel and Irish Sea. In 1858 the Government urged the London and North Western Railway to accelerate communications between England and Ireland and Parliament granted the company powers to use locomotives on the streets and pier at Holyhead.[3] To Morison, at least, it seemed illogical that the Government should help remove physical hindrances to through transport, while retaining, in the Railway Clearing Act, obstacles of a legal and commercial character to improved communications. By the terms of the Act membership of the Clearing House was confined to railway

[1] RCH 1/13: Minutes 170 and 171 of committee, June 11, 1851. Report of K. Morison to the committee, September 10, 1851. E. McDermott: *The Railway Clearing House*, London, 1890, p. 10.

[2] RCH 1/13: Minutes 344 and 347 of the committee, December 13, 1854. RCH 1/115 and 1/117: Decisions of Superintendents Conference, January 31, 1867, June 25 and September 10, 1879.

[3] London and North Western Railway: Directors' Report, August 19, 1859, *Herapath's Railway Journal*. For the Parliamentary powers see 21 and 22 Victoriae, c. 130-1.

companies. Through booking arrangements with steamship companies were not possible under Clearing House auspices. In the meantime Morison had been trying to bring in more of the Irish companies. The Dublin and Belfast Railway was an early member of the Clearing House but most of the southern lines remained aloof. In an endeavour to persuade them to co-operate, he chaired a series of meetings of representatives of the Irish companies in Dublin between July and November 1854. The response of the northern companies was encouraging but the Great Southern and Western Railway had already organised, at Kingsbridge, a clearing system for traffic between the north and the south and it refused to abandon these arrangements in favour of full participation in the Clearing House in London.[1] Eventually the Irish railway Clearing House was formally established by Act of Parliament in 1860. The failure of Morison's attempt to rope in more of the Irish Companies induced him to consider alternative means of encouraging through traffic across the Irish Sea.

In his report to the committee in September 1858, therefore, he advanced a new plan. The Clearing House should apply to Parliament to have the Railway Clearing Act extended to permit the admission to membership of canal and steamboat companies. The Committee gave the plan its backing and by the end of the year printed copies of a Railway Clearing Bill were in the hands of the companies.[2] After the September meeting, some of the delegates suggested to Morison that the Bill should be widened in scope to authorise membership by carrying concerns such as Pickfords and to permit agreements with continental and even colonial railways. This would serve to stifle any criticism that the Bill was mainly serving the interests of the London and North Western Railway Co. and it might save a subsequent application to Parliament to extend yet again the powers of the Clearing House.[3] Morison took this advice. Section one of the Bill, therefore, provided that 'all corporations companies, partnerships and bodies

[1] Irish meetings reported in RCH 1/383. By minute 199 of the committee held on September 10, 1851, it was decided that the City of Dublin Steam Packet Company was ineligible for membership under the Clearing Act.

[2] RCH 1/4: Morison's report to the committee, September 8, 1858, and minute 514 of committee, September 8, 1858.

[3] RCH 1/4: Morison's report to the committee, March 9, 1859.

of associated persons' engaged in any form of transport in 'any part of the world' were eligible for membership of the Clearing House. But these proposals were too sweeping for the Boards of the Great Northern, Midland and London and North Western Railways to accept and they sent petitions against the Bill to the Select Committee of the House of Lords which was considering it. Morison told this committee on April 7, 1859, that the principal grounds for their objections were that if membership was extended on the lines envisaged, the cost of administering the Clearing House would be greatly increased.[1]

In the light of this unexpected opposition of important railway companies, the sponsors of the Bill announced their willingness to strike out the offending clauses which permitted the admission of other carrying concerns, provided they could retain other clauses, which increased the legal powers of the Clearing House. The Lords' committee would not agree. As soon as the Bill had been printed copies came into the hands of various owners of colliery waggons who promptly organised a highly successful meeting in Nottingham. Two men who had attended this meeting Mr Harrison of the Moira Colliery Co. and Mr Dodson of the Kirk Lees Colliery Co. gave evidence before the Lords' Committee. They complained that on occasion the railway companies delayed the return of their empty waggons for up to two months, and that in consequence they were obliged to make uneconomic additions to their rolling stock. They asked for amendments to the Bill to permit the waggon owners to join the Clearing House which would inform them of the movements of all their vehicles and prevent undue delays. The Lords' committee saw the force of these arguments and agreed to amend the Bill accordingly. Faced with the possibility of having to admit hundreds of new members and to meet a great increase of administrative expenses, the sponsors of the Bill, on April 7, 1859, decided to withdraw it. The attempt to extend the legal powers and scope of the Clearing House had been a dismal failure.[2]

[1] House of Lords Record Office, H/L Papers, Box 6. Act for Extending and Improving the Railway Clearing System, and minutes of evidence of Select Committee, p. 39.

[2] H/L Papers 1859: Box 6, evidence of Messrs Harrison and Dodson, pp. 50–54, 69–73. Report of committee proceedings, p. 18.

In default of the greater powers sought in 1859 it was left to the individual railway companies most interested to make *ad hoc* arrangements for through traffic with Ireland and the continent. In the event the Clearing House recognised agreements made between the railways and the steamship companies for the division of receipts on through traffic, the railway companies accepting immediate responsibility for sums owing by those steamship concerns in which they were most directly interested.

The failure of the committee to obtain the greater powers which it sought in 1858–59 almost certainly encouraged rather than deterred new applications for membership. It is not surprising that the Great Western, with its broad gauge, should have declined membership until after Parliament had ruled in favour of the standard gauge by the Gauge Act of 1846; but it was not until eleven more years had passed that this company was formally admitted.[1] The Clearing House had been opened for ten years before any company from south of the river Thames applied for membership. The pioneer in this region was the London and South Western which sent a delegate to the committee for the first time in December 1851. The other southern companies were in no hurry to follow this lead. The South Eastern Board delayed its decision for a further eight years. The two other major companies of the south; the London, Brighton and South Coast, and the London, Chatham and Dover did not join until 1861 and 1863 respectively. An important reason for these delays was the absence of a through rail link between the railways north and south of the river until the line was built between Willesden and Old Kew Junction in 1854. Even then the new route was at first little used. Only with the opening of the West London extension from Kensington to Clapham Junction in 1862 was there a substantial expansion of through traffic in this area.[2] Nevertheless with the eventual recruitment of these important southern lines the percentage of route mileage of lines of member companies of the Clearing House to the country's total route mileage rose from 55.8 in 1850 to 88.7 in 1865. By 1900 it was up to 94.5.[3]

---

[1] RCH 1/14: Minute 456 of committee of March 11, 1857.
[2] Neele: *Railway Reminiscences*, London, 1904, p. 97.
[3] See Appendix 2 for details of membership.

II

For some months in the 1850s the Clearing House committee toyed with the ideas of trying to influence the decisions of Parliament through the employment of a Parliamentary agent. In 1839 a Railway Society had been formed in Westminster for the purpose, *inter alia*, of lobbying MPs whenever a Bill which affected the interests of railway companies was being considered in Parliament. But this organisation petered out in the following year when it was seen that the report of Lord Seymour's Select Committee on Railways presented no substantial threat to the companies' independence. George Hudson's mobilisation of the railway interest in opposition to important clauses of Gladstone's Railway Bill in 1844 is well known; but this was not the work of any formal organisation. Thereafter for some years interest in the subject waned. But after the railway companies had experienced several years of disappointingly low dividends in the late 1840s and the early 1850s the importance of Parliamentary influence to check excessive competition was again appreciated. In June 1851 the Clearing House committee, after a full discussion, resolved:

'. . . That is is expedient to appoint a Parliamentary agent in London, to watch, at the expense of the associated companies, any bills other than railway bills, which may be brought into Parliament in order that no clause injurious to the interests of railway companies may be passed unnoticed; and that steps be taken to ascertain whether the railway companies who are not parties to the Clearing System will unite in the object; the result of the enquiry to be reported at the next meeting.'[1]

At the following meeting, in September 1851, the replies of the companies were read out by Mr Morison. It may be implied that the majority were favourable to the plan, for the committee resolved:

'. . . that Mr Coates be appointed to act for the associated companies in the capacity just referred to, and be requested to communicate with the Secretary of the Clearing House on all matters,

[1] RCH 1/13: Minute 176 of committee of June 11, 1851.

connected with his office, whether relating to the interests of particular companies or to railway interests in general and further that companies communicate with Mr Coates through the same channel.'

Mr Coates was voted a salary of £200 a year.[1] Early in the following year Mr Coates warned Mr Morison that the Electric Telegraph and Permanent Ways Bill then before Parliament would, if passed, have serious repercussions on the interests of the companies. In March the committee concluded:

'. . . that as the powers proposed to be taken in the Bill introduce very objectionable principles and might prove in practice very oppressive to railway companies, it be opposed on the second reading and in committee under the authority of the companies represented at this meeting, unless they, within a fortnight, notify their dissent from the course proposed to be taken with reference to the Bill.'[2]

Despite his first having raised the subject, Mr Coates then began to have doubts whether the committee as such was in a position to influence decisions of Parliament. In June 1852 Morison reported that the Parliamentary agent was doubtful whether the committee had a *locus standi* on the measure. It was therefore decided to advise each company to petition against the Bill and to authorise Mr Coates to do all he could to co-ordinate their efforts.[3]

At the same meeting Mr W. Chaplin MP, a director of the London and South Western Railway, moved a resolution that the committee should make a united effort to persuade Parliament to abolish the passenger duty on all fares under a penny a mile. At this point Carr Glyn intervened from the chair. He considered Chaplin's motion as 'not being within the limits to which the Committee of Delegates of the Railway Clearing House should be confined. He thought the Committee would act wisely by rigorously restricting themselves to those functions.' The committee concurred.[4] Although over £1,500 was voted in fees to the

[1] RCH 1/13: Minute 188 of committee of September 10, 1851. Minute 203 of committee of December 10, 1851.
[2] RCH 1/13: Minute 223 of committee of March 10, 1852.
[3] RCH 1/13: Morison's report to the committee, June 9, 1852.
[4] *Ibid*. Report of committee meeting, June 9, 1852.

Parliamentary agent that year, much less is heard of his activities from the time of Carr Glyn's ruling.[1] In March 1853 his retaining fee was reduced in consequence of his services being less in demand.[2] In September 1855 he wrote a letter to the committee stressing the importance of a continuing watch over Parliamentary business. On his advice it was resolved:

'... to recommend to the Boards of Companies in connection with the Clearing System, and to any other inclined to join them, to form a permanent Committee for the protection of the general interests of the railway companies.'[3]

As a matter of fact eighteen months earlier at a meeting in the Kings Arms, Palace Yard, Westminster, Coates had brought together the representatives of twenty-three railway companies and had formed a committee which was, in effect, the forerunner of the short-lived Railway Companies Association which functioned between July 1858 and September 1861. It is significant that in March 1859 the Clearing House committee sanctioned Morison's acting as secretary to the Railway Companies Association at the same time as he was serving as secretary to the Clearing House—a remarkable indication of the liaison between the two bodies. A more permanent organisation, which eventually took the name of the Railway Companies Association was formed in June 1867 and survived for eighty years.[4]

Once this new organisation was well established there was no necessity for the Clearing House to continue dabbling in politics. Henceforward there was a division of labour. The Railway Companies Association protected the interests of the railways in Parliament: the Railway Clearing House confined itself to the business of organising the railway traffic.

### III

Although the legal powers of the Clearing House had been so greatly restricted by legislation, most railway companies soon

---

[1] RCH 1/13: Minute 252 of committee, September 8, 1852.
[2] RCH 1/13: Minute 366 of committee, March 14, 1855.
[3] RCH 1/13: Minute 386 of committee, September 12, 1855.
[4] P. S. Bagwell: 'The Railway Interest: Its Organisation and Influence, 1839–1914.' *Journal of Transport History*, November 1965, p. 65 *et seq*.

learned to appreciate the advantages of the central position of the Seymour Street building as a venue for railway conferences of all kinds. The meetings of general managers, passenger superintendents, locomotive engineers and many others became well known in the railway world as Clearing House conferences. But the decisions then reached lacked the binding force of arrangements for the division of traffic receipts which could be enforced by the Clearing House committee under the terms of the Clearing Act of 1850. The distinguished General Manager of the London and South Western Railway, Sir Charles J. Owens, explained the position very clearly in answer to a question from a member of the departmental committee of the Board of Trade in 1911:

Chairman: 'I suppose what have been loosely called by our witnesses Clearing House agreements really have nothing to do with the Clearing House properly speaking?
Sir Charles Owens: Quite so.
Chairman: They only happen to be the result of a conference which took place at the Clearing House?
Sir Charles Owens: Exactly: they are railway companies agreements but they are not Clearing House agreements.'[1]

Nevertheless this was not the whole of the story. Many decisions of the Conferences would have been quite unworkable without the full co-operation of the staff of the Clearing House. Strictly speaking the Conference of Superintendents which, each year, agreed on a long list of special excursion fares, was not a Clearing House Conference: it remained the fact that the clerks at Seymour Street were instructed to divide the receipts from excursion traffic according to the same rates as they divided receipts from ordinary fares. In the same way the decision of the general managers to remit the charge for the return of livestock unsold at agricultural shows was based on the assumption that the Clearing House staff would follow this ruling in the division of receipts. Furthermore the staff of the Clearing House performed valuable secretarial services for all the conferences.

From April 1842 until January 1847 the Clearing House committee dealt with all matters involved in the running of the new

[1] Departmental Committee on Railway Agreements and Amalgamation, 1910–11, minutes of evidence, Qs 11,747–8.

organisation. From the arrangements for the adoption of Edmundson's ticket system to decisions about the demurrage on goods waggons or the conditions of employment of the clerks, all came within its purview. Until January 1884[1] it was still the formal rule that the minutes of the conferences of general managers superintendents, etc., were not valid until approved by the Clearing House committee; but after that date it was decided that as business had become so vast, it was best to divide the agenda into two parts. All subjects which related directly to the carrying out of the Clearing Act and the settlement of accounts under the Act still needed the final approval of the Clearing House committee: all other matters were to be sent to a meeting of general managers for final approval. These general managers' meetings which began on December 1883 were quite distinct from the General Managers Conferences which had been held continuously from January 1851, and to emphasise their difference their minutes were printed on *white* paper (and hence known as the 'white minutes') to distinguish them from the conference minutes which had always been printed on *blue* paper and were thenceforward known as the 'blue minutes'.

It is scarcely surprising that the first conference to be held was that of the goods managers. The organisation of the goods traffic presented many more problems than did that of the passenger traffic, and whereas the Clearing House committee achieved a quick success in making arrangements for the through booking of passengers, it needed to call upon the expert assistance of the goods managers to tackle such complicated questions as the classification of goods, demurrage charges and the role of the private carriers. The first conference of this series was held on January 19, 1847,[2] and the delegates continued to meet monthly until July 1850 when it was felt that some of the most important tasks had been successfully tackled and that meetings held once in two months would be sufficient. From January 1884, when the Clearing House committee decided on the division of the agenda, there were both goods managers' meetings—to consider matters arising out of the Clearing Act—and goods managers' conferences

---

[1] RCH 1/118: Minute 5153 of Meeting of Superintendents, January 23, 1884.     [2] RCH 1/179.

which dealt with all other questions concerning goods traffic.[1] The last of the meetings of these two groups were held in December 1947, just before the British Transport Commission assumed responsibility for the railways.

The truth of the contention that the work of the conferences was not essential to the implementation of the Clearing Act is revealed in the early history of the Superintendents Conference. The first recorded meeting of this group of men, who had responsibility for the passenger services, was held at Normanton on November 14, 1850, though there is evidence in the minutes that earlier meetings of passenger superintendents of northern lines had been held. No reference whatever is made to the clearing house in the minutes of the November meeting and neither Mr Morison nor any member of his staff was present. It was not until the following meeting on December 19, 1850, that a proposal of Mr Denniston of the Great Northern, 'that the Clearing House should be asked to send a person down to attend all the meetings and take a record of the proceedings', was approved by all fourteen delegates present. From January 1851 onwards a senior member of the Clearing House staff was always present and in the early years this was Mr Macaulay. It was not until May 1851 that the first meeting was held in London. Thereafter the influence of the Clearing House over the proceedings of the conference increased substantially. On January 22, 1852 it was decided to hold alternate meetings in London on the same day as the goods managers met, and Mr Morison was asked to draw up a set of bye-laws for the conduct of the meetings. On March 19, 1852, at the first meeting held in the Clearing House building, these bye-laws were approved and the practice began of sending all resolutions to the secretary of the Clearing House for endorsement by the committee.[2]

The agenda of the Superintendents Conferences was characterised by its infinite variety. Besides questions of prime importance such as the establishment of a uniform code of telegraphic signals, members had to decide on a great number of questions of less fundamental moment. One would like to know, for example, how

[1] RCH 1/186: Minute 6018 of Goods Managers Conference, January 24, 1884.

[2] RCH 1/99: Superintendents Conference, minute 4 of December 19, 1850, and minute 84 of January 22, 1852.

long it took the conference, in April 1894, to decide that 'monkeys conveyed in charge of organ grinders etc., be charged as for one dog', or on what principle it was decided to reject the application for special concession fares for delegates attending the Primitive Methodist Conference at Brixton but to approve the application for reduced rate tickets to be issued to persons attending the Brewers Exhibition at the Agricultural Hall in London. In October 1894 delegates had to decide on an appeal for 'a rate for one dog to be charged for the conveyance of bitches (sent to act as foster mothers) and their puppies, the latter being destroyed on reaching their destination'. They concluded that this was asking too much and that a separate charge should be made for each animal even though the majority were of such a tender age and had so severely limited an expectation of life.

At the beginning of 1884 the agenda for consideration by the superintendents was divided into two parts in a similar fashion to the division of the agenda of the goods traffic managers.[1] Items which concerned the implementation of the Railway Clearing Act were dealt with at a superintendents conference whilst all other questions were to be discussed at the meeting. Separate meetings of superintendents under Clearing House auspices ceased after December 1947.

Regular conferences of the general managers were the outcome of demands from both the Clearing House committee and the superintendents. The managers met spasmodically at the request of the committee as early as 1849. In March of that year they were asked to meet for the purpose of determining the scale of terminal allowances. Just over a year later they were assigned the task of drafting a standard set of dimensions for railway waggons. But it was the coming of the Great Exhibition in Hyde Park, London, in the Summer of 1851 that transformed occasional *ad hoc* meetings into regularly held conferences. At their meeting on February 20, 1851, the Superintendents considered

'. . . that it would be exceedingly desirable that a meeting of General Managers and Coaching Superintendents be held to consider the question of excursion trains during the forthcoming exhibition with particular reference to fares'.

[1] RCH 1/118: Minute 5153 of Superintendents Conference, January 23, 1884.

The committee backed this up three weeks later with the more comprehensive request that the general managers should meet 'to fix arrangements for the Great Exhibition'.[1]

Thus the general managers began their regular conferences at the Clearing House early in 1851 and continued the series for nearly a hundred years. The last conference was held on December 11, 1947. After the division of the agenda at the beginning of 1884, a newly constituted General Managers Meeting dealt with those matters which had no direct bearing on the Clearing Act while all other questions continued to be discussed at the conferences. By this time the importance of the general managers in the railway hierarchy had greatly increased. In the typical railway company the chairman of the Board of Directors had yielded pride of place to the general manager as the person of greatest influence on policy. It was the outcome of the growth in size of railway companies and the increasingly complicated character of the administration. Thus from 1884 onwards on broad issues of railway policy, outside the narrow interpretation of the Clearing Act the general managers were final arbiters. After the minutes of conferences of goods managers, superintendents and others had obtained the approval of the general managers they could be effectively enforced with most companies. (Though of course each company retained its right to dissent from any conference ruling.) There was no longer any need to submit the majority of the conference decisions to the Clearing House committee for its approval. By the 1930s the roles of the Clearing House committee and the General Managers Conference had undergone a complete revolution when compared with the situation eighty years earlier. When it is recalled that the conference came into being as a result of a decision of the committee, it comes as a shock to read that in October 1939 the general managers reproved the committee for granting an increase of salaries to Clearing House staff and warned that in future no such decision should be taken without their prior approval.

In the case of the locomotive engineers and carriage and works superintendents, their conference, whose first meeting was not

[1] RCH 1/13: Minute of Clearing House committee, March 6, 1849; minute 121 of June 26, 1850 and minute 166 of March 12, 1851. RCH 1/99: Minute 21 of Superintendents Conference.

held until June 6, 1885, was brought into being mainly as a result of pressure from the Board of Trade. An accident at Penistone in January 1885 caused by the failure of an axle on a private owner's waggon, led Major Marindin, the Board's inspector, to write an adverse report on the general condition of private owners' waggons. The under-secretary at the Board of Trade then wrote to Mr Dawson, the secretary of the Clearing House, demanding that the whole question be given careful and urgent attention. The summoning of the Engineers Conference was the direct outcome. It continued to meet, though under varying designations, until the nationalisation of the railways.

In another category were a group of committees which directly served the interests of the Clearing House committee and its employees. Within fifteen years of its establishment the Clearing House had grown so large that Mr Morison thought it wise to establish an office committee over which he presided and in which he was helped by leading members of his staff. From its first meeting on May 4, 1867, to its closure in the course of 1941, its main task was to maintain the good discipline and welfare of the staff. While in theory its decisions required the approval of the Clearing House committee, in practice it enjoyed full autonomy. Mr Morison's successor, Mr Dawson, decided in May 1862 to summon regular meetings of the waggon inspectors who were directly responsible for the discipline and welfare of the number takers. The committee's work ranged from important tasks such as organising the inspectors districts and recommending scales of pay for the outdoor staff, to matters of detail such as putting pressure on the North Eastern Railways to provide proper waterproof shelters for the number takers at Stockton or dismissing the lad, J. Moses, from his part at Hereford on the grounds that he had 'no energy whatever' for number taking.[1] Very important for planning the work of the Clearing House was the Superintending Committee which held its first meeting on June 27, 1862,[2] and its last on May 14, 1955, the year in which the Clearing House was disbanded. It was set up by a resolution of the main committee following a special report on the internal management of the

[1] RCH 1/376: Meetings of Inspectors, minute 27 of December 23, 1862 and minute 32 of February 2, 1863.
[2] RCH 1/14: Minute 663 of Clearing House committee, June 11, 1862.

Clearing House which was ordered to be prepared soon after Morison's death in 1861. It was responsible for deciding how the costs of running the Clearing House should be divided between the different departments and shared out in an equitable manner between the member companies. It made recommendations on office management. Without its labours the costs of running the establishment would have mounted, alarmingly. The Premises Trust was formed in 1871 on the occasion of the Clearing House committee coming into possession of the freehold of the building in Seymour Street, after leasing it for many years from the London and North Western Railway. From the date of its first meeting on October 19, 1871, to the winding up of the Trust on August 4, 1948, after the property had been transferred to the British Transport Commission, it was responsible for maintaining the Clearing House premises in good condition and for making recommendations for extension and re-equipment of the premises.

In a category on their own were the rate conferences and pooling agreements, dependent on the Clearing House for their successful functioning, but in no way official Clearing House conferences. Their work was of such significance as to merit treatment in a separate chapter.

A large number of other conferences and committees which were associated with the Clearing House lacked the permanence and importance of those whose work has already been described. Perhaps the nearest approach to the better known bodies in importance was the Accountants Committee which met for the specific purpose of implementing the clauses of the Railway Regulation Act of 1868 concerning the standardisation of accounts, but which met more regularly after December 1870. From time to time it gave valuable advice about the better ordering of the accounts of the Clearing House as well as influencing the policy of the companies. The Parcel Post Conference met continuously after May 1883 to negotiate terms with the Postmaster General for the parcel post service; the Rules and Regulations Committee met from 1894 onwards to keep the Clearing House Rules up to date; a General Rates Conference in 1888 and 1889 was engaged in the vast task of redrafting freight charges; a Common User Committee functioned continuously after 1915 to organise the pooling of rolling stock; a Railway

Statistics Committee from 1919, supplied the Ministry of Transport with railway statistics and an Air Transport Committee met between 1934 and 1937 to deal with problems arising in the railway companies' air services. The list is by no means exhaustive, but is long enough to reveal how many and varied were the ramifications of the Clearing House.

## IV

In the first seventy years of its life the Clearing House was repeatedly under the urgent necessity of providing additional accommodation for its staff. It seemed that on every occasion when substantial additional seating space for clerks was provided, the volume of business expanded with remarkable rapidity and the employment of many additional men proved necessary. Congratulation on the provision of more elbow room had scarcely died down before there were renewed complaints of overcrowding. Before June 27, 1862, immediate responsibility for meeting the increased need for working space rested with the Clearing House committee, but for nearly ten years thereafter it was the job of the Superintending Committee, although final approval of the clearing house committee on important decisions was always necessary. From its foundation in 1871 until the closure of the Clearing House in 1955 the Premises Trust maintained the buildings and made arrangements for necessary extensions.

For the first five years the staff were housed in a small building at 11 Drummond Street nearly opposite the main entrance to Euston Station. But the number of companies in the Clearing House increased by over 400% in this period, and in February 1847 Mr Morison reported that a larger office would have to be provided 'without delay' if the work was to continue satisfactorily. The committee therefore accepted an offer of the London and North Western Railway to construct, in Seymour Street, a new £7,000 office building designed by the Company's architect Mr P. Hardwick. This work was completed early in 1849 and from that date until 1871 the committee rented the accommodation at a charge of £500 a year.[1] Scarcely more than two years later Morison

[1] RCH 1/13: Minutes of Clearing House committee, February 19, 1847.

was obliged to return to the subject of the office accommodation. In his report on June 11, 1851 he wrote:

'The additional office accommodation recently provided, is again found to be insufficient, and if the business of the Clearing House continues to increase, the office must be enlarged. It is also necessary that steps should be taken to improve the mode of ventilating the rooms; they cannot in fact be ventilated at present without producing cold currents of air, which are very injurious, and have, I fear, in one or two instances proved fatal to the clerks.'

The committee was convinced that the need was urgent. It ordered the preparation of a plan for the enlargement of the premises.[1] The outcome was the construction of the famous Long Office (illustrated between pages 96 and 97) and the Board Room for the meetings of the committee. The additional rooms were leased from the railway company.

At the end of 1855, membership of the Clearing House being more than double what it was in 1847, a sub-committee was instructed to prepare plans for yet more office space. This was duly made available on lease at the end of the following year. But once more it proved little better than a stop gap. In December 1858 Carr Glyn informed the committee that 'in consequence of the accession of new companies and the steady increase in business', more accommodation had to be provided. This particular emergency was met by leasing 99 Seymour Street, adjacent to the existing Clearing House premises.[2]

Additional nearby premises were leased in 1863 but the Superintending Committee reported, in May 1865, the need for still more room. Within the following twelve months the number of clerks employed rose by more than one hundred, and in April 1865 Dawson urged that in addition to building more rooms for the existing staff the committee should build at once extra rooms 'anticipating the future'.[3] The big improvement made in 1866 was the provision of a clerks' dining room and the extension of the office accommodation.

[1] RCH 1/13: Minute 182 of Clearing House committee, June 11, 1851.
[2] RCH 1/14: Minute 553 of Clearing House committee, June 8, 1859.
[3] RCH 1/23: Minute of superintending committee, April 20, 1865.

By 1870 the Board of the London and North Western Railway was becoming tired of dealing with repeated applications for new leases of property, and in July of that year the Superintending Committee was informed that the directors of the railway would be pleased if arrangements could be made for the Clearing House to purchase the freehold of all the leased buildings for a sum of £95,000. This plan was approved by the Superintending Committee in December 1870 after the consent of the majority of the companies to the change had been obtained.[1]

In the early 1870s the volume of work in the Clearing House reflected the rapid increase in railway traffic at the height of the boom. So great was the need for more desk space in these months that an arrangement was made with the Midland Railway to accommodate sixty clerks in two large rooms in St Pancras Station while the Rev. Thomas Stevenson, Vicar of St Mary's, lent the use of a school room in Clarendon Square for six months at a rental of £50. These temporary arrangements were brought to an end with the completion of new building work in March 1873.[2]

In 1874, under the Railway Clearing House Extension Act, Parliamentary powers were obtained for the borrowing of up to £150,000 to make possible the purchase of thirty-six more houses in Seymour Street and one in Bedford Street. Within a few days of the passing of the Act the Standard Life Assurance Company had advanced £80,000 for new building works. Repayment over a period of twenty-five years was undertaken by the companies in proportion to the value of work performed for them by the Clearing House, the London and North Western Railway, for example, making the sizeable contribution of £14,546 whilst the lesser known Portadown, Dungannon and Omagh Railway made the decidedly humbler contribution of £1.[3]

In the meantime the superintending committee had given serious consideration to a proposal that the Clearing House should move to a completely new site somewhere in the countryside north of London. The scheme was rejected on many grounds. Documents

[1] RCH 1/27: Report of superintending committee, December 14, 1870.
[2] RCH 1/27: Superintending committee, minute 2060 of June 29, 1871 and 2545 of March 27, 1873.
[3] RCH 1/15: Clearing House committee, minutes 1302 of December 10, 1873, 1335 of June 10, 1874 and 1346 of September 9, 1874.

would take longer to reach the Clearing House; London was the best meeting place for conferences of general managers and others; the existing building was ill suited to any other purpose and would have a poor market value and many clerks were in the process of buying their houses in the London area.[1]

In February 1881 the secretary submitted an 'urgent report' to the committee revealing a renewed threat of overcrowding. The committee responded in the following month by approving expenditure of £25,000, the money to be borrowed from the Clearing House Clerks and Number Takers Savings Bank Fund.[2] Within eighteen months the Clearing House had spread its tentacles many more yards northwards in Seymour Street. Although these extensions proved sufficient for nearly fifteen years, another 'urgent report' from the secretary, in February 1896, stressed that the provision of more space 'could not be long delayed', as the number of clerks in some of the offices was already 'in excess of standard accommodation'. To ease the situation a sum of £17,000 was voted to provide room for 250 additional clerks and to make necessary enlargements to the dining room and kitchen.[3] During the last six years of the nineteenth century the number of clerks employed in the Clearing House rose by over 400, to reach a total of over 2,000. In June 1900, therefore, additional office space for 600 clerks was provided by an expenditure of £36,000, to add another floor to the buildings purchased in 1896.[4] The number of staff employed again rose rapidly in 1912–13 and at the beginning of 1914 for the first time there were over 2,500 clerks employed in the London office.[5] But no permanent addition to the Clearing House premises resulted from this expansion in numbers which was checked in the course of 1914. In terms of accommodation the peak had been reached and the organisation entered its longest period of stability.

[1] RCH 1/28: Report of superintending committee, December 10, 1873.
[2] RCH 1/16: P. W. Dawson's report to the committee, February 24, 1881 and minute 1655 of March 9, 1881.
[3] RCH 1/17: Minute 2256 of Clearing House committee, March 11, 1896.
[4] RCH 1/35: Superintending committee report, December 31, 1899, and RCH 1/17: minute 3435 of Clearing House committee, June 13, 1900.
[5] RCH 1/11: Report of the superintending committee to the Quarterly Meeting of Delegates, December 10, 1913.

V

The cost of establishing the Clearing House was borne by the London and Birmingham Railway whose Board of Directors voted the money for the necessary publicity and correspondence and made available the first office accommodation. But one of the first tasks confronting the committee in April 1842 was to make arrangements for all member companies to make a fair contribution towards meeting the costs of the new organisation. The simple solution hit upon was for each member company to pay £5 per year to the Clearing House for each 'booking through' station on its line. If these sums proved insufficient, the residue of expenses was to be met by additional payments proportional to each company's share of the total through receipts from passenger fares, and the payments for carrying horses, carriages, dogs and parcels.[1] However, because some of the smaller companies complained that the charge of £5 per station was excessive, on the recommendation of Morison, in August 1844 the committee reduced the payment on account of intermediate stations to £2 a year while retaining the contribution of £5 in respect of terminal stations.[2] A further modification was made two years later when the charge for 'minor stations' was lowered to £1 a year.[3]

With the rapid growth in the clearing system the original simple method of financing the work of the organisation had to be substantially modified if injustice to individual companies was to be avoided. Morison therefore persuaded the committee, in March 1853, to adopt a different plan. The work was to be divided between four departments: mileage, through traffic, special traffic and publication. At the end of each half year the total expenses were to be divided between these four departments in the ratio of the number of clerks employed in each. In the mileage department member companies were to share the cost in the ratio of the number of entries for carriages, waggons and other stock made in the accounts for each company. For the other three departments no change was made in the method of distributing the costs between

---

[1] RCH 1/2: Minute 3 of Clearing House committee, April 26, 1842.
[2] RCH 1/2: Minute 32 of Clearing House committee, August 23, 1844.
[3] RCH 1/2: Minute 59 of Clearing House committee, August 26, 1846.

the companies, i.e. a sum proportional to each company's share of traffic receipts, but the costs of each department would be kept distinct and each company would be separately charged for each account.[1]

Although a sub-committee was appointed in December 1854 to enquire into the method of assessing the Clearing House expenses on the companies, it found the arrangements made in March 1853 'a fair compromise of conflicting interests and extreme views' and proposed only minor modifications.[2] This report by no means allayed the discontent which existed in some of the companies and on March 12, 1856, another sub-committee was appointed to re-examine the whole question. It reported that there was a wide-spread opinion that the existing method of dividing the expenses was 'unequal in its pressure on the companies' to an extent which was unjust, and it expressed some sympathy with this view. It recommended the adoption of a system of dividing the costs of the traffic department according to the time spent on each company's accounts. No change was proposed in the method of dividing the expenses in the mileage department. The committee accepted these recommendations and the new rule came into force on July 1, 1856.[3]

The death of Mr Morison on October 26, 1861, and the appointment of Mr Philip Dawson as his successor was made the occasion of a thorough review of the management of the Clearing House. In December of that year it was unanimously agreed that 'a committee be appointed to enquire into the working and establishment of the Clearing House and to report thereon to the Committee of Delegates'.[4]

Undoubtedly the most important outcome of the thorough investigation into the organisation of the Clearing House which followed the appointment of this special committee was an over-hauling and streamlining of the departments. From the time the

[1] RCH 1/3: Minute 277 of Clearing House committee, March 9, 1853.
[2] RCH 1/3: Report of sub-committee on division of Clearing House expenses, May 23, 1855.
[3] RCH 1/3: Minute 427 Clearing House committee, September 10, 1856.
[4] RCH 1/3: Minute 642 of Clearing House committee, December 11, 1861.

recommendations of the committee came into force on July 1, 1862, the work of the Clearing House was divided between three main departments. These were (a) the general or secretarial, (b) the traffic which was subdivided into the merchandise and coaching (or passenger train) sections, and (c) the mileage. There were many subdivisions within each of these three main groups but the general plan for the allocation of the work remained intact until after the First World War.[1] For more than fifty years, therefore, the method of dividing the expenses of running the Clearing House between the member companies was broadly as follows. The expenses of the general or secretarial department were distributed over the other two departments in the ratio of the number of clerks in each. The expenses of the traffic department—which took the lion's share of the costs of the whole establishment—were divided on the basis of the amount of time occupied in dealing with each company's accounts. Where companies had special traffic agreements with each other the cost of settling that part of their accounts was borne by the companies concerned. The expenses of running the mileage department were divided between the companies in the ratio of the number of vehicles of all kinds of each company booked through. Thus, if the London and North Western Railway had twice as many passenger coaches carried through over a given period of time as did the Midland, its contribution to the expense of this part of the department's work would be twice as great. As an example of how the division of expenses in the traffic department was effected we may take the six months ending December 31, 1865. The total expense of running the department in this period was £26,134 0s 9d, and the total time units, (i.e. hours) spent 484,553; 107,381 of these units were occupied in balancing the accounts of the London and North Western Railway which was therefore charged $\frac{107,381}{484,553}$ of £26,134 0s 9d or £5,791 10s 5d. 54,047 units of time were spent on the accounts of the Midland Railway which was charged £2,914 19s 9d for the work. At the other end of the scale, only one unit of time was taken up in dealing with the traffic account of the Fleetwood, Preston and West Riding

---

[1] RCH 1/14: Report of the sub-committee of delegates on the working and establishment of the Railway Clearing House, May 22, 1862 and minute 662 of the Clearing House committee, June 11, 1862.

Railway which paid one shilling and a penny as its contribution to the costs of the department.[1]

In the second half of the nineteenth century there was a persistent tendency for the costs of running the Clearing House to rise in relation to the traffic receipts cleared. This tendency, which is shown statistically in Appendix 9, was checked from time to time by administrative reforms, but it was never permanently reversed. By the 1860s the largest industrial and commercial centres of the kingdom had already been linked by railway. It was only to be expected that such new stations as were opened to traffic in the later part of the century would, in the main, bring relatively smaller additions to the goods and passengers carried. The type of traffic which increased most rapidly at this time was the carrying of parcels by passenger train. Compared with the heavy merchandise traffic, its organisation required a much larger expenditure in administration in relation to the value of the traffic. The three principal reasons for rising costs of administration can be illustrated from Clearing House figures for 1853 and 1873. In the first place the number of stations open to traffic grew more rapidly than did the through passenger receipts. Between 1853 and 1873 the number of stations increased from 1,600 to 6,392, or by nearly four times: through passenger traffic receipts grew from £1,235,000 to £3,263,356 or by little over two and a half times. Secondly the value of the through goods traffic receipts increased at a slower pace than did the average number of Clearing House monthly settlements for goods traffic. Over the same twenty years the value of through goods traffic receipts rose from £2,947,432 to £11,352,513, or by less than four times, while the number of monthly settlements mounted from 225,857 to 1,632,606 or by more than seven times. Thirdly, the number of pairs of stations booking parcels through grew at a very much faster rate than did the receipts from this form of traffic. In the twenty years they rose from 55,776 to 669,854, or by more than twelve times, while parcels receipts rose from £137,174 to £786,944, or by under six times.[2]

[1] RCH 1/24: Return showing sums due by respective companies for maintaining the traffic department in the six months ending December 31, 1865.

[2] RCH 1/15: Statement included in secretary's report to the Clearing House committee, April 1874.

It was one of the principal concerns of the Superintending Committee to devise administrative reforms which would offset these powerful influences in the direction of higher working costs. But before the Superintending Committee came into existence the special committee of investigation of 1861–62 made important recommendations which were brought into effect from July 1, 1862. The balancing of accounts for overcharges, allowances, claims and corrections was to be undertaken quarterly instead of monthly; where only two companies were involved, the Clearing House check on passenger, horse, carriage, and dog traffic was abolished; the period allowed the companies for the pointing out of errors was reduced from two years to six months and the independent Clearing House check on two company goods traffic was ended where the companies concerned had station returns of their own.[1]

Early in 1871, as a result of a special investigation into Clearing House administration by the general managers, the Superintending Committee agreed to substitute half yearly returns of the parcels traffic in place of the quarterly returns made up to that time. It was also agreed to accept Mr Dawson's proposal that mileage accounts should be prepared quarterly instead of monthly.[2]

Another way to cut down the amount of paper work in connection with the parcels traffic was to reduce the number of 'booking through' points. In June 1865 the Clearing House committee recommended that the companies should restrict the booking through of parcels to the principal and terminal stations only of other companies lines. It was further recommended that instead of the sum from each parcel being divided on the basis of mileage the gross receipts from parcels should be divided on a company to company arrangement based on percentages derived from periodic sample traffic surveys.[3]

In the average of the years 1880–84 the costs of running the Clearing House, as a percentage of total receipts, were 1·32% compared with 0·98% for the corresponding years of the previous

[1] RCH 1/14: Report of the sub-committee of delegates on the working and establishment of the Railway Clearing House, May 22, 1862.

[2] RCH 1/79: Minutes 1128 and 1129 of General Managers Conference, February 9, 1871.

[3] RCH 1/14: Minute 830 of Clearing House committee, June 14, 1865.

decade. This was a sufficiently rapid increase to worry the Super-intending Committee which made a special report to the Clearing House committee on the subject in 1885. The recommendations, which were made after prior consultation with the accountants of thirteen railway companies, were approved by the Clearing House committee for putting into effect from January 1, 1886. The most important change was that merchandise traffic receipts (other than livestock) of a value of 15s or under, in either direction, per pair of stations per month, was in future to be divided in the same pro-portions as the 'heavy traffic' between the same two stations (i.e. in accordance with mileage) after the deduction of the customary terminal charges. At the same time station abstracts were dispensed with, being replaced by station summaries, and special terminals on light traffic were abolished.[1] In February 1888 the problem of the high administrative costs on goods carried by passenger train was tackled in a fairly drastic way. The receipts of all parcels, horse, carriage, and dog traffic of under 5s a month in either direc-tion, per pair of stations, were to be divided in the same propor-tions as the receipts from heavy merchandise between the same pair of stations.[2] The reforms had the effect of bringing down the ratio of Clearing House running costs to total receipts from 1·32% in 1880–84 to 1·29% in 1885–89. Nevertheless the volume of work and the number of staff employed were both steadily increasing. The Clearing House committee, therefore, in December 1894, asked the General Managers Conference to consider whether any change in the existing methods of account keeping could be adop-ted which would result in a reduction in the volume of clerical labour required. After lengthy consultation with the accountants, the general managers came to the conclusion that so long as the existing regulations for the division of receipts remained, no further material economies were practicable although the labour of thirty clerks might be saved if a 20s limit for light goods traffic were imposed instead of the existing 15s limit. Their report was

[1] RCH 1/16: Minute 1844 of Clearing House committee, December 9, 1885.
[2] RCH 1/80: Minutes of General Managers Conference, February 9, 1888. RCH 1/16: Minute 1943 of Clearing House committee of March 14, 1888 and RCH 7/32: Regulations of the Railway Clearing House, 1890, p. 63.

adopted by the committee of the Clearing House on June 12, 1895.[1]

The total cost of running the Clearing House in 1895—the year in which the General Managers Report had been presented—was £244,817. By 1907 it had risen to £332,133, or by over 35% in twelve years. More distressing was the fact that costs as a percentage of total receipts were again rising. Once more the general managers were called upon to investigate and report. They found that no material economies could be effected so long as the companies' requirements remained the same. The two economies they did propose to effect a saving of £5,000 a year were adopted by the committee for implementation from January 1, 1911. These were the extension of the light merchandise limit from the existing 20s per pair of stations to 30s; the extension of the 'light' parcel traffic limit from 5s per pair of stations to 10s and the introduction of quarterly instead of monthly settlements for heavy merchandise traffic.[2] These were the last administrative changes of significance before the outbreak of war and they were effective in keeping within bounds the rise in the total cost of running the Clearing House. With the continued co-operation of the companies accountants and an overhaul in the methods of administration about once in every ten years it had proved possible to keep running costs from 1910 to 1913 at a lower percentage of total receipts than they had been in the 1880s.

One reason why it was not possible to reduce still further the cost of the work was the existence of 'suspense accounts' which involved the administration in much burdensome correspondence. The Clearing House Regulations explained what these accounts were:

'When companies differ as to any agreement into which they have entered, or as to the mode in which the receipts of their common traffic should be divided, the Clearing House is empowered to hold in suspense so much of the receipts as will cover the

[1] RCH 1/16: Minute 2224 of the Clearing House committee, June 12, 1894, with a report of the General Managers Conference, May 7, 1895.
[2] RCH 1/16: Minute 2851 of Clearing House committee, December 14, 1910, with appendix. Extract from the report of the superintending committee to the Quarterly Meeting of Delegates.

maximum amounts claimed by either party, and to divide the residue of the receipts in the customary way.'[1]

The origin of these accounts dates from the earliest days of the Clearing House. In his report to the committee in February 1846 Morison confessed that the payments for mileage and demurrage were so liable to be disputed that he could not 'with any degree of safety' divide the balances owing. He therefore kept large sums undistributed.[2] It was not until January 1853 that the practice was given official authorisation. The general managers then suggested:

'. . . That it be recommended to the committee of the Railway Clearing House to direct that when disputes exist between railway companies which prevent a division of receipts, the whole proceeds of the traffic in abeyance be paid to the Bankers of the Clearing House, to be held by them until the dispute is settled.'[3]

In the following twelve years both the number of the suspense accounts and the amounts held in them increased rapidly. By September 1865 £584,442 was being held, mainly on account of the English and Scottish traffic through disputes between the signatories to the pooling agreement. By March 1866 nearly £600,000 of suspense account money was being invested by Glyn's Bank and earning 6% but the superintending committee considered that the time had arrived when 'the responsibility for the proper investment and care of such an enormous and growing sum . . . should be borne no longer'.[4] The Clearing House committee responded by amending the Clearing House regulation in September of the same year. In future the Clearing House could refuse to receive either returns or traffic receipts in cases where the division was disputed.[5] Although the adoption of this firmer line led to some mitigation of the abuse it by no means brought the practice to an end. When in December 1868 two large companies, parties to the English and Scottish

<hr />

[1] RCH Regulations, 1866 edition, Regulation 135.
[2] RCH 1/2: Report of K. Morison to the Clearing House committee, February 25, 1846.
[3] RCH 1/70: Minute 78 of General Managers Conference, January 19, 1853.
[4] RCH 1/24: Superintending committee, minutes 756 and 772, February 22 and March 14, 1866.
[5] RCH 1/15: Minute 909 of Clearing House committee, September 12, 1866.

traffic agreement stated that they intended to put further large sums into suspense the superintending committee decided to inform them that the money would not be received.[1] This decision not only contributed to the dissolution of the English and Scottish Traffic Agreement but also helped to reduce very substantially the sums of money held in suspense. By 1887 amounts held had fallen to £93,681 compared with over £700,000 twenty years earlier; but it is doubtful whether the reduction in the costs of administration was proportional to the decrease in sums involved, as there were still sixty-seven separate suspense accounts to be managed.[2] It was government control over railways in wartime, exercised through a railway executive committee, which largely eliminated disputes over the division of traffic and caused a melting away of the suspense accounts. Early in 1915 the sum held was £41,447 but by December 1918 it had shrunk to under £20,000. The Clearing House maintained suspense accounts throughout the inter-war period but with the outbreak of the Second World War there was a rapid shrinkage in the number of accounts and the amounts involved. No accounts were held after October 1943.[3]

Glyn's Bank (later Glyn Mills and Co.) acted as bankers for the Clearing House throughout its entire history. It was an arrangement which contributed to the smooth and economical management of the organisation since this bank had more experience of railway finance than did any other of its contemporaries.

Before 1880 no charge was made for keeping the Clearing House accounts, but an arrangement existed under which the No. 1 Traffic Balances Account was never drawn below £13,000. On money credited to suspense accounts Glyn's allowed interest at rates advertised by London Joint Stock Banks. Overdrafts for purposes such as the extension of the Clearing House premises, were charged at 1% above bank rate with a minimum charge of 4%. Between 1880 and 1890 the arrangement for a minimum 'rest' of £13,000 was cancelled but it was agreed that interest on suspense accounts should only be paid on the aggregate in excess of £13,000.

---

[1] RCH 1/26: Minute 1448 of the superintending committee, December 9, 1868.

[2] RCH 1/16: Report of superintending committee, March 9, 1887.

[3] Railway Clearing House superintending committee reports, various dates.

Following an interview between Leslie Stephen, the chairman of the Clearing House, and Mr Glyn, at the bank in December 1890, it was agreed to substitute an annual charge of £300 for the requirement concerning the suspense accounts. The annual charge was halved in 1899 as it was argued that the bank profited from the lapse of time between the receipt of cash from the Seymour Street offices and the payment out to the companies. In July 1905 even this charge of £150 was cancelled.[1] Glyns still did very well out of the Clearing House accounts, for among other opportunities it possessed was the management of the parcel post funds. An average of six days elapsed between the receipt of substantial sums from the Postmaster-General and their distribution among the companies.

[1] RCH 1/37: Minute 11,379 of the superintending committee, February 22, 1905. Memorandum as to the banking arrangements with Messrs Glyn and Co.

# CHAPTER VII

# THE CLEARING HOUSE STAFF: THE CLERKS

## I

The six clerks who took up their duties as the first employees of the Railway Clearing House in the small Drummond Street premises on January 2, 1842, could scarcely have envisaged that in twenty years time the number of men on the books of their employer would have swollen to 800, or that by the end of the century more than 2,000 clerks would be employed at the one London office. By 1913 the Clearing House staff exceeded 3,000, the number of clerks having risen to 2,503, while there were 539 number takers and thirty-seven traffic inspectors also in the service. From being a tiny concern employing half a dozen men the organisation had grown in the space of fifty years to be one of the largest employers of labour in the country.

Although the growth in size of the undertaking was the consequence of the rapid expansion of the railway network and of the traffic which passed along it, the progress would have been a far more troubled one had it not been for the outstanding abilities and qualities of character of its first two secretaries.

Kenneth Morison had shown vision, persuasiveness and organising ability in advocating the clearing system and watching over its establishment. The delegates of the Clearing House committee were fortunate in having such a dedicated and capable man as chief officer of the new organisation from its foundation until his death on October 26, 1861. His quarterly reports to the committee were models of clarity, farsightedness and tact. The number of men under his charge grew to over 750, and it was no small part of his achievement to have standardised their salary structure and conditions of service so as to create a well disciplined and, on the whole, contented labour force at the service of the railway companies. To start with Morison was employed on a part-time basis at £200 a year,[1] his main employment being that of chief accountant of the London and Birmingham Railway, which paid him an annual salary of £300.[2] In February 1845, 'as an acknowledgement of the efficient manner in which he had performed his duties—and in consideration of the great increase of labour consequent upon the accession of new companies to the Clearing House' the committee increased his salary to £300 a year. Three years later the work at Seymour Street had so greatly extended that it was agreed that Morison should relinquish his employment with the railway company (by then the London and North Western Railway) to become the full time secretary of the Clearing House at a salary of £800 a year.[3]

One of the six clerks appointed to serve under Morison in January 1842, was a seventeen-year-old youth from Rochester, Philip William Dawson, who had worked for a year as a clerk for the London and Birmingham Railway, remained in the service of the Clearing House throughout the 'Morison era' and by 1861 was second in command of a greatly enlarged concern. Starting with a salary of £50 a year, in the next twenty years he acquired an intimate knowledge of every aspect of the work. On December 11, 1861, he was appointed to succeed Morison as secretary of the Clearing House. Though lacking the degree of insight and imagination possessed by his predecessor, he in every way matched Morison in devotion to his work, knowledge of the details of administration and concern for the good management of the men entrusted to his care. Those of his contemporaries who knew him best spoke of his sound judgement, wise experience and strict impartiality. The Clearing House was at the peak of its influence during his period of office of almost thirty years. He had very nearly completed fifty years of service for the organisation when,

[1] RCH 1/13: Report to the members of the Clearing House committee, April, 26, 1842.

[2] Glyn Mills Bank Archives. George Carr Glyn Letters, 1838/61: Report of the audit department to the Board of the London and Birmingham Railway, January 12, 1843.

[3] RCH 1/13: Committee minutes, February 19, 1845 and March 9, 1848.

leaving his office one Monday evening in October 1890, he collapsed and died.[1]

Long years of dedicated service to the Clearing House and administrative ability were the outstanding characteristics of many of Mr Dawson's successors. Mr Harry Smart had thirty years' experience of the work of the different departments before taking over the secretaryship in 1890 and serving in this new capacity for seventeen years. His son, Mr Harry Cuff Smart, who joined the staff in 1892, did an eight-year stint as secretary between 1911 and 1919. He was succeeded by Mr Percy Howard Price who gave the Clearing House forty-six years of his working life including sixteen as secretary. Mr Ernest Edward Painter had worked in the Clearing House for forty-five years before achieving the secretary's post in 1935.[2]

While Morison was secretary the method of recruitment of clerks was principally by recommendation of the leading directors of the companies in the Clearing House. The first staff book covering the years 1842–49 inclusive, contains 142 names. Seventy-five of these had been recommended by George Carr Glyn. Ten were proposed by George Hudson, six by Morison and four each by Creed and Dawson. Such exercise of patronage was by no means unusual. A similar method was followed at that time in the appointment of the railway companies' own clerks. But it is interesting to notice that the performance of the men nominated by Hudson was apparently far less satisfactory than that of Glyn's nominees. Four of the Railway King's men were subsequently classed as 'slow', one as only 'fair', and one other was dismissed.[3] Could it have been the case that he 'dumped' his less satisfactory clerks on the Clearing House?

Once a clerk had been accepted into the service his advancement largely depended on his own efforts. Before he was entrusted with the management of a particular company's account with the Clearing House he had to prove his competence by both written and oral examination. A sound knowledge of railway geography and mathematics, and a legible hand were essential.

[1] RCH 1/13: *The Railway News*, October 25, 1890, p. 705. RCH 1/77: Minute 2273 of the General Managers Conference, November 6, 1890.
[2] *The Railway News*, jubilee number 1914, p. 59.
[3] RCH 4/36: Staff Book.

The method of recruitment helped to generate the loyalty of the staff. Employment in the Clearing House was more secure than that of many a bank or city office in the 1850s and 1860s, even though in periods of prosperity these other employers were willing to pay more generous salaries. As it was something of a privilege to serve in the Clearing House, most clerks did not bite the hand that fed them. The practice of requiring all those who had the handling of cash to deposit large sums of money as security for their good conduct, helped to generate an attitude of reliability and dependence. In 1862 the secretary and accountant were required to deposit £4,000 each; the head of the merchandise department £2,000; the heads of the mileage and coaching departments £1,000 each, while inspectors and sub-inspectors who supervised the work of the number takers paid £150 and £100.[1] This practice was abandoned in the 1870s.

From September 1847 the Clearing House added a completely different class of men to the rapidly growing body of its employees —the number takers. The work of this group was so important that it deserves treatment in a separate chapter. It was the task of a small group of inspectors—never more than forty in number—to supervise the work of the number takers.

From September 1852 a few 'detective policemen' were employed by the Clearing House to ensure that waggons were not misappropriated and that goods were not pilfered. Although Morison commended their 'tact and perseverence' and reported that they had proved very efficient, their employment was resented by some of the companies, and in March 1855 the committee resolved against their continued employment.[2]

Until January 1912 the Clearing House was an entirely male establishment but in that month twenty-seven women, all relatives of the male clerks, were taken into the service. By the outbreak of the First World War they had been joined by more than 150 others and the superintending committee had reported that the 'experiment of their employment had proved a success'.

[1] RCH 1/122: Unnumbered minute of the superintending committee dated December 10, 1862.
[2] RCH 1/13: K. Morison's report to the committee, December 8, 1852, Minute 365 of March 14, 1855.

## II

As the Clearing House was entirely dependent upon the member companies for its income it was not given to lavish expenditure on wages and salaries. The committee expected value for money paid out. As early as 1844 Morison persuaded it to accept the following scale of payments to clerks:

Probationers
(Youths up to 18 years of age)   £30–70 per annum
3rd class clerks                 £80–100 per annum
2nd class clerks                 £110–140 per annum
1st class clerks                 £150–200[1]

Before a youth or man was allowed to transfer to a higher class he was obliged to pass an examination the result of which was by no means a foregone conclusion, as failure in subject railway topography was very common. By the early 1860s, with the increase in numbers and sub division of the work, the clerks in charge of departments were paid substantially more. Thus the clerk in charge of the goods department, immediately responsible for the work of 252 men and youths, was paid £350 a year, while the head of the parcels department with only fifty-two persons under his supervision received a maximum of £325.

Such improvement in rates of pay as the clerks were able to achieve in subsequent years were more the outcome of the scarcity of supply of clerical labour in London in times of booming trade than the result of any formal trade union action. Nevertheless the men were not slow to seize their opportunities. In March 1864 it was 'the very unusual demand for clerks by new banking companies and others' that persuaded the committee to take seriously a memorial for increased salaries received from the staff at Seymour Street.[2] In July 1864 the secretary revealed that clerks were leaving without giving proper notice and that one of them had sacrificed a month's pay in order to transfer to a better paid job at the London County Bank in Lombard Street. In the light of such happenings the committee had little choice but accept the superintending

[1] RCH 1/13: Morison's report to the committee, March 15, 1844.
[2] RCH 1/23: Minute 348 of superintending committee, March 24, 1864.

committee's proposals for an amended scale of salaries operative from March 1, 1864.[1]

The crisis caused by the desertion of well-qualified clerks in some of the top grades was met by awarding the senior men in responsible posts an increased salary, paid for in part by economies at the expense of the youngest employees. The salaries of fourteen heads of divisions, their assistants, and senior clerks were raised at a total cost of £1,435 a year, while the economies made at the expense of the youths amounted to £553, leaving the companies but £882 extra a year to find for the wages of the 873 clerks employed. The starting pay for boys of fourteen was lowered from £30 to £20 a year and the maximum pay for youths was not to be reached until twenty years of age instead of eighteen years as previously.[2] A year later Dawson was gratified to report that the new arrangements, which had been calculated to retain more of the best clerks, had been successful, since these men were 'comparatively satisfied to remain'. Rather it was the clerks 'of a lower scale of salary and of inferior experience' who were growing restless.[3] The case for these poorly paid men was being put by a Railway Clerks Association which had a brief existence in 1865–66. It was dealt with after a postponement of three months by a decision to pay a bonus of £5 a year to all clerks who had been on their maximum rate of pay for at least three years, provided their conduct had been satisfactory.[4]

The lower paid clerks submitted fresh memorials early in 1867, but by this time the demand for clerks in the city had slackened as a result of the commercial collapse of the previous autumn. Consequently, although Carr Glyn confessed in a letter to Dawson that he 'always thought the pay of the Railway Clearing House low', he saw little likelihood of the committee agreeing to further increases since they 'now had a most sufficient supply of candidates for vacancies'. His estimate proved correct since only minor adjustments were made to the salary scales that year.[5]

[1] RCH 1/23: Minute 426 of superintending committee, July 21, 1864.
[2] RCH 1/23: Minute 397 of superintending committee, June 8, 1864.
[3] RCH 1/24: Dawson's report to the committee, September 13, 1865.
[4] RCH 1/25: Dawson's report to the committee, June 12, 1867. RCH 1/25: Minute 1076 of committee, June 27, 1867.
[5] RCH 4/39: Letter from Carr Glyn to Dawson, March 16, 1867.

By the early 1870s, however, the market had again changed. No less than eighty clerks (out of a total of nearly 1,100) resigned from the service of the Clearing House in the first six months of 1872 alone.[1] In June 1871 small increases of £5 and £10 a year had been granted to most of the clerks, but the cost of living was rising rapidly and in less than three weeks of July 1872 the price of coal in London rose from 21s to 29s a ton.[2] When the clerks in the second lowest grade presented a memorial at the end of February 1872 the committee turned down the request for further rises. But early in July hundreds of clerks signed a petition demanding a 20% increase in their salaries, using as one of their arguments the fact that rents in the Kings Cross area had risen by between 20% and 30% over the preceding decade. From his home in Stanmore Park the ageing Glyn wrote on September 8th that 'the low scale at which they stand demands some immediate increase for all'. Dawson therefore drafted a circular letter to the member companies in which he maintained that the price of fuel and provisions were much higher than they had been at the time of the last salary increase. Resignations of clerks 'to enter more lucrative employments in the Banks, the Civil Service and Merchants' Offices' increased and had made 'more urgent the settlement of the claim'.[3] The result was an improvement in salaries right through the grades from the £5 a year increase for youths aged eighteen to twenty to the £100-a-year rises granted to the four heads of departments.

During the years of the 'Great Depression' of trade in the last quarter of the nineteenth century the clerks showed a growing concern at the slowing up of the rate of promotion. A letter from the £90-a-year clerks written to Mr Dawson on February 11, 1880, refers to 'serious hardships . . . suffered during the late protracted period of commercial depression . . . due as much to alterations in the methods of working the traffic which have tended to retard

---

[1] RCH 1/27: Minute 2374 of superintending committee, September 11, 1872.

[2] RCH 1/15: Minute 1184 of committee, June 14, 1871.

[3] Minute 2340 of superintending committee, July 18, 1872. RCH 1/27: Minute 2338 of superintending committee, July 18, 1872. RCH 4/39: Letter from Glyn to Dawson, September 8, 1872. RCH 1/27: Minute 2340. Special report of the superintending committee. RCH 1/27: Minute 1234 of committee, September 11, 1872. This was the last committee attended by Glyn (by then Lord Wolverton).

promotion as to the stagnation in trade'. The committee showed some sympathy for their case and granted an addition of £5 to those clerks at the top of the £90 scale who had passed the examination for taking charge of an account.[1]

Fear of redundancy and the slowing down of promotion as a result of the substitution of working agreements for competition in many railway regions, prompted the salary demands of the years immediately preceding the First World War. In 1912 the rank and file of the clerks were demanding the scrapping of the grade system and its replacement by a single scale with automatically granted annual increments rising to a maximum of £170 at the age of thirty-seven. When they were granted small increases within the existing salary structure, they complained that 'a large number of clerks were barred, through lack of vacancies, from entering the class above them'.[2] It was only when this stage had been reached that they gave serious attention to trade unionism.

Although Clearing House clerks worked a 'normal' eight-hour day and in this respect were far better placed than the operating grades on the railways, the performed frequent obligatory overtime. In 1862 a special report to the Clearing House committee declared overtime working 'unavoidable and . . . if kept within proper limits, more economical than maintaining a larger staff for which, owing to the fluctuations in traffic, there might not always be full employment'. During the months of summer and autumn when the value of clearances was greater than in the winter and spring, there was always some overtime working. In December 1865 the committee was told that there had been 'an enormous increase in Clearing House work . . . consequent upon the opening of additional lines, further development of through invoicing by companies . . . and a general increase of through traffic all over the kingdom'.[3] On such occasions the eight-hour day seemed a distant aspiration rather than a present reality to many of the staff. For many years there was no consistent ruling on overtime pay which was granted as a favour by the committee. In two months of the summer of 1862 a total of 15,000 hours overtime was worked by the clerks who requested extra payment. The committee decided

[1] RCH 1/3: Minute 4485 of superintending committee, April 28, 1880.
[2] *The Railway Clerk*, March 15, 1912, p. 53.
[3] RCH 1/14: Report to the committee, December 13, 1865.

that 'a moderate gratuity be allowed them, and that the Secretary be requested to report to the next meeting thereon'. A month later 'a gratuity of £500, being at the rate of about 8d an hour' was voted.[1] This was, of course, well under the normal rate per hour for some of the clerks though above the hourly rate paid to youths. When extra work was done in November 1870 Dawson promised the clerks extra pay for overtime but reassured the superintending committee that the amount he would pay out 'would not exceed the salary which would have been paid for the extra number of clerks required'.[2] It is evident that from time to time, when there was an exceptionally rapid increase in railway traffic, the principal reason for overtime working was the difficulty of increasing Clearing House accommodation sufficiently quickly to provide the extra desk space for new clerks. This was the reason given for the overtime working of the mileage clerks in November and December 1867.[3]

Clerks were allowed a fortnight's holiday a year but there is no indication in the records as to whether they were paid for those weeks of absence. It also became the tradition that in addition to Good Friday and Christmas Day the Saturday following Good Friday and Boxing Day might be counted as holidays providing the clerks got the work of those days completed by 'working extra hours without pay beforehand'. On February 26, 1863, it was ruled by the superintending committee 'that the secretary be permitted to close the office on the day of the Prince's [the Prince of Wales, later King Edward VII] wedding, provided the clerks by working extra hours without pay anticipate the work falling by the programme to be done on that day'.

In the early years of the Clearing House a clerk who fell sick was entirely dependent on the charity of the committee for any income he might be granted while absent from work, but in January 1860 a set of rules was approved. Men with less than a year's service were not allowed any sick pay. Those who had between one

[1] RCH 1/22: Minutes 72 and 79 of superintending committee, September 25 and October 30, 1862.

[2] RCH 1/26: Minute 1917 of superintending committee of December 14, 1870.

[3] RCH 1/26: Minute 1211 of superintending committee, January 23, 1868.

and three year's service were entitled to one month on full pay; with between three years and seven years of service a man would be paid for up to two months' absence, while for those who had worked in the Clearing House for more than seven years' paid sick leave of up to three months was allowed.[1] Despite such rules the superintending committee still had to judge occasional individual cases on their merits. A clerk who was absent from work for a month in the autumn of 1863 'in consequence of lodgers in his house having been attacked with scarlet fever' was paid half his salary but warned that such an excuse would not be accepted in the future.

One of the dangers to the health of the clerks which emerged with each trade boom was that of overcrowding in the office. In May 1864 Mr Dawson warned the committee that an increase in accommodation had become 'absolutely necessary' since 'the cubic amount of breathing space per clerk was considerably less than that required to preserve a good state of health'. Such a deterioration in working conditions was scarcely surprising in the light of the fact that the number of clerks had increased by 128 since the last building extension had been completed in 1860.[2]

Long hours of checking over accounts which were not always very legibly written were a constant threat to eyesight. The adequacy of the office lighting, and even the colour of the paper used for the companies' returns, were matters of vital importance to the welfare of the clerks. In 1880, as an economy measure recommended by the London and North Western Railway, the Clearing House introduced a yellowish coloured paper for one of the most frequently used returns. The clerks protested that it caused undue eyestrain. Mr Dawson therefore sought the opinion of Mr Haynes Walton, an eminent occulist, who declared that the change was to be deprecated, and in March 1881 the superintending committee accepted his advice and decided to revert to the use of the more expensive bluish tinted paper.[3]

From the beginning of 1861 when there were close to 500 men

[1] RCH 1/14: Minute 451 of committee, January 2, 1860.
[2] RCH 1/23: Dawson's report to the superintending committee, May 26, 1864.
[3] RCH 1/30: Minute 4784 of the superintending committee, April 27, 1881.

on the establishment, the superintending committee decided to appoint a part-time medical officer at a salary of £250 a year and it was one of his routine duties to test the eyesight of new recruits to the staff. He was also responsible for visiting the sick clerks and number takers in their own homes. In April 1868, in claiming a salary rise of £100 a year, he reminded the committee that the staff of the Clearing House had increased by 31% since his appointment and that he had been obliged to incur 'an increased annual expenditure on horseflesh' in visiting his patients.[1]

In January 1890 it was one of the pleasanter tasks of the medical officer to visit the famous 'Long Office' in the Clearing House building to report on the electric lighting installed there as an experiment during the preceding month. He found the room 'everywhere illumined with a steady, equable, and by no means too dazzling, light', and could read by it as easily as he could in daylight. Since the clerks had already expressed their approval of the change, it was decided to invite tenders for the installation of the electric light in all fifty-nine of the rooms. The work was undertaken by the Planet Electrical Company and completed in January 1893 at a cost of £3,052, power being supplied from the mains of the Electrical Department of the St Pancras Vestry.[2] From the viewpoint of the well-being of the clerks it was money well spent.

### III

To relieve the main committee of its responsibility for detailed administration and the disciplining of the staff, Kenneth Morison decided in May 1857 to establish an office committee with himself as chairman, Mr Zachary Macaulay as secretary, and five senior members of the staff (mostly heads of departments) as additional nominated members. The clerks do not appear to have had any voice in the composition of the committee. It was thus very much of an 'establishment' concern even though it was designed to promote the welfare of the staff. At the first meeting Morison outlined its most important tasks as follows:

[1] RCH 1/24: Minute 602 of the superintending committee, May 25, 1865.
[2] RCH 1/32: Superintending committee, minutes 7323 of January 29, 1890, 8016 of April 27, 1892, and 8221 of January 25, 1893.

1 Kenneth Morison
Secretary of the Railway
Clearing House, 1842–
1861

George Carr Glyn, first Baron
Wolverton, Chairman of the
Railway Clearing House Com-
mittee of Delegates, 1842–1873

2 Goods Transhipment (in the absence of through traffic arrangements)
*Illustrated London News* 17 August 1847

Transferring horses at a railway junction
*Illustrated London News* 17 August 1847

3 Drawbacks of the absence of through traffic arrangements. (Although this lithograph, reproduced from the *Illustrated London News* of 17 August 1847 depicts the situation arising from the break of gauge at Gloucester, it typifies difficulties which must have been common before the Railway Clearing House organised through transport of goods and passengers)

The 'Long Office' of the Railway Clearing House in 1864 (Reproduced from *Cassell's Illustrated Family Paper*)

4 An early Railway Clearing House Classification of Goods. The first classification, published in 1847, did not include the class for minerals. By 1879 the classification fitted a 129 page book

5  The Railway Clearing House building in Seymour Street (later renamed Eversholt Street)

The original offices of the Railway Clearing House at 11 Drummond Street, Euston. Destroyed by enemy action in 1941

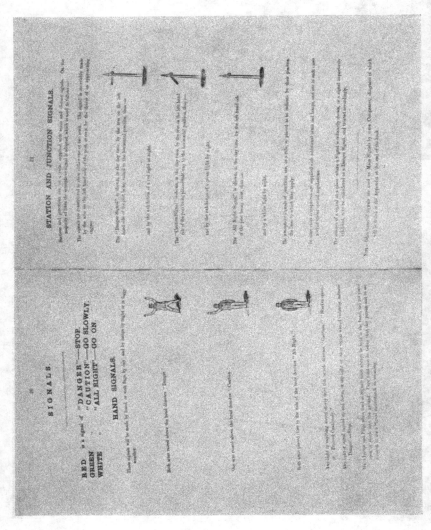

6 From the first book of Railway Clearing House, Rules and Regulations, 1867

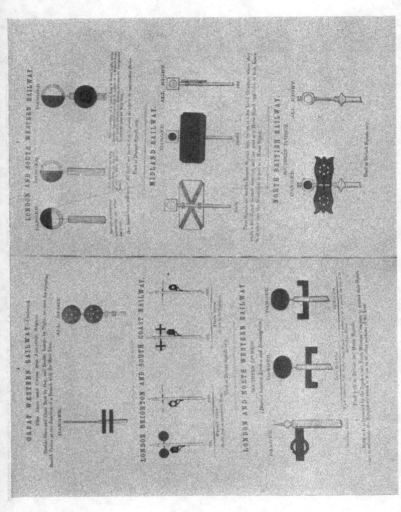

7 The Railway Clearing House Rules and Regulations, 1867 (illustrating the diversity of practice, before Railway Clearing House rules prevailed). N.B. the Great Western Railway disc signal for 'All Right' and the London and North Western Railway disc signal for 'Danger' were both painted red

(1) That by having a formal investigation of complaints and a record of precedents, a more uniform system of carrying on the discipline of the office might be obtained.

(2) That suggestions from the heads of departments and from the clerks with regard to the mode of carrying on the work might be received and discussed.

(3) That the various agreements now in the office or hereafter brought in might be discussed and any points of doubt or difficulty cleared up.'[1]

If employment at the Clearing House had the advantage of a reasonable security it had the great drawback of monotony. Sometimes the tedium was so great that a clerk felt he simply had to 'let off steam'. The minutes of the committee for March 24, 1849, solemnly record that a Mr Tyson 'was called in to answer a complaint against him for having thrown an apple against a fellow clerk'. The case having been proved to the satisfaction of the committee, it was ordered that the offender be deprived of his holidays for that year and that the case should be made known to the clerks as a warning. Just over two years later another offender, Mr F. Russell, not only threw things about the office but also 'made peculiar noises' which brought upon him the additional punishment of deprivation of occasional leave for a period of six months.[2] Two years later still Messrs Metcalf and Glover sought light relief with some 'platoon drill' in the office before the start of the working day—Glover having recently joined the Third City of London Rifle Corps. Believing his rifle to be unloaded, Glover pointed it towards his friend and pulled the trigger while Metcalf stared down the barrel. Nothing happened. But the rifle was then aimed at the office clock and the trigger again pulled, this time with devastating results. In the event, the pair were lucky to be let off with a fine of 50s plus the cost of repair of the clock.[3]

To incur the displeasure of the members of the Clearing House committee might be a matter of no great consequence when railway traffic was booming and clerks were in short supply: it was a different matter when trade was slack or the work of the Clearing

---

[1] RCH 1/56: Minutes of office committee meeting, May 4, 1857.
[2] RCH 1/56: Office committee minute 865 of June 3, 1861.
[3] RCH 1/58: Office committee minute 1174 of October 22, 1863.

House was being streamlined. Thus in February 1905 new arrangements for dealing with some of the passenger traffic accounts created redundancies and seven clerks 'who had for some time failed to give satisfaction' were given notice.[1]

The records of the office committee reflect changing social habits and conditions. Before the First World War the most common cause of serious complaint against both clerks and number takers was that of drunkenness. After 1918 it was the improper use of a privilege ticket.

## IV

Of greater importance than the activities of the office committee in keeping the clerks contented with their lot was the far-sighted policy of the superintending committee in the support given to welfare schemes. The Clearing House athletic club, established in 1858, was the earliest of its kind to be formed for the recreation of the employees of the railways. But the first of the 'social security' schemes was the Contingent Sick Fund founded in 1860 with the object of augmenting the income of staff who had exhausted their rights to sick pay under Clearing House rules. For a subscription of 6d a week members were entitled to allowances varying from 12s to 30s a week in the first year and 12s to 15s a week during the second year of sickness. From 136 in 1860 membership grew to 1762 by the year 1900 when over £1,000 was paid out in benefits. Moreover the fund was the first democratically managed one in the Clearing House since an elected committee of eighteen, plus a president and treasurer, had been responsible for its management. From the start the scheme had the backing of the superintending committee which voted an 'annual donation' to the fund.[2]

At its meeting on March 9, 1863 the superintending committee recommended:

'. . . that for the comfort and convenience of the numerous body of clerks (of whom many are mere youths) employed in the Clearing

[1] RCH 1/64: Office committee minute 4003 of February 10, 1905.
[2] Anon: *The Railway Clearing House: Its Origin, Objects, Work and Results*, London, 1901.

House, and to avoid the necessity now existing of their being compelled to resort to public houses, and other equally objectionable places, to obtain their dinners, a dining room be provided for them at the expense of the committee at a cost, including cooking apparatus, etc., not exceeding £750.'

The superintending committee was wrong both in its estimate of the capital expenditure involved and in its belief that not more than 200 clerks would use the new service. The cost of equipping the new dining room was over £1,200 and, in addition, a loan of £200 over a period of four years was made to the clerks to enable them to buy the necessary cutlery. Double the expected number of clerks took their midday meal in the Clearing House. Carr Glyn was very gratified. He told the Clearing House committee that 'the benefit of the service would undoubtedly be great. The good morals of the clerks were more likely to be preserved, and there would be a greater disposition on the part of the clerks to remain in a service where they are well cared for.'[1]

Initially the cost of the two-course meal was ninepence, but already by 1865 some of the clerks were suggesting that a lower priced meal should be provided for the benefit of youths on a low scale of salary. The proposal was eventually adopted in 1869 when 'a very good, though moderate, dinner of hot meat, vegetables and pudding at a cost of 5d' was provided as an alternative to the more ample ninepenny meal.[2]

By 1899 the number of 'Junior class' clerks had risen to 702 and the cost of the low priced dinner had risen to 6½d. The medical officer was distressed to find that very few of those, whose salaries were between £20 and £30 a year were dining in the canteen. Believing that such a state of affairs was 'prejudicial to good health and efficiency', the superintending committee, at its meeting on June 14, 1899, decided that clerks whose salaries ranged between £20 and £30 would be entitled to a rebate of 3d a day, and those on the scale £30–£50 a year, one of 2d a day, from the 6½d charged for the cheaper midday meal; 80% of the 529 clerks entitled to this privilege availed themselves of it.

[1] RCH 1/5: Minute R 750 of Clearing House committee, December 9, 1863.

[2] RCH 1/25: Minute 1688 of the superintending committee, December 8, 1869.

The Clearing House Clerks' Literary Society, which held meetings and ran a library was formed as early as 1849. When the premises were extended in the course of 1864 provision was made for a reading room with space both for bookshelves and reading desks. From time to time grants to the Society were made from Clearing House funds, for example, one for £50 being made in June 1868 and another for £100 in March 1874, by which time the library had 6,576 books. In June 1875 a full-time librarian was appointed at a salary of £70 per annum, half of which was found from Clearing House funds and the other half from the clerks' subscriptions.[1] The main responsibility for the management of the library rested with an elected committee of clerks.

Another organisation run entirely by a committee of the clerks was the Co-operative Supply Association, founded in 1868. From the first its business was by no means confined to the sale of groceries, but also included sales of drapery, boots and shoes, hardware and furniture. Although the Association started business in a room in the Seymour Street premises, it soon asserted its independence, renting a store quite apart from the Clearing House premises. Its annual turnover rose from £1,318 in 1868 to over £24,000 in 1900.

In the spring following, the period not inaptly called 'the coal famine of 1872–73', some enterprising clerks set up the Coal Supply Association which bought coal in bulk at wholesale prices and retailed it on a strictly cash basis at prices considerably under those charged by the coal merchants. An elected committee of twelve was in charge. By 1900 sales reached the impressive figure of 4,000 tons a year.[2]

Before 1873 when the Railway Clearing House Superannuation Fund Association came into being, most employees of the Clearing House must have looked forward to the date of their retirement with more apprehension than relief. In the absence of a state-provided old-age pension, those clerks and number takers who

[1] RCH 1/23; Report of superintending committee, December 14, 1864. RCH 1/26: Report of superintending committee, June 10, 1868. RCH 1/8: Minute 1317 of Clearing House committee, June 11, 1874. RCH 1/28: Minute 3144 of superintending committee, June 9, 1875.

[2] Anon: *The Railway Clearing House: Its Origin, Objects, Work and Results*, London, 1901, pp. 48–49.

outlived the compulsory retirement age of sixty-five were entirely dependent on their own savings if they wished to retain their independence.

As early as October 1839 Carr Glyn's company, the London and Birmingham, had sponsored a Railway Friendly Society for the benefit of its employees. It offered old-age allowances of from 5s to 20s a week, depending on previous earnings. The company subsidised the funds from the proceeds of the sale of lost luggage and the rent of a newspaper stand. It also helped to promote good discipline and loyalty among the staff, for its members forfeited all their claims if they were proved guilty of 'misconduct'.[1] It was this scheme, taken over by the London and North Western Railway when it superseded the London and Birmingham line in 1845 (and modified in 1853) which proved the inspiration for the first proposals for a General Railway Superannuation Fund, Widows Fund and Friendly Society submitted by Kenneth Morison to the Clearing House committee on September 14, 1849. It was intended that railway company or Clearing House employees joining the society should provide, by their subscriptions, two-thirds of the necessary revenue of the society's funds and that the railway companies and the Clearing House committee the remaining one-third. Pensions were to be payable to those reaching the age of sixty-six.

In a circular to the companies dated March 5, 1850, Morison explained that the success of the proposed society largely depended on whether or not a sufficiently large number of companies gave it their support, since even the largest railway in the country would not, on its own, be able to provide enough members to finance a self-supporting scheme. It is recorded, however, that 'the opposition on the part of the employees, notably those of the Railway Clearing House, was so determined that the scheme had to be abandoned'.[2] The explanation of this hostility on the part of the staff to a plan supposedly drawn up for their benefit can be found in those very features of it which Morison considered worth commending to the companies in his circular:

---

[1] BTHR, HL 2/18 R 411: Circular Euston Station, November 1839, and London and Birmingham Board resolution, October 10, 1839. Letter from K. Morison to C. E. Stewart Esq., July 9, 1849.

[2] Anon: *The Railway Clearing House, etc.* London 1901, pp. 37–40.

'We have been induced to acquiesce in the suggestion that the companies should become partially subscribers to the fund by considering that the companies would be thereby exonerated from the responsibility of guaranteeing the solvency of the funds. That it would give them a perfect right to compel their officers to become members of this fund, and that it would relieve them of the chief part of the burden of maintaining servants disqualified by age or accident, or contributing to the support of the families of persons killed in their service. . . . If established these funds would prove the means of permanently retaining at moderate salaries the services of faithful and efficient servants, and of punishing with increased severity those who may betray their trust'.[1]

Few railwaymen, apparently, favoured a scheme which meant compensation on the cheap combined with tighter discipline and new impediments to deter them from moving to other employment.

Between December 1851 and June 1853 the Clearing House committee spent £700 in a vain endeavour to gain support for a General Railway Association for providing Superannuation and Guarantee Funds backed by Mr Laing, chairman of the London and Brighton Railway, but based on the earlier plan of Morison. The attempt was abandoned because it failed to win the support of more than three companies.[2]

It was the goods managers who took the next initiative. At their meeting in January 1860 they appointed a committee of ten to confer with representatives of the Superintendents Conference in devising a new superannuation scheme. In July that year they accepted a draft prepared by Mr Ansell, an eminent actuary, and forwarded it to the general managers of the leading companies for their comments. It was only at this stage that the rank and file of the staff were consulted. As their suspicions of a plan which emanated solely from the management could not be dispelled it is not surprising that this further attempt came to an untimely end.[3]

[1] BTHR, HL 2/18 R 411: Report of the Railway Clearing House, March 5, 1850.
[2] RCH 1/2: Clearing House committee minute 211, December 10, 1851; 249 of September 8, 1852; 260 of December 8, 1852, and 294 of June 8, 1853. (RCH 1/3).
[3] RCH 1/165: Resolution of Goods Managers Conference, January 26, July 26, and August 9, 1860.

Five years later the Clearing House clerks themselves formed a provisional committee with the object of making arrangements for a superannuation fund to be opened. More than 500 men expressed themselves in favour of a contributory scheme, but on this occasion there was an unfavourable response from the Clearing House committee 'as it was considered that railway affairs were not in such a satisfactory state' as to warrant further action being taken at that time.[1]

The clerks were more fortunate with their next effort which was made at a time of booming trade and buoyant railway revenues. At a mass meeting of the staff held in the dining room of the Clearing House on April 3, 1872, a committee was elected and an appeal was made to the superintending committee for support. The response both from the Clearing House management and from the companies was encouraging, and by the close of that year, printed copies of the proposed general rules of the fund and of the Parliamentary Bill were in the hands of the companies. Under the Railway Clearing System Superannuation Fund Association Act of 1873 all newly appointed clerks of the Clearing House were obliged to contribute $2\frac{1}{2}\%$ of their salaries to the fund to match the $2\frac{1}{2}\%$ paid in by their employers. Clerks already in the service were given the option of joining and of making back payments to augment their pensions, but number takers were not at that time eligible to join. The pensions scale was a generous one, rising to a maximum of two-thirds of average salary of the five years preceding retirement in the case of a man with forty-five years' completed service. On the other hand the rules were clearly designed to encourage the clerk who made the service of the Clearing House his lifelong career and to discourage the 'bird of passage'. Those who resigned the service were paid back only half the contributions made in their name with no interest on the capital. Those who were dismissed the service through redundancy were repaid all contributions made in their name but were not given any interest. Only those resigning through ill health had the benefit of $4\%$ interest on their previous premiums. Despite these drawbacks, there was good support from the clerks. At the end of 1874 1,011 out of a total 1,325 clerks were contributors to the fund as well as other staff from four large

[1] RCH 1/ Anon: *The Railway Clearing House etc.*, p. 40.

railway companies which had co-operated. By 1900 the individual membership of the fund was 13,204, with the majority coming from the sixty railway companies or managing committees which were associated with it.[1]

In January 1897 in consequence of the accumulation of a credit £500,000 in the fund the Clearing House committee approved a revised and more generous Superannuation Fund Scheme with enhanced death grants and increased minimum pension rates. Pensions were to be based on the average salary of the last seven years of service instead of the average for the entire period of service. But the actuaries who had advised them were wrong in their forecasts of future life expectancy. Subsequent actuarial reports revealed, among other startling facts, that the mortality of pensioner clerks after 1903 was nearly 30% lighter than during the previous ten years and that withdrawals from the fund, through change of occupation or ill health, were 29% lighter than had been anticipated. From June 1905 therefore the future pension rates were reduced by about one twelfth of the levels ruling since 1897 and to cover the existing pensioners position, the committee agreed to meet the cost of the difference between the old and the new rates, amounting to about £1,300 a year. However, the Board of the Midland Railway took exception to this decision. Meeting in December 1906 it resolved;

'That this Board does not approve the principle that the pensions payable under the scheme of the Railway Clearing System Superannuation Fund should be guaranteed by the railway companies, or of the proposal that the 1897 scale of pensions to present annuitants should be maintained at the cost of the ordinary shareholders of the railway companies.'

The Boards of the Great Northern and Great Western Railways had similar objections.[2] After prolonged controversy the matter was eventually settled under the Railway Clearing System Superannuation Fund Act, 1914, which provided for the continuance of

[1] RCH 1/27: Superintending committee minutes 2262 of April 18, 1872, 2414 of October 31, 1872, 2461 of December 11, 1872, and 2984 of December 9, 1874. Minute 1296 of Clearing House committee of September 10, 1873. Anon: *The Railway Clearing House etc.*
[2] RCH 1/17: Minute 2682 of committee of December 12, 1906.

the existing scale of contributions and benefits for those already in the service and an increased scale of contributions for those recruited from July 1, 1913.[1] In the meantime the railway clerks' confidence in the solvency of superannuation funds managed by the railway companies and by the Clearing House had been seriously undermined. This disillusionment was expressed in the rapid growth of the Railway Clerks Association after 1909 and in the evidence given by Mr A. G. Walkden and others to the Board of Trade Departmental Committee of enquiry into the superannuation funds in 1909–10.

From the summer of 1874 an additional avenue for thrift was open to the clerks who could invest in the Clearing House Savings Bank which offered them interest at the rate of 4% per annum. It was a fund started on the initiative of the clerks and managed entirely by them, though the Clearing House committee gave £50 a year to the funds 'with the view to encouraging habits of prudence and economy among the junior clerks'. Within a year of its foundation it had nearly five hundred members.[2] The Clearing House Deposit Bank founded in June 1885 was equally successful and had accumulated reserves of over £155,000 by May 1914.[3]

The widows of Clearing House clerks were grateful for sums outstanding in the name of their late husbands, for no arrangements were made for the payment of pensions to the widows of Clearing House clerks until after 1937 and then it was only through a reduction of the man's pension rate.

v

Although some hundreds of clerks were crowded together in one location with many interests in common and with rates of pay which did not always compare favourably with those given in other London offices, it was not until more than sixty years after the first

---

[1] RCH 1/18: Minute 2953 and Appendix B of committee, December 10, 1913.

[2] RCH 1/15: Minute 1327 of committee of March 11, 1874, 1333 of June 10, 1874 and report of P. W. Dawson to the superintending committee, June 9, 1875.

[3] RCH 1/39: Minute 13,521 of superintending committee, May 27, 1914.

clerks were signed on that a trade union branch was formed in the Clearing House. That there was such a long delay is a tribute to the success of the numerous welfare schemes which the committee supported. There were spasmodic rumblings of discontent from a much earlier date but it is difficult to assess how far these were generally supported. A 'Clearing House clerk' complained in a letter to the *Morning Herald* in October 1855 that preference had been given in new appointments to men coming from Kendal, the constituency which Carr Glyn, the chairman of the Clearing House, represented in Parliament. Although *The Railway Times* also claimed that

'Mr Glyn brought men down from Kendal, where he is MP and converted these very clerks into Shrewsbury proprietors, and obtained for them occasional holidays, so that they could proceed to Wolverhampton to Shrewsbury or to Chester to discharge the important duty of voting in favour of London and North Western Railway proposals', the allegation was strenuously denied by Mr Morison in a letter published a week later.[1]

For a brief period in 1865–66 some of the clerks gave their allegiance to a Railway Clerks Association which campaigned for better pay for the lower paid members of their grade, but the organisation disappeared in the commercial crisis of October 1866. Early in the following year the lower grades of the Clearing House clerks petitioned again for a rise, but made no headway. It was at this stage that George Potter, the well-known trade unionist and editor of the working class newspaper *The Beehive*, wrote to the leaders of the movement as follows:

'*Gentlemen*,

It has been suggested to me that some lasting benefit might be derived from your combined efforts in forming an association with the object of meeting together at stated periods for the discussion of your present position with a view to its amelioration. I have been induced to address you on the subject by several gentlemen interested who inform me that there is a sufficiently strong feeling existing amongst you to ensure the success of the undertaking. I

[1] *The Morning Herald*, October 25, 1855. *The Railway Times*, October 27 and November 3, 1855.

may mention that all business of the association would be entirely of an independent character, the secretary unshackled in by any official connection other than that of the proposed association who would receive private communication from any of your members, put them into shape, and himself assume all the responsibility of placing them before the members at the meeting. As entering into particulars here might destroy the object in view, I would suggest that those who are disposed to become members should send me their names in the course of the next few days by post. I will then call a meeting at an early date and undertake to show the advantages to be derived from uniting together to protect your mutual interests which have become neglected through your not having a qualified person to take the helm when your just and equitable claims are at stake. Whilst no one is to be eligible as a member whose salary exceeds £120 per annum, everyone from the youngest junior clerk to those in receipt of the above amount will, it is hoped, reap the advantages of the movement which he is earnestly invited to support, and therefore trusting that the benefit to be derived from similar societies will be a sufficient inducement to enlist your hearty co-operation,

I am, Gentlemen,
Your faithfully,
George H. Potter
April 17th 1867[1]

No evidence survives of any meeting being held as a 'follow up' to this invitation. It seems possible that Potter's correspondent had been over optimistic about the degree of support for trade unionism among the Clearing House clerks.

If the railway clerks employed directly by the railway companies had felt strongly enough to form a national union, the likelihood of the Clearing House clerks organising themselves would have increased. But it was not until 1897 that discontent about the slow rate of promotion, the result of the amalgamation movement among the railway companies, led to the formation of the Railway Clerks Association. Some timely concessions by the superintending

---

[1] RCH 4/39: File of Clearing House letters. RCH 1/23: Minute 703 of November 30, 1865, reads 'Laid on the table . . .' Memorial from the Railway Clerks Association.

committee at this time helped to dampen the discontent in Seymour Street. The adoption of the 'unification principle' by which a clerk became eligible for promotion in *any* department and not only the one in which he had been trained, at least appeared to bring more prospect of promotion. The option of retirement between the ages of sixty and sixty-five instead of uniformly at sixty-five opened new opportunities for promotion to younger members of the staff. A bonus of £10 a year to clerks who had been on a salary of £140 a year for at least ten years completed the concessions.[1]

In the course of 1908–9 much more ambitious plans for the elimination of competition were being considered by such giant concerns as the London and North Western Railway, the Great Northern and the Great Central. *The Railway Clerk*, journal of the Railway Clerks Association, noted that the Clearing House clerks were, 'becoming alive to the fact that the sweeping changes now developing in the railway world (might) seriously affect their position'.[2] The first general meeting of the Clearing House branch of the Railway Clerks Association was held at St Marys school, Clarendon Square, Euston on January 12, 1909, with A. G. Walkden, general secretary of the organisation, as principal speaker. In July that year a further meeting carried by a large majority the motion that 'The R.C.A. represents the best interests of the Clearing House clerks', the report of the meeting stating that 'Mr Romeril [one of the leaders of the R.C.H. branch] fully proved R.C.H. staff are in great danger through impending amalgamations'. By the end of 1912 the Clearing House branch of the Railway Clerks Association with 815 members was the largest of any of the 195 branches in the country. A year later, although pride of place had been yielded to the Glasgow branch, whose membership had shot up to 1,168.[3]

When the Board of Trade Departmental Committee on Railway Agreements and Amalgamations met in 1910 a recently formed

---

[1] RCH 1/35: Superintending committee minutes 9422 of March 10, 1897.

[2] *The Railway Clerk*, January 15, 1909, p. 15. I am very grateful to Mr R. F. Ayliffe of the Transport Salaried Staffs Association for allowing me to see files of this journal.

[3] *Ibid*. February 15, 1909; July 15, 1909. Railway Clerks Association annual report and balance sheet, 1912, p. 80, 1913, p. 8.

'R.C.H. Clerks Central Watch Committee' which had the backing of 1,700 of the men at Seymour Street, persuaded the committee to hear one of its members as a witness. Mr Romeril, who was chosen for this task, claimed that the Clearing House clerks would have 'very great difficulty' in finding alternative employment as the experience gained in the service of the railways 'would have little or no value in ordinary commercial offices'. Together with the witness from the Railway Clerks Association, Mr A. G. Walkden, he helped to persuade the departmental committee to recommend that in all measures of railway amalgamation adequate compensation should be paid to men unavoidably discharged.[1]

Although these were impressive achievements for such a recently formed body, little headway was made in the direction of genuine collective bargaining at Seymour Street. The first formal application by the Railway Clerks Association to the superintending committee on behalf of the clerks was made, as late as June 11, 1913.[2] The letter from Mr Walkden was simply 'laid on the table'. Similar treatment was given to other applications made in the course of the First World War during which the Clearing House simply followed the lead of the Railway Executive Committee in granting war bonus increases.[3]

---

[1] Departmental committee on Railway Agreements and Amalgamations, 1910–11, BPP 1911, Vol. XXIX ii, minutes of evidence 1658–1669 and report. Railway Clerks Association: *The Railway Clerks Association and the Path to Progress*, 1928, p. 22.

[2] RCH 1/38: Minute 13,310 of superintending committee, June 11, 1913.

[3] RCH 1/39: Minute 13,838, 14,007, 14,061 and 14,078, September 1915, September 1916.

# CHAPTER VIII

# THE CLEARING HOUSE STAFF: THE NUMBER TAKERS

## I

Of all those employed on British railways few were less well known to the general public than the number takers. They were a small group—never more than 536 of them were on the books of the Clearing House at any one time before 1918—and yet their work was pivotal to the smooth working of the entire railway system. Without the results of their conscientious labours at junction points all over the country, reporting the movements of every waggon and carriage and every tarpaulin, the clerks in Seymour Street would have been quite unable to balance the companies' claims against each other. Without number takers there would have been no clearing system and without a clearing system much of the internal trade of the kingdom could not have developed. On the occasion of the jubilee of the Clearing House a reporter from *The Times*, who had visited many of the railway junctions, paid an appropriate tribute to these key men:

'Night and day throughout the year they are engaged in recording the number, name and owner, and intended destination of every railway company's waggon, passenger carriage, van or tarpaulin which passes from one company into the hands of another company, the same process being gone through when the vehicle or sheet is returned. The making of this record is unquestionably one of the most arduous as well as one of the most important duties in connection with the system. The number takers must be capable of bearing exposure to all kinds of hard weather, and possess the requisite amount of smartness and intelligence to enable them to perform their different duties with the utmost accuracy and dispatch. It is to them in great measure that the efficiency of the Clearing House is due.' [1]

[1] *The Times*, January 26, 1892.

174

Number takers had been employed even before the foundation of the Clearing House. As early as December 1840 the London and Birmingham Railway had found it necessary to employ 'a responsible person resident at Derby for the purpose of regulating the proper return of carriages, trucks, waggons, horseboxes, etc.' [1] Many other men had been appointed by this and other companies before the Clearing House took over responsibility for their employment in September 1847. As the rail networks of the major companies extended and grew more complicated the managements found it convenient to employ some number takers solely on their own lines.

The job of the number taker was one of the most dangerous on the railways. The night shift was often busier than the daytime and it brought added risks. Shunting yards were often ill lit or without any form of lighting, so that extra care was needed to avoid tripping over exposed points, cables or rods. The greatest danger was being crushed between the buffers or run down when crossing the rails to inspect waggons. In a special report to the committee in November 1897 Mr Smart, the secretary, conceded that night work was 'a greater tax upon the men than day work' and that it was generally 'heavier, certainly more hazardous and necessitated greater expenditure for food and, at certain seasons, for clothing also'.[2] When number taker Casey was squeezed between the buffers and severely injured in March 1865 the superintending committee decided to make up his pay, less the 7s 6d a week obtained from the Passenger Assurance Company, for a period of one month. In the case of William Warnock who was injured on duty in November 1876, the cost of an artificial leg, £7 10s 0d, was met by the committee; while in the case of William Stacey who lost both his feet while in the performance of his duty, the sum of £10 was voted to cover the cost of artificial feet provided by the Surgical Aid Society. When a man was killed on duty it was the rule that his widow should be paid the rest of the wages for the month in which the accident occurred, and that a small lump sum should be added. This was done in the case of J. Whyman, killed in February 1877, his widow receiving

[1] LBM 1/95: Minute 640 of the London and Birmingham Railway, Coaching and Police Committee, December 30, 1840.
[2] RCH 1/35: Secretary's report to the committee, November 24, 1897.

a lump sum of £5. In the case of a man killed at Retford, almost exactly a year later, the balance of funeral expenses, £5 16s 6d, was paid by the Committee.[1]

Exposure to inclement weather and irregularly taken and ill digested food were features of the number takers' working life which undermined their health. For many years a number of the railway companies did not consider it necessary to provide any form of shelter for these men. In December 1850 Kenneth Morison, in a report to the committee, urged that adequate shelter should be provided at the junctions so that the men could make out the returns they were required to send daily to the Clearing House. He doubted whether accommodation would be provided until the committee undertook to pay for any buildings erected at a rent proportional to the outlay, which need not exceed £30 to £40 per junction.[2] No action was taken on this recommendation. A report on the same subject presented nearly ten years later again exposed the inadequacy of the accommodation provided.[3] Improvement came only very gradually thereafter. The minutes of the superintending committee from time to time reveal the consequence of this lack of consideration for the men. Thus at the end of November 1862 it was recorded that the foreman number taker at Wakefield 'has been unable to attend to his duties since 29th September in consequence of severe illness brought on by having got wet through while in the performance of his duties'. [4] A frequent cause of getting a soaking or sustaining an injury was rummaging around the waggons looking for the serial numbers on tarpaulins. The number of occasions for bad language was reduced after 1892 when the goods managers, on the recommendation of the secretary, issued a circular to the companies with suggestions on improved methods of marking

[1] RCH 1/29: and 1/31: Minutes of superintending committee 573 of March 30, 1865, 3546 of November 30, 1876; 3605 of February 22, 1877, and 3857 of February 28, 1878, 5819 of September 10, 1884.
[2] RCH 1/42: Minute 150, report of K. Morison to committee, December 11, 1850.
[3] RCH 1/14: Minute 589 of the committee, June 13, 1860.
[4] RCH 1/22: Minute 102 of the superintending committee, November 27, 1862.

so that the numbers could easily be read when the sheets were tucked up.[1]

With the increase in the number of men in this group to over 400 in 1890 more consideration was given to their welfare than had been the case with their predecessors in the service. By the 1880s most number takers had heated offices or shelters to which they could resort in particularly bad weather or when they had to make out returns. Arrangements were made between the Clearing House and the railway companies for regular supplies of coal to be delivered to the number takers' quarters. Thus in 1885 an agreement was reached with the London and South Western Railway to supply coal at 40s per annum at each of the number takers' offices on the line.[2]

## II

In 1848 the committee decided that the cost of paying the wages of the Clearing House number takers should be divided among the companies on the same principle as the other portions of the expenditure, i.e. £5 per junction per year to each company passing traffic through. If this did not prove sufficient, the balance was to be met by additional payments proportional to the volume of through traffic in each case. This method was abandoned in 1858 because it did not work fairly. In its place the cost was shared on a junction by junction basis, each company bearing that proportion of the cost which corresponded to its proportion of the number of waggons passing through.[3]

Possibly because their ultimate paymasters were not their immediate employers, the Clearing House number takers tended to fare worse in respect of wages and hours of labour than did their contemporaries employed by the companies. Unfortunately no record of wage rates survives for the period before 1865. At that time all youths entering the service between the ages of sixteen and nineteen were paid 10s a week. Between the ages of

[1] RCH 1/87: Minute 6663 of the Goods Managers Conference, October 27, 1892.

[2] RCH 1/32: Minute 6066 of the superintending committee, June 10, 1800.

[3] RCH 1/2: Resolution of the committee, March 9, 1848. RCH 1/14: Minute 485 of committee, December 1857.

nineteen and twenty-three wages rose to a maximum of 18s 6d, except in the case of foremen who were paid up to 23s and inspectors who were on a scale rising to 30s.[1] Until nearly the end of the century improvements in the wages scale were granted principally in times of trade boom. At such times the payment of higher wages was found imperative to prevent too great erosion of the labour force into the service of the companies where the prospects were brighter. One disadvantage of working as a Clearing House number taker was that there were very few opportunities of promotion to better paid employment since the number of vacancies for foremen and inspectors was very small. In the service of the companies, on the other hand, the porter might qualify for upgrading for shunter, and the shunter had prospects of appointment as goods guard; the engine cleaner could hope to become first a fireman and then a driver. Hence whenever railway traffic expanded sufficiently rapidly to create a labour shortage, Clearing House number takers would desert in large numbers. In November 1865 the men employed at Crewe were resigning 'so frequently as almost to endanger the proper performance of work' and the superintending committee decided to raise wages, at that junction only, by 2s a week. Within six months, however, it was found necessary to grant increases to the men at fifteen other centres. In the midst of the next trade boom in 1873 Mr Dawson reported that resignations had become so numerous that difficulty was being experienced in filling vacancies. Unless increases in wages were given promptly, the work of recording the exchange of rolling stock could not possibly be maintained. He was not exaggerating. On March 11, 1874 it was revealed that 135 men out of a total staff of 420 number takers had resigned during the previous twelve months. The increases of from 1s to 3s a week for the men and 1s to 2s a week for the youths given in the autumn of 1873 were inescapable if the work of the Clearing House was to continue efficiently.[2]

[1] RCH 1/23: Minutes 704–5 of superintending committee, November 30, 1865.

[2] RCH 1/23: Minutes 704 and 822 of superintending committee, November 30, 1865, and May 24, 1866. RCH 1/23; Minutes 2591, 2746 and 2791 of superintending committee, May 29, 1873, January 22, 1874, and March 11, 1874.

There were other occasions when the superintending committee considered that it could safely reduce the rate of wages of some of the number takers. In April 1887, for example, it was decided to revise the scale of pay for youths entering the service after January 1, 1884. In place of the old maximum of 21s reached at the age of twenty-one there was to be a new maximum of 20s not attainable until the age of twenty-three. There is no record of any resistance to this change introduced at a time of falling prices and a glut in the labour market.[1]

It was not until the closing years of the nineteenth century that there is any clear evidence of concerted action by the number takers in each of the ten regional groupings into which they were divided. In July 1897 Mr Smart received a petition from a large proportion of the men in all areas claiming an increase in the maximum for adults from 23s to 27s per week, overtime payment for all work in excess of ten hours daily and time and a half rates for Sunday duty. Faced with these united demands the committee made some concessions. It was agreed to pay overtime rates after eleven hours and to pay time and a quarter rates for Sunday duty.[2] With the turn of the century new, concerted demands were submitted with increasing frequency. General petitions were received in March 1903, October 1907 and January and November 1911. By the outbreak of the war the maximum for adult number takers had risen to 26s while assistant foremen were paid up to 28s and foremen between 30s and 34s 6d, according to grade.[3]

The Clearing House number takers had to wait longer for a reduction of their hours of duty than did any other grade of men employed on the railways. One reason for their failure to match even the slow progress made by the other grades was that goods traffic was being moved throughout the twenty-four hours of the day. Until the eight-hour day became a compulsory maximum early in 1919 and a three shift system was introduced, two shifts—

[1] RCH 1/32: Minute 6569 of superintending committee, April 27, 1887.
[2] RCH 1/35: Superintending committee minutes 9559 of July 28, 1897 and 9652 of November 24, 1897.
[3] RCH 1/36: Minute 10,987 of superintending committee, March 25, 1903. RCH 1/37: Minute 11,999 of superintending committee, October 30, 1907, and RCH 1/38: Superintending committee minutes 12,753 of January 25, 1911, 12,946 of November 29, 1911, and 13,001 of February 28, 1912.

one for night and one for day—seemed to the management to be the only practicable alternative. In 1897 Mr Smart summarised the organisation of the work which, in its essentials, had remained unchanged for half a century:

'With few exceptions . . . each man and boy is one week on day duty covering eleven hours or more, including meal times, and the next week on night duty covering eleven to thirteen hours (without meal times) throughout the year. This unequal division of hours originated at the men's own request, and through long custom a day of eleven hours and a night of eleven to thirteen hours have come to be regarded as the normal hours.'[1]

As the volume of goods traffic passing at night tended to increase at a faster rate than the day traffic it was not always possible to keep to the regular cycle of alternating shifts of day and night duty. A man might at any time be called upon to work on fourteen consecutive nights. In May 1887 the superintending committee recognised that where this was demanded of a number taker he should be rewarded by an extra shilling a week pay in the second week of working a night shift.[2]

It is scarcely surprising, in view of the way the duties were organised, that the number takers had the longest average working week of any railwaymen. In a typical week of November 1897, of 203 men who were on night duty, 17 worked 66 hours; 19 others between 66–70 hours; 105 between 71 and 75 hours; 57 between 76 and 80 hours, and 5 between 81 and 85 hours. The pattern of day shift working does not make such grim reading, for the large majority of the men and youths (198 out of 257) were working no more than an 11-hour shift. But even in this case there were 17 men whose weekly hours exceeded 70, including one case of a man working 96 hours.

The storm which blew up on the question of overwork on the railways at the time of the Scottish railway strike of 1890–91 and the Select Committee on Railway Servants' Hours of Labour in 1890–91, passed by the number takers without having any appreciable effect on their working hours. Nobody giving evidence before the select committee bothered to mention them. In July

[1] RCH 1/35: Superintending committee, special report on the number taking staff, November 24, 1897.  [2] *Ibid.*

the standard night shift to the same length as the day shift, viz. eleven hours, with overtime payment at normal hourly rates for any time worked in excess of eleven hours. The men would in practice, continue to work the same number of hours per week

4  An early Railway Clearing House Classification of Goods. The first classification, published in 1847, did not include the class for minerals. By 1879 the classification fitted a 129 page book

the standard night shift to the same length as the day shift, *viz.* eleven hours, with overtime payment at normal hourly rates for any time worked in excess of eleven hours. The men would, in practice, continue to work the same number of hours per week as before, but an average of seven and a half hours weekly would qualify for extra pay. If this improvement were combined with Sunday duty payment at time and a quarter rates, the men's demand for an improvement in the basic rate of pay could safely be ignored. As he believed that the men 'did not really desire an actual shortening of the hours of labour', he considered that his proposals had the additional merit that 'the payment for overtime would make it to the interest of the men for the present two shifts arrangement to remain undisturbed, as an increase of staff would withdraw their overtime'. The committee accepted these cleverly conceived proposals unanimously.[1]

The dramatic change in the length of the working day of Clearing House number takers did not come until March 1919. As a result of an agreement between the Associated Society of Locomotive Engineers and Firemen and the President of the Board of Trade, reached in August 1917 and given full backing by the executive of the National Union of Railwaymen immediately the armistice was signed, the eight-hour day came into force on the railways of Britain on February 1, 1919. This time the Clearing House number takers were not forgotten. By increasing the numbers on the books from 536 in March 1918 to 726 a year later, it proved possible to organise the work into three equal shifts of eight hours and to bring to an end the anomaly of the thirteen-hour night shift which had survived for over seventy years.[2]

### III

As was the case with the clerks, the co-operation of the staff with the management was secured partly by means of the enforcement of a disciplinary code and partly by the provision of social welfare benefits.

[1] RCH 1/35: Minutes 9558 and 9652 of superintending committee of November 24, 1897. Also secretary's report on the number takers.

[2] RCH 1/54: Superintending committee report to the Railway Clearing House committee, March 12, 1919.

The responsibility for the good discipline of the number takers was shared between the office committee and the inspectors. Considering the arduous nature of the work, it is surprising that so few cases of breach of discipline occurred. During the first five years in which the inspectors held separate meetings, *viz.* 1862–67, they dismissed fifteen men for making careless returns, thirteen for drunkenness, six for absenting themselves without warning; five for absconding, and two for being unsuited for the work.[1] It is, however, reasonable to assume that the provision of improved social security benefits did more to enhance the self respect and good discipline of the number takers than did the enforcement of a code of punishments for misdemeanours.

Between 1847 and 1887 there were two principal agencies through which the number taker who was unavoidably absent from work might avoid resort to poor relief. In return for an annual premium of 4s per man insured, the Passenger Assurance Company undertook to pay a weekly pension to those injured at work or a lump sum to the next of kin of those fatally injured. But these premiums—which were paid by the Clearing House committee—did not cover sickness. To meet this contingency the rules of the Clearing House provided that a man with more than a year's service would be given sick pay from Clearing House funds, the amount of pay varying with the length of service.

In November 1887 a more comprehensive scheme of insurance was approved by the superintending committee which at the same time terminated the arrangement with the Passenger Assurance Company. In return for contributions of twopence a week from each employee and a like amount paid by the committee, the benefits shown on p. 184 were made available.

At the same time the committee undertook to make up the full wages of a man during the first month of his absence through sickness or injury. From the management's viewpoint it was a most economical arrangement for, by comparison with the old scheme, the net additional cost was only £6 per annum.[2]

At its meeting in November 1897 the superintending committee decided to seek a solicitor's opinion as to whether the Clearing

[1] RCH 1/15.
[2] RCH 1/32: Minute 6725 of the superintending committee of November 30, 1887.

### SICKNESS ALLOWANCES

| | |
|---|---|
| For the first twenty-six weeks | 10s |
| For the second twenty-six weeks | 7s 6d |
| For the next fifty-two weeks | 5s |
| In case of fatal accident at work | £100 |
| In case of death through other causes | £10 |
| In case of loss of two limbs or two eyes | £100 |
| In case of loss of one limb or one eye | £50 |
| Payment during absence through injury | £50 |
| 10s a week up to a maximum of | £50 |

House committee was liable to pay compensation to its employees under the Workmen's Compensation Act passed that year. A month later Mr Smart was happy to report that although the Act applied to the railway companies individually it did not affect the men directly employed by the Clearing House and that therefore the arrangements of the Provident Fund established ten years earlier could remain undisturbed. The exclusion of Clearing House employees from the scope of the Workmen's Compensation Act led to a number of anomalies. When a number taker employed by a railway company was killed at work, his widow was entitled to a minimum compensation of £150 under the Act. If a similar disaster befell a Clearing House number taker his widow was only entitled to £100 under the rules of the Provident Fund. In March 1901 Mrs Bowie claimed compensation on behalf of her late husband, a Clearing House number taker fatally injured in an accident on January 24th of that year. The superintending committee, on the advice of a solicitor, denied the liability but voted a gratuity of £100 in addition to the £100 to which Mrs Bowie was entitled under the Provident Fund Rules. Mrs Bowie then withdrew her claim.[1]

On October 25, 1901, within a few months of Bowie's death, a nineteen-year-old youth, Matthew Delaney, was killed by a Great Central Railway express at Godley, Cheshire, while number taking for the Clearing House. His parents promptly claimed compensation under the Act of 1897. When the case was

[1] RCH 1/36: Minutes 10,470 and 10,486 of superintending committee meetings, March 13 and 27, 1901.

argued at the Hyde County Court the judge denied the claim that the Clearing House was acting as a sub-contractor for the Cheshire Lines Committee (on whose rails the accident happened). The sole responsibility of the Railway Clearing House was the balancing of the companies' accounts with each other. The claim was therefore dismissed. In this case the committee voted a gratuity of £50 in addition to the £100 to which Delaney's parents were entitled under the rules of the Provident Fund.[1]

After the passing of the Workmen's Compensation Act in 1907 the Clearing House incurred an equal liability to that of the railway companies to pay compensation when its employees were injured or killed at work. Thus the anomaly of the past twenty years was removed. In May that year the superintending committee accepted a proposal from the number takers that the balance of £2,169 outstanding in the Provident Fund should provide the nucleus for a new Sickness and Provident Fund. At the same time it was decided to continue the men's contributions at 2d per week per member. The Clearing House contributions ceased but an annual gratuity of £50 was voted to augment the new fund.[2]

In the concluding months of the First World War the number takers shared in the growing militancy of the general body of railwaymen who looked for a transformation of working conditions, especially in regard to hours of labour, once the war was over. Early in 1918 a small negotiating committee was elected by the men to bargain with the superintending committee on a very wide range of topics including scales of pay, overtime rates, hours of duty and the introduction of a London allowance. In a memorial submitted to Mr H. Cuff Smart on April 4, 1918, protests about the 'utter inadequacy' of the rates of pay were coupled with a claim to be recognised as members of the salaried staff. It was asserted that 'the status and nature of the number takers work had been misconceived by the Superintending Committee'.

'We are of opinion [the memorialists continued] that as a grade we have suffered because our designation as number takers has caused us to be confused with the similarly named grade employed

[1] RCH 1/36: Minutes 10,679, 10,768 and 10,801 of the superintending committee, December 1, 1901, April 30 and June 11, 1902.
[2] RCH 1/37: Minutes 11,881 and 11,899 of superintending committee, May 1907.

by the companies, and therefore our work has been quite erroneously thought to be comparable to that performed by them. In order, therefore, that this obstacle may be removed, and our designation be brought into relation to the actual duties we undertake, we ask that the name "record clerks" be in future substituted for that of "numbertakers".' [1]

The most that the superintending committee felt able to concede at the time was a reduction in the number of years taken to reach maximum pay on the basic scale. It refused to budge on the important question of the number takers' status.

It was at this stage that an interested party, the Railway Clerks Association, took up the cudgels on behalf of this much neglected grade of railwaymen. In July the superintending committee received a letter from Mr W. R. Southeard, the solicitor for the Railway Clerks Association, raising the question of the status of number taker T. Bell who had been in the service of the Clearing House since 1897. It was admitted that this was a test case on behalf of all of the men in the grade. The union's claim was that Bell was a salaried officer of the Railway Clearing House since he had been obliged to contribute to the Superannuation Fund. The Railway Clearing House Superannuation Fund Corporation Act of 1873 had defined membership as limited to 'all officers, clerks and other servants remunerated by annual or monthly salaries'to the exclusion of those paid by weekly wages'. Because the Clearing House paid contributions to the Fund on Bell's behalf it was, by implication, admitting that he was a member of the salaried staff. The superintending committee was, however, reluctant to admit the logic of this and other arguments. It played for time by referring the matter to the General Managers Conference. This, in turn passed on the question to the solicitors of the Railway Companies Association who eventually reported in favour of Bell and Southeard. Finally, in October 1918, Mr H. Cuff Smart, the secretary of the Clearing House, wrote to Mr Southeard recognising the claim of Bell and all other number takers to be classified as members of the salaried staff.

This triumph, and the equally important concession of the

[1] RCH 1/39: Memorial from Railway Clearing House number taking staff, April 4, 1918.

eight-hour day, implemented four months later, came at a time when the work of the number takers—for many decades vital to the smooth operation of the railway system—was of somewhat different significance. The common user scheme for railway waggons, introduced in January 1917, greatly reduced the amount of clerical work required at the junctions. Whereas before all waggons had to be worked home to the parent system, under the simplified arrangements of wartime the waggons were pooled and all that had to be adjusted was a balance of waggons at regular weekly intervals. Nevertheless, it was because of the earlier work of the Clearing House and the labours of the small group of number takers in particular that the transition to the new method of waggon use was made so smoothly.

# CHAPTER IX

# STANDARDISATION: ROLLING STOCK
# AND LOCOMOTIVES

## I

The establishment of a neutral organisation with a large and well-trained staff of clerks provided a magnificent opportunity for railway management to share advances in technology and to standardise equipment and methods of railway operation. Would this opportunity be seized? The answer to the question depended on the influence of individual reputations and company prestige on the one hand and the need for a large degree of uniformity for the efficient through working of traffic on the other.

Even before the Clearing House was founded the disadvantages of the unplanned expansion of railway services were being experienced. As soon as a railway company's lines ceased to be isolated and became, willy-nilly, part of a *system* of communications, difficulties were encountered. To cite one example: as soon as the rails of the Liverpool and Manchester Railway joined those of the Grand Junction Company complications arose from the differing dimensions of the rolling stock. Some of the Liverpool and Manchester line's waggons were only 3 feet 9 inches wide and were obviously ill-matched with the 7-foot-wide waggons of the Grand Junction.[1]

On September 21, 1842, not many weeks after the Clearing House had started business, Captain Cleather of the Manchester and Birmingham Railway wrote an aggrieved letter of protest to Mr Burgess of the Coaching Committee of the London and Birmingham. Passengers travelling from Manchester to London, he complained, were obliged to change carriages at Birmingham because the two companies' coaches could not be attached to the

[1] Francis Whishaw: *The Railways of Great Britain and Ireland*, London, 1840, pp. 132, 204–5.

same train. The centre point of the buffers of some of the London and Birmingham coaches was 3 feet 8 inches above the rails—almost 4 inches higher than the centre point of the buffers of the Manchester company's coaches.[1]

To Captain Mark Huish, general manager of the London and North Western Railway, must be given the credit for first raising, in the Clearing House, the subject of standardisation of the companies' rolling stock. At a meeting of the committee, held on February 25, 1846, he drew attention to the want of uniformity both in the dimensions of goods waggons and in the mode of coupling them. The committee responded by drafting the first Clearing House recommendation on this subject:

'That this Committee are of opinion that it is highly expedient that goods waggons should be constructed according to some generally recognised standard and that all railway companies who are parties to the Clearing House be recommended to adopt, both as regards their waggons and carriages, some uniform principle of construction so that, when arranged in trains, the buffers of all vehicles may be in line and one mode of coupling may prevail throughout. The London & Birmingham, the Grand Junction and the Midland Companies now keep these objects in view in the construction of their waggons, and if the new waggons in use on the lines of these companies were taken for a standard of construction by all other companies the uniformity which the committee feel to be desirable would be established.' [2]

There was no rush by waggon superintendents on other lines to follow this excellent advice. Six months after it was given, the Committee was again pleading that 'carriages, waggons and other railway conveyances should be constructed in accordance with the same generally recognised standard'.[3]

Because many of the early waggon's couplings were easily detachable there never seemed to be enough of them when trains were being assembled. To try to remove this cause of friction

[1] BTHR, HN 2/9 R219: London Midland and Scottish collection of historical documents.
[2] RCH 1/13: Minutes of the Clearing House committee, February 25, 1846. [3] Ibid., minutes for August 28, 1846.

between the companies, the committee, in February 1846, appointed an assistant waggon inspector with the special responsibility of ensuring that loose couplings were returned to their rightful owners. It was not an enviable assignment. Six years after the first inspector was appointed there were still difficulties. On one occasion the general managers were informed that 'parties had been detected in the act of taking away coupling irons from stations to sell as old iron'.[1] The nuisance was only eliminated as more and more companies took the advice of the committee, given in September 1847, and substituted permanently attached couplings for the troublesome and evasive loose ones.[2]

Nevertheless it was easier to achieve a workable degree of uniformity in some of the essential dimensions of the passenger coaches than it was of the goods waggons. For more than a century before the coming of the steam locomotive, goods waggons had been hauled along wooden or iron rails in many parts of the kingdom. Hence there was ample time for a bewildering variety of types of waggon to have come into use before 1842. The better-class passenger carriages were, however, modelled on the stage and mail coaches of the early nineteenth century and were far more uniform in pattern. Moreover, the desire to attract customers for through services and the liability to pay compensation to injured passengers encouraged standardisation in coupling facilities and in the overall dimensions of the rolling stock. From the end of March 1850 the Clearing House kept a file of the plans and specifications of the different companies' passenger coaches to which any locomotive and waggon superintendent might refer for information and guidance.[3] Although there were frequent and bitter complaints about the quality and safety of many of the goods waggons, few general managers appeared to have many worries, after the 1850s, about the suitability of the passenger rolling stock for through working. In August 1875, Henry Oakley, the distinguished general manager of the Great Northern Railway, rejected the idea that any committee was needed to achieve better

---

[1] RCH 1/70: Minutes of the General Managers Conference, February 4, 1852.
[2] RCH 1/13: Minutes of the Clearing House committee, September 22, 1847.    [3] *Ibid.*, March 15, 1850.

standardisation of passenger coaches though he was highly critical of the condition of many of the goods waggons.[1]

Although Clearing House committees did not need to spend much time considering the overall dimensions of passenger carriages they did become involved in a big way in the prolonged controversy over the communication cord.

On July 1863 *The Times*, in a leading article, gave a frightening description of the characteristic passenger train of the day:

'As a railway train is now constructed in England there is no machine so cruelly inexorable. Once put yourself into it, and you cease to have any power of action, and must surrender yourself in practice to its iron will. It is composed of a set of closed boxes chained together without the least communication with each other, dragged on by an irresistible force along an inevitable iron path, helpless in the grasp of a giant.

One of them may break or get on fire or jump off the line, but the engine and the engine driver need know nothing of what is going on, and may drag it mercilessly to destruction. Each of the boxes, too, is itself divided into smaller boxes, which are part indeed of the same construction, but like adjoining prison cells, have no further communication with each other. The prisoners who occupy these cells have no means of communicating with their neighbours, and they have not even the relief of knowing that they can apply in the case of necessity, to their gaolers; for the gaolers; are prisoners too, and are shut up by themselves—it may be several boxes off.'

At the same time the editor of *The Engineer* commented that the prisoners on the railway were in a worse plight than the inmates of Pentonville Prison who could at any time communicate with the warders by means of a large bell or gong in the centre of each line of cells.[2]

This situation had arisen because the earliest railway companies, in building their passenger carriages, copied the pattern of the stage coach. Its long survival is explained by the Englishman's

---

[1] Royal Commission on Railway Accidents, minutes of evidence, August 4, 1875, BPP 1877, Vol. LXVIII Qs 33,535 and 33,481.

[2] *The Engineer*, July 31, 1863.

fixed determination to remain as isolated as possible from those who have the effrontery to travel on the same train as himself.

But isolationism also had its dangers. Whenever a fearful accident or a violent attack by one passenger on another was reported, which could have been avoided if only the passengers had been able to communicate with the driver or guard, there was the inevitable demand for action to prevent the recurrence of such a disaster. In October 1847 Lady Zetland and her maid were lucky to escape with their lives when their private carriage, in which they were travelling on the Midland Railway, was set on fire by a spark from the engine. Until the train stopped at the next station neither the driver nor the guard were aware of the frantic efforts that had been made to attract their attention. The incident led to the Commissioners of the Railways issuing a circular to the companies drawing attention to the rule of the Great Western Railway that a travelling porter, seated high upon a box at the back of the engine tender, was to notify the driver of any sign of mishap to the train.[1]

The Clearing House first gave attention to this problem early in 1852. The Board of Trade had asked the companies to examine the feasibility of the use of continuous footboards on passenger trains as a means by which the guard could reach all parts of the train when it was in motion. A committee of general managers responded by sending a questionnaire to the railway companies, inviting comment on the Board of Trade proposals. Of the thirty-five companies that sent in replies, twenty-three opposed the scheme because the existence of bridges, tunnels or other permanent structures near the track would make it dangerous for the guard to be on the outside of a moving train. Most companies had a further objection. Continuous footboards would enable second-class passengers to transfer to first-class compartments![2] Although the Clearing House committee endorsed these objections in December 1852 it asked the general managers to consider alternatives. During the first three months of 1853 a sub-committee of the general managers made enquiries of all British, and several

---

[1] Captain Tyler's report to the Board of Trade reported in *The Engineer*, July 7, 1865.

[2] RCH 1/70: Report of a sub-committee of general managers, February 1852.

foreign, railways. Among the proposals they examined were a metallic rod worked by an endless screw to operate a steam whistle in the drivers cabin; a whistle at the end of a gutta percha tube; an air whistle in the guard's van; an electric telegraph bell, and a continuous rope attached to a bell in the drivers cabin. They even considered the plan for vestibule coaches but rejected it, giving their reasons:

'As regards the American arrangement (i.e. the corridor), it is obvious that it is so opposed to the social habits of the English, and would interfere so much with the privacy and comfort they now enjoy that these considerations, apart from others, nearly as important, would forbid its adoption in this country.'

Although the sub-committee saw no mechanical difficulty in the way of the continuous cord working efficiently, they were not prepared to recommend its general adoption until the legislature had 'specially guarded against the abuse of privilege by making it penal'. Without such a safeguard the drawbacks of the scheme would outweigh any advantage it might confer.

'It requires little acquaintance with railway travelling to be convinced that its dangers would be greatly increased if the train were to be stopped wherever and whenever a passenger, under the influence of fear or levity, chose to make a signal. The Committee is not, therefore, prepared, in the first instance to recommend any arrangement or regulation, which would put it in the power of the timid or reckless to control the discretion of the guard or engine driver, and put the safety of the whole train in peril'.[1]

The accidents resulting from the absence of contact between different parts of the train did not cease merely because of the hesitations of the general managers. The demand for an adequate means of communication between passengers, and guard remained unabated. In 1858 a Select Committee on Railway Accidents had recommended that it should be 'imperative on every railway company to establish means of communication between guards and engine driver'. In the early weeks of 1863 the General

---

[1] RCH 1/70: Report of a sub-committee of general managers, March 9, 1853.

Managers Conference appointed another sub-committee to re-examine the question. The conclusion they reached was that

'the mode of communication by means of a cord wound on a wheel, and adjusted by a compensating weight in the last brake van in the train, and extending through rings or loops under the locked doors on the right hand side of the carriages to a bell on the tender, or whistle on the engine, was the one best suited to general adoption'.[1]

Little action followed this recommendation as the practice of the companies varied greatly and not all engineers and passenger superintendents were convinced of the reliability of the method of communication suggested.

In the event, the Board of Trade's intervention was intensified as a result of an item of news which gripped the public imagination. On Friday July 17, 1863, there occurred one of the most gruesome incidents in the history of passenger travel on British railways. In an express train travelling from Bletchley to Camden Town an insane man suddenly attacked a fellow passenger with a large clasp knife, wounding him seriously. There was no means of summoning help from the driver or guard. Fortunately there was a third man in the carriage who came to the rescue of the victim of the assault; but the attacker was so powerful that it required the utmost exertions of the two men to keep the assailant at bay until the ticket collector opened the door at Camden Town and saw one wounded man holding down another on the floor of a blood-bespattered compartment.[2]

When a murder occurred in another train not long afterwards a state of panic afflicted the travelling public. Ladies who were 'unable to discriminate between those they should avoid, and those who would be their best protectors' shunned all alike. Gentlemen passengers 'refused to travel singly with a stranger of the weaker sex, under the belief that it was only common prudence to avoid . . . all risk of being accused for purposes of extortion or insult or injury.'[3] On July 8, 1864, a circular letter to the railway companies

---

[1] RCH 1/79: Report of a sub-committee of general managers, April 2, 1863.     [2] *The Times*, July 20, 1863.
[3] Captain Tyler's report to the Board of Trade, February 6, 1865, quoted in *The Engineer*, July 7, 1865, pl.

from the Board of Trade cited 'recent occurrences of a criminal nature' as justification for urging speedier action by the railways to establish a communications system.[1] But another committee of general managers, reporting in the following March, confessed that 'no mechanical device, so far demonstrated, could be relied upon and recommended for general adoption'.[2] Although yet another sub-committee meeting in October 1867 reached the same conclusion, the Government was under strong pressure to legislate on the matter. Under Section 22 of the Regulation of Railways Act of 1868, every train which travelled more than twenty miles without stopping was to be provided with 'such efficient means of communication between the passengers and the servants of the company in charge of the train as the Board of Trade might approve'. When the general managers discussed this section of the Act at their meeting on August 29, 1868, they abandoned all their former hesitations and resolved unanimously to recommend to Mr John Bright, President of the Board of Trade, the cord and pulley system which had been tried out on the North Eastern Railway. The Minister then gave full sanction to the adoption of this system from August 1, 1869, despite contrary advice by the Board's inspecting officers.[3]

Subsequent experience was to confirm the inspectors' doubts about the efficiency of the bell and cord system. Its repeated failure to 'communicate' led to Board of Trade sanction being withdrawn in January 1873. But most companies continued its use for the next twenty years. In the meantime the Manchester, Sheffield and Lincolnshire Railway introduced the method—still in use—whereby the pulling of the cord operated the continuous brake. In 1890 the Board of Trade gave this new scheme provisional sanction and, three years later, its full approval. The old bell and cord system was finally condemned in the report of a departmental committee of the Board of Trade in 1898. By the end of the century it had been entirely superseded by the newer

---

[1] Captain Tyler's report to the Board of Trade, February 6, 1865, quoted in *The Engineer*, July 7, 1865, pl.

[2] RCH 1/72: Minute 568 of General Managers Conference, adopting a sub-committee report.

[3] RCH 1/79: Minute 893 of General Managers Conference, August 29, 1869.

and safer method.[1] The Clearing House engineers, having burned their fingers by an over-hasty endorsement of an imperfect system, were content to be interested bystanders of these later developments.

As early as November 1861 successful experiments were carried out at Wolverton to heat railway carriages with the waste steam from the engine. Although one of the leading technical journals of the day praised this 'clever and economical'[2] arrangement, it was many decades before the Clearing House engineers considered its general adoption. In the meantime the use of the inefficient and time consuming footwarmers was continued. By December 1893 when the engineers first came to consider the question, many trains were steam heated, but the conference concluded that the time was 'not yet ripe' for recommending a standard system of coupling for heating pipes.[3] Eighteen months later the gold pattern of coupling was recommended for future fittings although there was no attempt to impose uniformity.[4] A sub-committee examining the situation in the early months of 1903 found that where the same type of coupling was used there was no difficulty in connecting one company's steam heating pipes with those of another. They recommended that in all future fitting of non-vestibule stock 'the steam heating pipes should be fixed at a distance of twelve inches from the centre of the drawbar on the right hand side of the vehicle when facing the end'.[5] Two years later another sub-committee reached the wholly praiseworthy conclusion that it was desirable 'to prevent passengers getting overheated'. That they were thinking in physical, rather than in metaphorical terms, is indicated by their further recommendations that the temperature to be aimed at was fifty-five degrees centigrade and that the maximum steam pressure should be fifty pounds per square inch.[6] These Clearing House engineers could at least claim to have

[1] H. Rayner Wilson: *Railway Accidents*, London, 1925, pp. 9–10.
[2] 'Railway Appliances and the Public Health', *The Engineer*, November 29, 1861.
[3] RCH 1/551: Minute 4 of LECWS, December 7, 1893.
[4] *Ibid.* minute 60 of LECWS, May 2, 1895.
[5] RCH 1/552: Report of a sub-committee of LECWS, February 26, 1903, approved in minute 332 of main committee, July 3, 1903.
[6] *Ibid.*, minute 460 of LECWS, May 17, 1905.

made it possible for railway passengers in the Edwardian age to travel more comfortably than did their predecessors in Victorian times.

## II

Nearly a century of effort was devoted to the struggle to achieve some order out of the chaos of goods waggon dimensions and fitments. Only partial success was achieved and many of the problems were still awaiting solution in the 1920s. At the end of the First World War the outstanding impression gained by the Advisory Council of the Ministry of Reconstruction was of 'a riot of individuality'. There were still over 200 different types of axle boxes, over forty varieties of waggon hand brakes, and a remarkable diversity of types of wheel tyres, springs and axles. Individuality in waggon design had been given more scope in Great Britain than in any other country.[1]

One of the reasons for this unsatisfactory state of affairs was that the Clearing House committee had no power to compel a strongly opinionated engineer in the service of a railway company to comply with the recommendations of the conferences held in Seymour Street. A minority of the companies could always be counted upon to defy a resolution of the locomotive engineers or the general managers or even the Clearing House committee itself. In December 1856 a sub-committee of general managers, after an investigation lasting eighteen months, reported 'very serious differences' in the patterns of waggon stock. While they held out no hope that any sudden change for the better could be expected, they did submit dimensions and specifications for a limited number of standard types of waggon. The Clearing House committee promptly accepted these proposals and caused them to be printed and circulated to the companies. At the very next meeting a letter was read from the Board of the Great Northern Railway indicating its refusal to accept any precise dimensions for its rolling stock.[2] When the chief traffic manager

[1] Ministry of Reconstruction, Advisory Council: Report on the standardisation of railway equipment, July 4, 1918. BPP 1918, Vol. XIII, pp. 16–18.

[2] RCH 1/13: Report of a committee of general managers, appointed under minute 375 of Clearing House committee, July 13, 1855, and minute 451 of Clearing House committee, March 11, 1857.

of the London and North Western Railway was asked, nearly twenty years later, whether the railway companies had agreed to a uniform classification for their own waggons he was obliged to confess that they had not. He claimed that when his company tried to secure compliance with Clearing House specifications for waggons it was frustrated because the Midland, Great Northern, Manchester, Sheffield and Lincolnshire, and other companies 'did not think it necessary or desirable' to make such an attempt.[1]

The greatest obstacle to the standardisation of the goods rolling stock of the railways was the private owners' waggon. By 1911, 4,000 different private owners had invested some £20 million in no less than 650,000 waggons, approximately 46% of the waggon stock of British railways.[2] In the circumstances it proved easier for the railway companies to combine, through the Clearing House, in complaints about the unsatisfactory state of the private owners' waggons, than it was for them to attempt to put their own house in order. Although there were honourable exceptions, there were many grounds for discontent with the standards of construction and maintenance of the privately owned waggons. One general manager, in November 1900, described this part of the rolling stock as 'the bane of the English railways'. They hindered progress, involved risks to safety and were 'a constant source of unprofitable expenditure'.[3]

The particular complaints that were made about the private owners' waggons were that they were often constructed of inferior materials and according to obsolete specifications; they were sometimes overloaded; they were kept in service too long; the standards of maintenance were poor, and they were more frequently run empty—and therefore uneconomically—than were the waggons of the railway companies. Most numerous and notable for their 'bewildering variety' were the coal waggons. Although a large number of these were made by the one firm, the Gloucester Railway Carriage and Waggon Company, an historian who

---

[1] Royal Commission on Railway Accidents, minutes of evidence, July 7, 1875. BPP 1877, Vol. LXVIII, Q. 30,950, 30,948.

[2] *The Railway Engineer*, July 1911, p. 38.

[3] John A. G. Aspinall, general manager, Lancashire and Yorkshire Railway—reported in *Proceedings of the Institute of Civil Engineers*, Vol. CLXXIX, p. 103.

examined the photographs of 171 made by this firm between the years 1881 and 1893 found difficulty in discovering two which were identical.[1]

The general manager of the Midland Railway estimated that accidents to the private waggons arose 'from the use of inferior materials'. His contemporary on the Great Northern admitted that his company had to reject the private waggons 'very frequently indeed because of some defect such as a tyre being loose or a coupling being imperfect'. The general manager of the London and North Western Railway took an even more pessimistic view. He claimed that the accident rate of private waggons was three times that of the Company's stock.[2] Complaints of overloading were more frequently heard in times of booming trade than in years of depression when waggons were standing idle. The general managers noted, in February 1906, that some firms were ceasing to indicate on their waggons the maximum weights they were permitted to carry. They therefore issued a circular to inform the private owners that waggons improperly marked would not be accepted for transit.[3] In the boom years of the early 1870s the general manager of the Great Northern Railway found that the private owners worked their waggons to a 'greater extremity' than the company's stock was worked and after they required repair.[4]

On many occasions when it was proved that a major railway accident had been caused by a defect in a privately owned waggon the Board of Trade inspector expressed concern at the railway companies' failure to impose stricter standards on the private owners. When Captain Tyler reported on an accident which had occurred near Bishops Stortford on September 11, 1873, he declared that

'sooner or later it will be found necessary for the railway companies to own all the waggons employed for different purposes on their

[1] L. Tavender: 'Structural Features of Private Owners' Coal Waggons,' *Historical Model Railway Society Journal*, Vol. 5, no. 8, October 1966.

[2] Royal Commission on Railway Accidents, minutes of evidence, BPP 1877, Vol. LXVIII. Evidence of Messrs Allport, Oakley, and Findlay. Q. 31,689, 33,481 and 30,945.

[3] RCH 1/87: General managers meeting, minute 400 of February 6, 1906.

[4] Royal Commission on Railway Accidents, 1877, evidence of H. Oakley, BPP 1877, Vol. XLVIII, Q. 33,267.

line. It is very desirable that they should look forward to the accomplishment of this result and should pave the way for carrying it out with as little delay as possible.'[1]

Had Captain Tyler's advice been followed it would have made possible the speedier improvement in the standard of the rolling stock. It would also have made possible its more economical use. The accident rate of shunters and goods guards would have been reduced. Mr Allport, general manager of the Midland Railway, favoured such a solution. Mr Oakley of the Great Northern, while admitting that outstanding benefits would have resulted from such a policy, felt that it would only be practicable if all the main companies agreed. He would need to be sure that the London and North Western Railway, the Great Western Railway and the Midland were taking similar action before he could recommend to his directors that they should co-operate. Unfortunately such a coincidence of views did not exist. The chief traffic manager of the 'senior line'—the London and North Western Railway—did not think that it would be a good idea to buy up the private waggons. If his company bought out all the colliery waggons used on its rail network it would require 'the maximum number of waggons for doing the minimum amount of work'. This would be an unprofitable business. It would be better for the Clearing House to make the bye-laws and regulations and insist on the specification of private waggons being carried out.[2]

As early as June 1855, Captain Mark Huish, general manager of the London and North Western Railway, had proposed that there should be a systematic and regularly repeated inspection of all private waggons. The committee of the Clearing House, on his recommendation, appointed six general managers as a sub-committee to prepare detailed specifications of waggon dimensions and components but it proved impossible at the time to gain the compliance of the private waggon owners because the railway companies themselves could not agree on a policy of standardisation.[3]

The companies' concern about the state of the private owners' waggons increased or diminished in direct proportion to the

[1] Royal Commission on Railway Accidents, 1887, evidence of G. Findlay, Q. 30,951.     [2] *Ibid.*
[3] RCH 1/3: Minute 375 of Clearing House committee, July 13, 1855.

number and seriousness of accidents to goods trains caused by the defective condition of that part of the rolling stock. When the number of such accidents increased markedly in the early 1870s, Captain Tyler, for the Board of Trade, wrote numerous reports on the dangers to goods trains of faultily constructed wheel tyres, axles and axle boxes. At a meeting of the general managers in August 1870, therefore, Mr Findlay of the London and North Western Railway urged that the Clearing House should insist on private owners conforming to minimum standards of safety for their waggons. In November of that year a sub-committee was appointed to make detailed recommendations. But its labours proved as abortive as did those of its predecessor fifteen years earlier. In November 1872 the General Managers Conference, by this time less perturbed about the accident rate, resolved 'that the question referred to the sub-committee be dropped for the present'.[1] In February 1874, following Captain Tyler's report on an accident caused by the breaking of an axle of a coal waggon near Bishops Stortford, the subject was again raised at the General Managers' Conference by Mr Swarbrick of the Great Eastern Railway. He urged the adoption of a uniform specification as the only alternative to the companies' buying up all the rolling stock. But it was not long before the sense of urgency again passed by and it only required the absence of Mr Swarbrick from the November 1874 meeting for the other general managers to agree to drop the whole subject once more.[2]

It was only after another very outspoken report from another Board of Trade inspector, Major Marindin, that the Clearing House was induced to take more effective action. No less than 141 axles of goods waggons had been broken in 1883 and the inspectors were becoming increasingly critical. Then on January 1, 1885, near Pennistone, there occurred another serious accident caused by the breaking of the axle of a colliery waggon. The following strongly worded report from the Board of Trade was the inevitable outcome:

---

[1] RCH 1/79: Minutes 1099, 1127, 1247 of General Managers Conference, August 11, 1870, February 9, 1871, and November 7, 1872.

[2] RCH 1/79: Minutes 1346 and 1394 of the General Managers Conference, February 12 and November 12, 1874.

'Too great a case cannot be taken to ensure, first, that all waggon stock is built of such materials and dimensions that it is fit for running at high speed; and secondly that such stock is not at any time allowed to deteriorate and get into a bad running condition. . . . It is highly desirable that all waggons commencing to run on any line should either be the property of the railway company, or should be carefully inspected before being permitted to enter upon the line, that care should be taken that all materials of which they are constructed are of good quality, and that there should be a systematic periodical inspection of waggon stock of every description, including a rigid examination of all axles after they have run for a specified time. All waggons should bear a label to show that they have been passed for running by some railway company, and should be legibly marked with the date when they were last thoroughly overhauled. Such regulations to be effectual must be common to all railway companies, and can be enforced only by legislation or by the united action of the railway managers.' [1]

As early as 1847 the goods managers had recognised the need to subordinate individual preferences to the collective will for the benefit of the goods traffic as a whole. The general managers came to a similar decision for their sphere of influence four years later. But a further thirty-four years of frustration, inefficiency and needless slaughter of railway staff passed before the locomotive engineers were persuaded to meet as a separate group. Their prolonged independence of action was detrimental to the interests of the railways as a whole.

To forestall more positive government intervention on the question of privately owned waggons the general managers summoned the first meeting of the locomotive engineers and carriage and waggon superintendents on September 10, 1885. Their task was to draw up a uniform specification of private waggons and to prepare a code of regulations for both an initial and periodical examination of such vehicles. It is clear that this action was seen as an alternative to legislation, for Major Marindin's report on the Pennistone accident was included in the minutes. Within a month, a sub-committee, meeting at Derby, was engaged on the detailed task of specifying measurements, standards of

[1] RCH 1/551: Quoted in minutes of LECWS, March 9, 1886.

material to be used, etc. The outcome, by the end of the year, was a businesslike document: 'Proposed Standard Specification for the Construction of 8 or 10 Ton Private Owners' Waggons, to Work Upon the Lines of the Railway Companies.' It was impossible to maintain that the specification was not sufficiently detailed. Not only were exact dimensions laid down but also the quality of the wrought iron used for the metal parts of the waggon. The tyres were to be of Bessemer or Siemens steel. There were very detailed requirements for axles and axle boxes. Waggons which came up to the required standard were to have a register plate, according to the following pattern, attached to the bodywork:

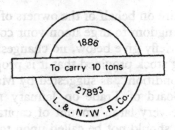

1886
To carry 10 tons
27893
L. & . N . W . R . Co.

At their meeting on November 11, 1886, the general managers gave unanimous endorsement to these proposals for adoption in the following year. Where privately owned waggon stock differed from the new specifications it would have to be modified. All new stock was to be built in conformity with the new regulations. On August 4, 1887, the general managers agreed on the wording of a circular to be sent to all parties sending private waggons over the companies' lines. The companies' engineers, through the Clearing House, had at last thrown down the gauntlet.[1]

Years of bickering followed. The engineers in the Clearing House had to fight the determined opposition of the Railway Carriage and Waggon Builders Association (with headquarters at 8 Great Queen St, W.1—a convenient address for lobbying purposes) and the Association of Private Owners of Railway Rolling Stock. The opening shots of the campaign were fired in April 1858 when Messrs Hargrove and Co., acting on behalf of the waggon builders, wrote to the general managers wanting to know what was implied

[1] RCH 1/551: Meetings and resolutions of LECWS including relevant minutes of general managers' meetings.

in the 'rebuilding' of waggons. They were informed that it included the replacement of inferior axles and tyres by others conforming to the new standards.

This answer gave the cue for the main campaign launched at a 'largely attended meeting of owners from all parts' held at Derby on May 14, 1890. The resolution, which received the unanimous endorsement of the meeting, began by giving lip service to the objective of uniformity and safety of operation of private waggons, but it went on to express the reluctance of the owners to spend money in altering their property to meet the requirements of the Clearing House:

'We therefore desire on behalf of the owners of private waggons in all parts of the kingdom to urge upon your committee that for reasons which we briefly give below, no changes are necessary in their existing rolling stock provided that it is properly maintained "in good running condition", as suggested by Major Marindin in his report to the Board of Trade on January 17, 1885, and in consideration of the very large amount of capital invested in it, such private owners should not be called upon to make structural alterations in their rolling stock, a gradual reduction in the number of accidents having followed the presentation of his report.'

'The number of failures of axles and tires (namely an average of 51 axles and 611 tires per year) is so rapidly diminishing and is so small compared with the number of waggons running as to show, we submit, that no change in design is called for.' [1]

In November 1890 it was the turn of the waggon builders to take delaying action. A deputation of ten men from the Railway Carriage and Waggon Builders Association came to the Clearing House where they were interviewed by a sub-committee of the general managers. Their plea was that if the journals of axles were worn down more than $\frac{1}{8}$ inch below the specified thickness, the waggon owner should be permitted to mark down the carrying capacity of his waggon to the next lower tonnage. They also hoped that the general managers would agree to a relaxation of the regulations for the fixing of wheel tyres by permitting the continued use of rivets. The general managers would not give way on either of these points. For reasons of safety they were par-

[1] Reported in RCH 1/155.

ticularly reluctant to agree to the suggestion that tyres could be attached by riveting.

Being thus obliged to 'rebuild' their old waggons, the private owners endeavoured to stifle criticism by replacing the worn out woodwork in the hope that the unsatisfactory condition of the ironwork might be overlooked. But the Clearing House engineers were not to be fobbed off with such cheese-paring tactics. They told Mr Taynton, Secretary of the Association of Private Waggon Owners, that putting new woodwork to old ironwork did not constitute the rebuilding of a waggon. Seven out of every eight accidents to private owners' waggons were due to defective ironwork, so that the condition of the ironwork was infinitely more important than that of the woodwork. Mr Taynton, in his reply, put his finger on the weakness of the railway companies' cases. The companies were not practising what they preached:

'I am desired to point out that the specified design and dimensions not only of axle boxes and bearing springs but also of the underframe and many other parts of a waggon are shown not to be of importance by the fact that the railway companies themselves are not adhering to the provisions of the standard specification with regard to them in reconstructing their own waggons, or even building new waggons'.[1]

Possibly Mr Taynton had been informed of the London and North Western Railway Company's dissent from the Clearing House specifications for axle lengths and methods of tyre fixing, expressed at a meeting of general managers on June 5, 1888.

By March 1, 1893, the sub-committee of engineers felt that they had gone to 'the fullest extent compatible with safety' in meeting the wishes of the private owners. They could not accept any further relaxation of standards. The other side then replied with open defiance. On May 17th Mr Taynton, on behalf of a joint committee of both builders and owners' organisations, wrote that 'compliance with the specification would lead to the needless sacrifice of a large number of good and safe waggons'. They therefore thought it unreasonable to advise the members of either association to comply with the terms.[2]

[1] Reported in RCH 1/551, sub-committee of LECWS, October 26, 1892.
[2] *Ibid.*, minute of meeting of LECWS, June 13, 1893.

Undoubtedly the fiercest battle between the railway companies and the private owners was fought on the issue of eliminating dumb (i.e. unsprung) buffers from railway waggons. In a standard specification for waggons issued by the Clearing House in September 1889 it was decided that, in the interests of the waggon owners, as well as in the interests of safe working and the prevention of accidents to railway companies' servants and others, all future waggons to be put on the railways should be provided with spring buffers. This was a tall order, as there were approximately 200,000 dumb-buffered waggons belonging to the coal owners alone in the closing years of the nineteenth century. In South Wales, as an economy measure, the coal owners had had their waggons built with spring buffers at one end and dumb buffers at the other. When a train was assembled the waggons were so arranged that the spring buffers were placed opposite the dumb buffers throughout its length.

Acting on behalf of its many customers who were reluctant to incur the expense of converting dead buffers into the spring variety, the Gloucester Railway Carriage and Waggon Company in the early weeks of 1894 deliberately built a waggon with dead buffers and axle (grease) box not conforming to Clearing House specifications. When the Great Western Railway would not accept this vehicle on its lines its action was challenged by the Waggon Company in the Court of the Railway and Canal Commission on April 20, 1894. The railway company was in a morally weak position. At the same time as it was refusing to accept waggons from the private owners because they did not conform to Clearing House specifications, it was accepting hundreds of dead-buffered waggons from the Midland Railway and even keeping some of its own in service. On the other hand the attitude of the general manager of the waggon company, Mr Alfred Slater, was not very encouraging for those who hoped, one day, to achieve a greater degree of standardisation in design and construction of waggons:

*Sir Richard Webster:* Do you agree that some standard or period must be arrived at when reconstruction should take place, or the waggon should be deemed as reconstructed, or not?
*Mr Slater:* No, I do not think there is any.

*Sir Richard Webster:* Then the view that you present to the court is, however old a waggon is, however obsolete its type is, if it is repaired so as to be as you consider safe, the Railway Company should be bound to recieve it?

*Mr Slater:* Practically that is the proposal; if it is safe for traffic it should be received.

*Sir Richard Webster:* And your view is that the Railway Company should not have any right to impose any condition with regard to safety of which they are to be the judges, however old the waggon may be?

*Mr Slater:* That is it.

*Sir Richard Webster:* I only want to get your view.

*Mr Slater:* They have a statutory right I suppose to issue regulations.

*Sir Richard Webster:* I am not asking you about the statutory right. I am asking you upon the merits, you have just told me you consider, however old a waggon is, however obsolete it is, if it is considered as good as it was before the Railway ought to take it?

*Mr Slater:* If it is safe for traffic they ought to be bound to take it.[1]

After two days in which charges and counter–charges were exchanged the two parties agreed to try to settle the matter out of court and the proceedings were adjourned indefinitely. In the following June the engineers decided to meet the waggon owners half way by agreeing to an alteration in the specification for axle boxes to make the reconstruction of waggons less expensive.[2]

In the course of 1903 no less than 333 accidents attributable to the use of dead-buffered waggons were reported on the railways of Britain. There can be little doubt that the knowledge of this high accident rate influenced the decision of the engineers, at their Clearing House meeting on November 21, 1903, to ban the use of dead-buffered waggons on the railways from January 1, 1910.[3] The decision was unpopular with most of the private

[1] The case is reported verbatim in RCH 1/386 with the minutes of the LECWS, May 3, 1894.
[2] RCH 1/386: Minute 28 of LECWS, June 13, 1894.
[3] RCH 1/552: Minute 379 of LECWS, March 16, 1904, minute 312 of LECWS, November 21.

waggon owners and led to immediate protests. A deputation of ten from the Mining Association of Great Britain, interviewed by the engineers in the Clearing House in January 1904, claimed that the alteration of the 200,000 waggons involved would make it difficult to maintain sufficient waggons in service to meet traffic needs. They urged extension of the time limit to December 31, 1913.[1] Because neither the London and North Western Railway nor the Scottish companies were prepared to agree to the earlier date, and the pressure from the private owners was strong, the Clearing House engineers gave way. The new regulations, issued later in 1904, provided that no dead-buffered waggons would be accepted by the companies from the beginning of 1914.[2]

Even after these concessions had been made, the railway companies did not present a united front. The representative of the London and North Western Railway told the meeting of engineers in March 1904 that his company reserved liberty of action to accept dead-buffered stock even after January 1914. The last straw was the announcement made by the Scottish companies in December 1913, within a few weeks of the projected enforcement of the new regulations, that they would allow the condemned waggons on their lines until the end of 1915. Not surprisingly another year's grace was allowed by the Clearing House, the private owners being granted until December 31, 1914, to make the necessary alterations to their rolling stock.[3] The declaration of war against Germany proved a godsend to those concerns which still had not felt able to afford the capital outlay for the necessary modification. In November 1914 the secretary of the Association of Private Owners of Railway Rolling Stock wrote to the Clearing House pleading 'existing trade conditions' as an excuse for a further twelve months' postponement. Though the engineers formally declined the request they were in an even weaker position in wartime, than they were in peace, to obtain compliance.

[1] RCH 1/387: Minute of sub-committee of LECWS, January 13, and February 26, 1904.
[2] Ibid., minute 373 of LECWS of March 16, 1904.
[3] RCH 1/78: General managers' minutes 994 of December 5, 1913, and RCH 1/388: Minute 1260 of LECWS, November 18, 1913.

The difficulties that the Clearing House companies had experienced in trying to persuade the private waggon owners to modify existing rolling stock should not blind us to the fact that progress was made towards uniformity of design for the construction of the railway companies' new waggons. Standard specifications were agreed for eight-, ten- and twelve-ton waggons in 1904, with some revisions in 1907. In 1902 and 1907 agreement was reached on a set of specifications for ten-ton tank waggons for inflammable liquids and there were similar agreements for twenty-ton goods waggons and tank waggons in 1903–4 and 1907.[1]

In the early 1900s both private waggon builders and some railway companies were depending to an increasing extent on continental manufacturers for the tyres and axles of their rolling stock. The cheapness of the foreign-made basic steel in comparison with the British-made Open Hearth or Bessemer steel was the great attraction. Nevertheless there were doubts about the quality of the imported components and a number of railway companies had by 1904 appointed their own inspectors to check the products concerned at the place of manufacture. The difficulty was that there was no liaison between the companies to ensure common standards. In March 1904, therefore, the engineers in their Clearing House meeting agreed that the companies should, in rotation, appoint an inspector on the continent. 'With the view of avoiding any possibility of axles and tyres which had been rejected at one inspection being accepted on a second inspection'.[2] This decision did not check the increasing flow of orders to foreign firms, a circumstance which greatly disturbed British steel manufacturers. On March 1909 the Clearing House engineers received a letter from Cammell Laird and Co., pointing out that private waggon owners were being supplied with foreign made tyres and axles of basic steel though the Clearing House specification since 1906 had stipulated that they should be made of acid steel. Shortly afterwards, when they interviewed a deputation of five from the steel manufacturers, the engineers were told that the foreign-made tyres wore out in nine years while the British variety lasted as long as twenty-one years. It was there and then decided to

---

[1] RCH 1/387: Minutes 377, 392, 401, 409, 411, 416, 436, 455, 485, 587, 660, 676 of LECWS, various dates 1902–7.

[2] RCH 1/387: Minute 387 of LECWS, March 16, 1904.

appoint a Clearing House inspector of all axles and tyres manufactured on the continent for importation into Britain. Four months later it was agreed that the salary of the inspector should be met by debiting the firms for whom the material was being tested in proportion to the time spent on the work.[1] The arrangement worked smoothly until the outbreak of war caused it to be brought to an end on December 31, 1914.[2]

In the case of cattle waggons, uniformity in design was achieved with less delay than was experienced with the less specialised vehicles. Nevertheless, the early history of construction of these waggons was far from promising. A report from the general managers to Kenneth Morison on April 24, 1861, referred to the many 'serious evils' arising from the great diversity of sizes of waggons in use:

'A glance at the Clearing House list of sizes of cattle waggons in use, even in 1858, and which has since been extended, will at once show the immense difficulty there is in dealing with it so as to establish even an approximation to uniformity and equity in arranging the rates between different companies.'

Encouraged by a circular letter sent to all railway companies by the War Office which urged a standard specification for cattle waggons, the general managers appointed a sub-committee to make precise recommendations. There was undoubtedly need for quick action.[3] The goods managers had recently discovered that there were eighty different types of cattle waggon in service on the railways, with linear dimensions ranging from the 10 feet 4 inches by 6 feet 7 inches of the Monmouthshire Railway to the 15 feet 6 inches by 7 feet 2½ inches of the Lancaster and Carlisle.[4] In February 1862 the general managers made their recommendation. In future the inside measurements of the standard cattle waggon were to be 15 feet by 7 feet 4 inches with a doorway giving

[1] RCH 1/387: Minutes 723 and 741 of LECWS, March 30, and July 14, 1909.
[2] RCH 1/387: Minute 1344 of LECWS, December 16, 1914.
[3] RCH 1/71: Minute 419 of General Managers Conference, August 8, 1861.
[4] RCH 1/180: Minute 1210 of Goods Managers Conference, January 28, 1858.

6 feet 2 inches clearance. Sprung buffers were to be fitted.[1] Two years later the general managers were told that the principal companies had accepted the new recommendation. But early in 1866 it was revealed that the principal Scottish companies and the Great Northern were still not complying with the regulations. Although the three Scottish companies had fallen into line by the end of that year the Great Northern had not. By 1873 the goods managers realised that it had proved impossible to gain complete uniformity and they therefore proposed a compromise with three standard sizes in the place of one. The small cattle waggon was to have a length inside of 13 feet 6 inches; the medium waggon was to measure 15 feet 6 inches, and the large waggon 18 feet. The general managers quickly endorsed this proposal and the large majority of the companies were happy to agree.[2] Compared with the tedious progress of the negotiations for goods waggons, this was a remarkable success.

As soon as through goods traffic began to assume substantial proportions in the 1850s railway companies were making frequent complaints that the ropes used to secure goods to the waggons were not being returned to their rightful owners. This source of annoyance was as much due to difficulties of identification as to downright dishonesty. The companies could have met the difficulty by instituting a common user system for ropes similar to that adopted for waggons in 1917. Instead the goods managers, in July 1858, resolved (in ungrammatical language):

'That each company may introduce a particular mark in their ropes, and must report the same to the Clearing House; and that the Clearing House suggest any alteration that may be needed in consequence of more than one company using the same mark.' [3]

In July 1861 the goods managers published a list of identification marks for the different companies' ropes. With so many independent companies in being it was difficult to avoid duplication.

[1] RCH 1/72: Minute 449 of General Managers Conference, November 6, 1862.
[2] RCH 1/79: Minute 1286 of General Managers Conference, May 8, 1873.
[3] RCH 1/180: Minute 1329 of Goods Managers Conference, July 29, 1858.

It requires little imagination to appreciate that for the harassed porter to distinguish between dirty ropes of the Newcastle and Carlisle Railway (one red and two black strands) and the Great Eastern Railway (one red strand) was no easy task. The ropes of the Great Northern (a red, a white and a black strand) must have, on occasions, been mistaken for those of the London and South Western (two red strands and one black). However, identification was helped by the requirement, from July 1861 that a metallic ferule, stamped with the initials of the company, was to be attached to the middle of each rope.[1]

Tarpaulins were less frequently 'mislaid' than ropes. Even before the foundation of the Clearing House it was the general practice to stamp them with the companies' initials. Early in 1886 the accountants suggested that it would simplify the settlement of accounts between companies if a common user scheme for sheets was introduced. The general managers promptly vetoed the proposal.[2]

In 1881–82 both the superintendents and the general managers looked into the question of head, tail, and side lamps, and lamp brackets for rolling stock. A sub-committee of the superintendents reached agreement on dimensions for the lamp brackets but reported that the sockets on the South Eastern and Brighton Companies' lamps were so different from the rest that they could not be brought within the specification. The full meeting of the superintendents then reluctantly concluded 'that it was not practicable to adopt generally any uniform pattern of tail lamp or tail lamp iron'. Another attempt at standardisation had ended in frustration.[3]

## III

One item which never appeared on the agenda of any Clearing House committee, was 'standardisation of locomotive design'. In view of the fact that innumerable hours of discussion were devoted

[1] RCH 1/180: Minute 1563 of Goods Managers Conference, October 27, 1859.

[2] RCH 1/79: Minute 2086 of General Managers Conference, February 11, 1886.

[3] RCH 1/109: Minutes 4348, 4658 of Superintendents Conference, April 27, 1881, and April 26, 1882.

material to be used, etc. The outcome, by the end of the year, was a businesslike document: 'Proposed Standard Specification for the Construction of 8 or 10 Ton Private Owners' Waggons, to Work Upon the Lines of the Railway Companies.' It was impossible to maintain that the specification was not sufficiently detailed. Not only were exact dimensions laid down but also the quality of the wrought iron used for the metal parts of the waggon. The tyres were to be of Bessemer or Siemens steel. There were very detailed requirements for axles and axle boxes. Waggons which came up to the required standard were to have a register plate, according to the following pattern, attached to the bodywork:

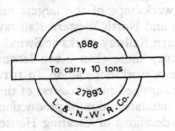

1886
To carry 10 tons
27893
L. & N.W.R. Co.

At their meeting on November 11, 1886, the general managers gave unanimous endorsement to these proposals for adoption in the following year. Where privately owned waggon stock differed from the new specifications it would have to be modified. All new stock was to be built in conformity with the new regulations. On August 4, 1887, the general managers agreed on the wording of a circular to be sent to all parties sending private waggons over the companies' lines. The companies' engineers, through the Clearing House, had at last thrown down the gauntlet.[1]

Years of bickering followed. The engineers in the Clearing House had to fight the determined opposition of the Railway Carriage and Waggon Builders Association (with headquarters at 8 Great Queen St, W.1—a convenient address for lobbying purposes) and the Association of Private Owners of Railway Rolling Stock. The opening shots of the campaign were fired in April 1858 when Messrs Hargrove and Co., acting on behalf of the waggon builders, wrote to the general managers wanting to know what was implied

[1] RCH 1/551: Meetings and resolutions of LECWS including relevant minutes of general managers' meetings.

locomotives were seldom built more than 13 feet 4 inches high or 9 feet wide, although, on tracks no wider than the British, American engineers could build to heights of 15 feet 6 inches and widths of 10 feet 9 inches with beneficial effects on the power of the locomotive. Given the varying physical conditions on British Railways before 1914, the problem of standardisation was 'bristling with difficulties'.[1]

By 1885, when the adverse reports of the Board of Trade inspectors shamed the engineers into holding regular monthly conferences, the amalgamation movement on British railways had reached an advanced stage. The majority of new locomotives were being built in the workshops of the largest railway companies, notably the London and North Western Railway works at Crewe and the Great Western Railway works at Swindon. By the end of the nineteenth century more than 4,000 locomotives had been produced in the Crewe workshops alone. In 1914 only 250 out of the 700 locomotives supplied in the course of the year came from private firms. Such standardisation of production as was achieved came not from any decisions of Clearing House committees but from the initiative of celebrated railway engineers in the huge company workshops. Thus, between 1852 and 1872, John Ramsbottom at Crewe supervised the production of 943 standard type goods locomotives.[2]

With the railway companies meeting most of their own requirements there was little scope for the private manufacturers to plan for economies of scale and standardisation of design. The orders they received were not large enough or regular enough to warrant the substantial capital outlays such policies required. There was little scope for mass production even in the fulfilment of foreign orders. Emigrant British engineers were found in large numbers on the railways of the Argentine, South Africa and other important markers and they took with them their characteristic traits of individuality and eccentricity. The tendency of the American locomotive manufacturing firms to decline orders for less than

[1] P.E.P. *Locomotives: A Report on the Industry*, London, 1951, p. 4; *The Railway Gazette*, February 1, 1918, p. 133.
[2] *The Railway Engineer*, December 1918, p. 236. S. B. Saul: 'The Market and the Development of Mechanical Engineering in Britain, 1860–1914', *Economic History Review*, April 1967, p. 114.

fifty locomotives of one pattern, left the British firms with a large number of orders for small quantities of a great variety of designs.[1] These historical circumstances brought about a situation before 1914 which has been ably summarised by a recent historian:

'The British engine was a high quality product with a long life, relatively expensive and difficult to service, closely tailored to the needs of the line for which it had been specifically designed. . . . For their type of engine the British makers were unsurpassed. Their works were well equipped: standardisation within the runs they were given was a commonplace, but by the last decade of the 19th Century not only had they no sound market basis for producing standard engines cheaply for stock, but the engineering traditions which the market had built into them would have made it well nigh impossible for them to adopt the practice anyway.' [2]

In the early years of the twentieth century there was increasing awareness of the shortcoming of some of the British traditions in locomotive building. In 1903 the Engineering Standards Committee reported in favour of the construction of standard pattern locomotives for the Indian Railways. During the next seven years 841 engines of one basic design were built for the 5 feet 6 inches gauge lines and 472 for the metre gauge lines of that country. In its third report on 'Standard Locomotives for Indian Railways', published in March 1910, the committee claimed that 'the standardisation of Indian locomotives has undoubtedly benefited all concerned and has reacted favourably towards the builders in this country'.[3] The Committee's comment reflected the private manufacturers delight in a long run of orders and the companies' greater willingness to learn from each other, rather than any concern to establish a Clearing House agreement for standardised designs. In August 1910 Lord Stalbridge, Chairman of the London and North Western Railway, noted that there was 'active co-operation between the railway companies to secure the best results'.[4] In the two years 1909 and 1910 six companies took part

---

[1] P.E.P. *Locomotives*, p. 52. Departmental committee on the engineering trades: report on standardised locomotives, printed in *Board of Trade Journal*, February 7, 1918, p. 150.        [2] Saul: *op. cit.* p. 117.
[3] *The Railway Gazette*, March 18, 1910, p. 302.
[4] *The Railway News*, August 20, 1910, p. 442.

in trials in which locomotives were exchanged to test their performance on different routes from those for which they had been designed. Perhaps the most celebrated of these exchanges took place in August 1910 when the Great Western Railway's *Polar Star* was employed on the route from Euston to Crewe while the London and North Western Railway's *Worcestershire* was tried out between Paddington and Plymouth. The tests showed that while the London and North Western Railway's locomotives were 'meeting all reasonable demands made on them by their own company' they were 'not performing with anything approaching the efficiency of Great Western Railway locomotive power'. The trials had 'no measurable influence' on the design of London and North Western Railway locomotives. Only after further exchanges between engines of the London and North Eastern Railway and Great Western Railway in 1925 had again demonstrated the superiority of the locomotives designed in Swindon did adjustments take place in the 'Pacific' type locomotives which immediately reduced their coal consumption from 50 lb. to 38 lb. per mile.[1] Before the advent of British Railways there was a great improvement within the regions of all four main-line companies in the fitting of interchangeable boilers, cylinders and other smaller components.

Such incidents disclosed what *might* have been achieved through the Clearing House, given wholehearted co-operation to improve the design and performance of the locomotives of the nation. The absence of such co-operation meant that Britain in the early twentieth century was a train 'spotters' paradise rather than a country that led the world in railway engineering.

IV

Although Clearing House committees had nothing to say about the design of the locomotive, they did eventually interest themselves in train brakes—a matter of concern to those who drove the locomotive as well as to passengers and guards who were dependent on its safe working.

In 1876 there was still a great diversity of practice among the companies. The London and North Western Railway favoured

[1] C. J. Allen: *The Locomotive Exchanges, 1870-1948*, pp. 33,54.

the use of Clark's brake modified by the company's chief mechanical engineer, F. W. Webb. The Midland were experimenting with the Westinghouse Automatic although most of its locomotives were fitted with the same firm's air brake. The Great Northern was awaiting the report of the Royal Commission on Railway Accidents. The Great Western, in the view of one writer, had decided 'to wait until the problem had been worked out on other lines, and then to benefit by the experience gained'.[1] By the late 1870s the best informed engineers were in little doubt that there were only two systems worthy of serious consideration: the Westinghouse Automatic and the Smith Vacuum. Following a series of trials held in December 1876 between Edinburgh and Glasgow, *The Engineer* claimed that the superior efficiency of the Westinghouse system was 'incontestable'.[2]

The consensus of opinion among leading engineering writers was one thing: willingness of locomotive superintendents to abandon cherished beliefs was another. Progress in the introduction of continuous brakes was painfully slow.

The initiative in pressing for the uniform adoption of a system of continuous brakes in the 1870s and 1880s came from the Board of Trade rather than from the Railway Clearing House. Following a series of graphic reports on railway accidents written by Captain Tyler of the Board of Trade in 1870–71, the Railway Companies Bill, which contained clauses making compulsory the absolute block system and continuous brakes, was introduced in the Commons in 1871. This and another bill introduced in the Lords in 1877 were squashed largely because of the successful mobilisation of the railway interest in Parliament.[3] The principal argument of the companies in resisting compulsion by legislation was that good progress in the installation of continuous brakes was being made by their engineering departments. Yet as late as June 1887 a return issued by the Board of Trade revealed that of a total rolling stock of 8,472 engines and 52,808 coaches, only 2,688 engines and 23,729 coaches had brakes which conformed to five requirements recommended by the Board in a circular sent

[1] *Engineering*, October 13, 1876, pp. 323–4.
[2] *The Engineer*, January 5, 1877, pp. 12–14.
[3] P. S. Bagwell: 'The Railway Interest: Its Organisation and Influence, 1839–1914,' *Journal of Transport History*, November 1965, pp. 73–75.

to all companies on August 30, 1877. Because of the absence of any lead from Clearing House committees at this stage and the failure of attempts at a legislative remedy, some of the companies most involved in the through passenger traffic sought an alternative way out. They fitted locomotives and coaches with *both* the principal braking systems. But this was no real answer. An imposed uniformity of pattern was imperative. On July 28, 1887, an accident occurred through a train leaving the rails at Aviemore on the Highland Railway. The whole train was fitted up with various kinds of brakes and some of the coaches had two kinds, yet none of them could be fitted up and used. Under the Regulation of Railways Act which became law on August 30, 1889, the fitting of continuous brakes on passenger trains at last became compulsory; but both Westinghouse and Vacuum systems were permitted. The dangers which remained despite the improvements resulting from the Act were exemplified in an accident at Ramsgate on August 31, 1891. A London, Chatham and Dover Railway engine, running tender first and hauling some empty Great Northern Railway coaches, could not hold the train on a gradient of 1 in 75 and carriages and engine crashed through the end wall of a tunnel. Although the carriages had the vacuum brake and the engine was 'dual fitted' it had no vacuum pipe at the leading end. In consequence no brake connection could be made with the coaches. The driver apparently realised this after he had narrowly escaped death by jumping clear of his engine.[1]

The Engineers Conference of the Clearing House did not attempt to adjudicate in the controversy over the two braking systems. Its members did see fit to intervene in important matters of detail. The positioning of the brake pipes on railway carriages varied greatly from company to company. A return sent in to the Clearing House by the companies in 1900 revealed that pipes of the vacuum brake were placed in the centre of the drawbar on the Caledonian Railway's stock while on the Furness Railway they were placed over 2 feet 6 inches from the centre. There were many other variations with other companies which fitted the vacuum brake and at least as many differences between the stock

[1] C. F. Dendy Marshall: *A History of the Southern Railway*, London, 1936, p. 472. I am grateful to Mr Edwin Course for drawing my attention to this incident.

of companies using the Westinghouse system. At Clifton sidings, York, in July of the following year, a selection of vehicles from the different companies were examined by a sub-committee of the Clearing House engineers who subsequently made recommendations on standard positioning for all Westinghouse and vacuum pipes. Although the new regulations, which came into force in 1902, applied only to newly constructed stock, and it was left entirely to the companies to decide whether or not they altered existing stock, they were at least an important contribution to safety. Accidents which arose from the galling situation of incompatible brake fitments were now less likely to occur with each year that passed.[1]

Although shunters and goods guards would have welcomed it the law did not require the installation of continuous brakes on goods trains. No Clearing House committee considered this problem until 1905. In February of that year Mr Inglis of the Great Western Railway persuaded the general managers to ask the companies for statistics of the number of vehicles fitted with the different kinds of brakes. When the information was received it was considered by a sub-committee of the general managers of ten of the larger companies. Its members examined the problem intermittently for more than two years but finally 'postponed' consideration of the subject in November 1907.[2] Their failure to make any firm recommendation is not difficult to explain. The presence of over 600,000 waggons belonging to private owners made the difficulty of introducing a general system of continuous brakes for goods waggons almost insuperable. Most companies by 1905 had some waggons fitted with continuous brakes and an increasing number of fast goods trains were being run. But when the engineers considered the subject in December 1905 they made recommendations for the dimensions of draw hooks, screw couplings and buffers of waggons already fitted for continuous braking. They had no suggestions for speeding the conversion of the vast majority of waggons which still had hand-operated brakes.[3]

[1] RCH 1/386: Minute 20 of a sub-committee of LECWS, February 7, 1902, and Appendix of returns from railway companies, January 19, 1901.
[2] RCH 1/87: Minute 336 of general managers, February 7, 1905, and Minute 523 of general managers, November 5, 1907.
[3] RCH 1/387: Minutes 487 and 521 of LECWS, July 27, 1905, and February 14, 1906.

The consequence of the inability of the Clearing House to tackle the problem of the inadequately braked goods train was excessive running costs. Because of deficiencies in brake power the Board of Trade regulations required the provision of run away catch points on all lines where the rising gradient was more severe than 1 in 260. These requirements were to prevent a major disaster when waggons broke loose (with continuous brakes, the disconnection of a waggon automatically led to the application of its brakes). As late as 1950 there were over 4,000 of these run away catch points on the British railway network. At over 1,000 places the regulations required the stopping of trains for the application of the hand brakes. The process of application and release of brakes occupied at last 10,000 hours per week, whereas with continuous brakes, 250,000 engine hours in steam would have been saved. Through the faster speed of goods trains fitted with continuous brakes, between 20% and 30% of train engine hours would have been saved.[1] It was a heavy penalty to pay for the continued survival of the private owners' waggons. It was only possible to tackle the problem in earnest after all waggons came under the ownership of the State in 1948.

[1] S. E. Parkhouse: 'Railway Freight Rolling Stock,' *Journal of the Institute of Transport*, September 1951, p. 215.

THE RAILWAY CLEARING HOUSE

# CHAPTER X

# STANDARDISATION: RAILWAY
OPERATION

I

In the first four decades of the nineteenth century when the first
public railways were being opened in widely scattered parts of
Britain, railway engineers had no precedents to go by when they
came to frame a set of rules for the safe working of the traffic.
Devising a reliable method of railway signalling proved a happy
hunting ground for all those with any pretentions to inventive
capacity. Inevitably a bewildering variety of systems were in
operation by the time the Clearing House started business.

Mr J. Entwistle, a director of both the Brighton and the Greenwich Railways, pointed out to a Parliamentary committee in 1841
that the signals of some railways 'were almost the converse of those
on others', and that the signal for 'safety on one line was that for
danger' on another.[1] Understandably directors were reluctant to
appoint engine drivers or pointsmen who had previous experience
on lines with different signalling systems. When Rowland Hill
(later Sir Rowland Hill) took up a directorship of the Brighton line
in 1843, its trains were still obliged to use the rails of other railway
companies on the last part of the route from Brighton to London.
The driver of a through train had to be familiar, therefore, with
three separate signalling systems and had to be particularly careful
to remember when he passed from the tracks of one company to
those of another. It was a situation fraught with great danger.[2]

As the number of independent lines grew, the directors of some
companies considered it prudent to glean what information they
could on the signalling systems in use on other railways. Thus on

[1] Select Committee on Railways, 1841, minutes of evidence. BPP 1841,
Vol. VIII, Q. 1177.
[2] George Birkbeck Hill: *Life of Sir Rowland Hill*, London, 1880, Vol.
2, pp. 19–20.

December 28, 1840, Mr W. H. Booth, secretary of the Liverpool and Manchester Railway, wrote to his opposite number, Mr C. A. Saunders, on the Great Western Railway:

'I perceive by the Public Prints that you have lately established a new or revised code of signals on your line. If you have the regulations in a printed form, and would favour me with a copy, I would feel much obliged. We want all the light that we can get from the four corners of the railway world.'[1]

Not all those who had influence in railway management were so enlightened. When Saunders sent a copy of his company's rules and regulations to the Board of the Newcastle and Carlisle Railways a few weeks later he received back a bare acknowledgement together with the comment: 'The directors consider that the working of their line requires, from its situation, regulations peculiar to itself.'[2]

The earliest railway signalling was done by hand. On the Liverpool and Manchester line railway policemen were stationed at regular intervals between the termini. Each man 'signified a clear road by assuming an erect position with arms outstretched' and indicated danger by adopting the 'stand at ease' position.[3] Other companies used a flag system, manually operated, but found it costly and inefficient. Mr Fred Clarke, from Bristol, wrote to Mr Saunders of the Great Western Railway, on October 19, 1841, bewailing the fact that 'the consumption of flags on the Exeter line was enormous'.

'The flags will not stand a week. These last few windy days have, I believe, put every flag on the line out of repair.'[4]

It was not long before the need for more substantial and reliable signals was recognised. In the course of the 1840s various devices made of wood or iron replaced the flag and the railway policeman on almost all lines. But there was still no attempt to achieve uniformity. In October 1856 *The Engineer* listed six different kinds of

[1] BTHR, HL I, 16D.
[2] Select Committee on Railways, 1841, minutes of evidence, BPP 1841, Vol. VIII, Q. 2135.
[3] Richard Blythe: *Danger Ahead: The Dramatic Story of Railway Signalling*, London, 1951, p. 27. Quoting *The Railway Companion*, 1833.
[4] BTHR, HL I, 16D.

signalling systems in use on British railways. Very common was the disc system in which a red painted disc facing the driver indicated 'danger' and a green painted one 'caution'. 'All clear' was indicated by the edge of the disc facing the driver. There were both double vane and treble vane systems. The Bouch patent had one white disc for 'clear', one green square for 'caution' and two red circles for 'danger'. A sort of fish-tailed pointer was used on the parts of the Great Western Railway. The semaphore described as 'the most distinct of all signals' was gradually gaining the ascendancy. Under this system 'danger' was shown with the arm at right angles to the post, 'caution' with the arm at an angle of 45°, and 'all clear' with the arm within the post.[1]

That the inconveniences of such a diversity of practice should have been tolerated so long was partly due to the general rule that for many years most drivers only rarely took their locomotives beyond the lines of the company that employed them. Hence the standardisation of signals was not seen as a matter of practical urgency. A foremost engineering authority of the day blamed 'the self sufficiency of the railway fraternity' who were 'a law unto themselves' for the reluctance to listen to the proposals of reformers. He considered 'the predominance of the practical spirit which pervades all English institutions alike, which is supposed never to make a mistake, when in truth the whole practice may be one continuous mistake' as a major stumbling block to uniformity. Directors and managers who had this outlook distrusted 'scheming' and 'theorising'.[2]

With the remarkably rapid growth of through traffic in the years 1858–62 the number of drivers who were obliged to work their engines on foreign lines increased sharply. Uniform signalling now became much more a practical necessity. Nor were there wanting advocates of reform. In November 1860, Thomas Wrigley, a man with long experience of railway management, wrote to *The Times* advocating, as the sheet anchor of railway travelling, 'one uniform description of signals used throughout the kingdom'. Only by these means could an engine driver, passing from one line to another, have no difficulty in reading and understanding the messages sent to him by the signalman.[3]

[1] *The Engineer*, October 3, 1856, p. 535.
[2] *The Engineer*, August 8, 1856, p. 422.      [3] *The Times.*

These sentiments first found reflection in the Railway Clearing House at a meeting of the Superintendents held on April 24, 1862. Mr Walter Leith, superintendent of the Great Northern Railway, asked for the appointment of a sub-committee

'. . . for the purpose of suggesting concise regulations for general adoption, for the guidance of engine drivers and guards when working the trains of one company over the railways of another company, to obviate the necessity of supplying them with a book of the regulations of each company over whose line they may be called upon to work'.[1]

There is no indication that the eight men then nominated ever met as a sub-committee. If they did, no record of their meeting survives.

Credit for reviving the discussion of signals, rules and regulations was claimed by Mr G. P. Neele, superintendent of the London and North Western Railway and a member of the Conference of Superintendents almost continuously from 1856–95.[2] But the general managers were also becoming more concerned with the question because of the increasing practice of companies acquiring running powers over neighbouring lines. There was also concern lest the Royal Commission on Railways, appointed in 1865, might recommend legislation imposing uniform regulations if the companies did not produce them themselves through the Clearing House. At their November 1865 meeting, therefore, they appointed a sub-committee of seven 'to report on the advisability of having uniform rules and regulations for the working of railways'.[3] The committee, which was in close consultation with a small group of the leading superintendents, proceeded by very easy stages. Its report was dated May 1, 1867. After some modifications by the General Managers Conference, it appeared in its final form as 'Rules for Working over Foreign Lines', on June 12, 1867.

Far from forming a set of compulsory regulations such as had

[1] RCH 1/101: Minute 619 of Superintendents Conference, April 24, 1862.    [2] G. P. Neele: *Railway Reminiscences*, London, 1904, p. 155.
[3] See the evidence of Captain Mark Huish on the increase of running powers. Royal Commission on Railways, 1865–7. BPP 1867, Vol. XXXVIII, Q. 15,943, and 15,952. RCH 1/79: Minute 607, General Managers Conference, November 9, 1865.

been adopted by a conference of railway engineers of the German States and the Austrian Empire as early as 1850, the rules comprised the gist of the accumulated rules of the principal railways. According to Neele's account, 'the form adopted was carefully compiled so as to avoid any interference with existing rules'. The main idea was that the set of Clearing House rules should be bound up as an appendix to the separate companies' own rule books.[1] It was hoped that Clearing House recommendations would eventually take precedence over variants from them.

The semaphore system of signalling was printed at the beginning of the document as being the recommended common standard; but there was included an appendix, printed partly in colour, showing the signalling systems of important companies which had not adopted, or only partially adopted, the semaphore. The important discrepancies which still existed between the companies were all too manifest. The Great Western, Bristol and Exeter, Somerset and Dorset, South Devon and Cornwall Railways all used the red disc, at least on some of their lines, to indicate 'all right', while on the London and North Eastern and North Eastern Railways the same symbol indicated 'danger'. The Brighton line's danger signal, on the other hand, comprised *two* red discs. The thirty-seven page publication also revealed what a long way there was to go before block signalling by means of the electric telegraph became general. Under the heading 'General Regulations for Officers in Charge of Stations and Others', it is made clear that the time interval method of controlling the movement of trains was still predominant:

'The "Danger" signal is shown for five minutes after the passing of any engine or train and the "Caution" signal is shown for a further five minutes, after which the "All Right" signal is shown. The exception to this rule is, when it has been ascertained

---

[1] German engineers regulations included in Royal Commission on Railways, 1865–67. Report, Appendix CA, BPP 1867, Vol. XXXVIII, ii, p. 202. G. P. Neele: *op. cit.* p. 155. Note also minute 757 of General Managers Conference, May 9, 1867. It was also resolved that the various companies, parties to the clearing system, be recommended to put the regulations into force as from July 1 next, and that each company print them for the use of its own servants when working over other companies' railways.

by telegraph, that the line is clear to the next station ahead, in which case the "All Right" signal is shown.'

The continued absence of an effective communication cord on most railways was revealed in rule 32:

'Enginemen and firemen must, on starting, and frequently during the journey, look back and see that the whole of the train is following in a safe and proper manner.'

The revision of the 'Rules for Working over Foreign Lines', undertaken in the Clearing House between 1874 and 1876, took place under the threat of greater legislative interference to ensure safe working of the railways. The reports of Captain Tyler, one of the government inspectors for the railways, for the years 1872 and 1873—following an alarming increase in the number of fatal accidents—and Board of Trade circulars to the railway companies, all acted as stern reminders that the patience of Parliament was becoming exhausted. In a letter sent to all the railway companies on November 18, 1873, with which Captain Tyler's report for 1872 was enclosed, it was claimed by the Board of Trade that safer methods of working traffic and appropriate mechanical contrivances had been 'too slowly introduced'. The government was therefore 'considering the expediency of legislation' and called the attention of the companies to the whole question in the hope that they, 'in whose hands the means of improvement mainly rested', would 'make every effort to meet the reasonable demands of the public and of Parliament'. The final spur to action was the appointment of the Royal Commission on Railway Accidents in 1874 which, according to Mr Galt, had the effect of 'stimulating the principal companies to unwonted exertions in order to avoid the necessity of any legislation.'[1]

Five out of the ten members of the Clearing House sub-committee appointed in November 1874 came from companies on whose lines serious accidents had occurred during the preceding

[1] Royal Commission on Railway Accidents, 1875–77. BPP 1877, Vol. XLVIII, Appendix K, p. 130 *et seq.* 'Circulars issued by the Board of Trade Relative to the Working of the Railways in the Matter of Public Safety.' See also H. Raynar Wilson: *The Safety of British Railways*, London, 1909, p. 108.

five months.[1] 'The Rules and Regulations to be observed by all persons in the service of the Railway Companies', approved by the General Managers Conference in March 1874, besides being far more comprehensive and detailed than the 'Rules' of 1867, which they superseded, were also expressed in more confident and authoritative terms: Concessions still had to be made to meet the peculiarities of individual company working, but the supremacy of the Clearing House rules was stressed by the general managers,

'That the special requirements of each company be met by such instructions as may be, from time to time, found necessary, the instructions, however, to be framed so as not to be inconsistent with the General Rules and Regulations now approved.'[2]

Neele claimed that the absence, in the Rules of 1876, of the appendix illustrating the varieties of signal in use was due to the general adoption of the semaphore signal over the preceding nine years. Certainly the new rules showed the semaphore (with the fish-tail end for the distant signal) as the standard. But uniformity of practice was still not nearly as complete as Neele suggested. Board of Trade inspectors Hutchinson, Tyler and Yolland, were all agreed that there were still great differences in the codes of signals and regulations of the various companies, though Colonel Hutchinson conceded 'a gradual tendency to assimilation' and Captain Tyler did not believe that the differences were a cause of accidents, even though he cited a case where an 'all right' signal on one line was a 'danger' signal on another.[3]

The inclusion of no less than fifteen rules (numbers 88–102) under the heading 'General Rules for Working the Absolute Block Telegraph' reflected the progress made by the companies in this direction since 1867 when the block system was mentioned as an exception to the general practice of working by time interval.

The companies were approaching unanimity in the types of

[1] Royal Commission on Railway Accidents, 1875–77, Report of Captain Galt. BPP 1877, Vol. XLVIII, p. 62.
[2] RCH 1/79: Minute 1482 of the General Managers Conference, of March 16, 1876.
[3] G. P. Neele: *op. cit.* p. 212. Royal Commission on Railway Accidents, 1875–77. Minutes of evidence, BPP 1877, Vol. XLVIII, Q. 415–423, 1331–1337, and 2147.

signals in use; it was another matter to give such signals precisely the same significance. Colonel Yolland told the Royal Commission on Railway Accidents that there was a great diversity of practice in the observance of distant danger signals. Some companies allowed their drivers to pass danger signals without any appreciable reduction in speed if the line immediately ahead was seen to be clear; others ruled that the train was to be brought to a halt. The rules of the London and North Western Railway were the exact opposite of the Great Western Railway in this case.[1] In the Book of Rules of 1876, Rule No. 276 reflected this diversity of practice and marked something of a compromise between the two extremes.

'When an engine driver finds a distant signal at "danger" he must immediately shut off steam, and reduce the speed of his train, *so as to be able to stop at the distant signal post*, but if he sees that the way in front of him is clear, he must proceed slowly and cautiously within the distant signal, having such control *as to be able to stop it short of any obstruction* that may exist between the distant signal post and the home signal and must bring his train to a stand as near the home signal as the circumstances of the case will allow.'

The new rules were far more specific in respect of the discipline of the labour force. Railwaymen were to devote themselves 'exclusively' to the service of the company that employed them (Rule 1); they were to be 'prompt, civil and obliging' (Rule 9); no money or gratuity in the shape of fee, reward or remuneration 'was allowable from passengers or other persons under any pretence whatever' (appropriately, rule No. 13). Most draconian was Rule 15:

'The company reserve the right to punish any servant by immediate dismissal, fine or suspension from duty, for intoxication, disobedience of orders, negligence, misconduct or absence from duty without leave; and to deduct from the pay of their servants, and retain, the sums which may be imposed as fines, and also their wages during the time of their suspension or absence from duty from any cause.'

Guards were required to show a tender regard for members of

[1] Q. 172, 359.

the female sex, who were not to be placed in compartments reserved for smokers (Rule 238). Rule 242 was the epitome of gallantry:

'When ladies are travelling alone, the guards are to pay every attention to their comfort; and in placing them in the train, they must, if requested, endeavour to select a carriage for them (according to the class of their tickets) in which other ladies are travelling; and if they wish to change carriages during the journey, the guards must enable them to do so.'

In contrast was the treatment of railwaymen travelling to or from their place of work. Guards had to prevent any embarrassing mixing of the classes. Under Rule 246, they were to ensure that 'platelayers and other workmen of the company, holding third class passes, were kept as separate as possible from the passengers'.

Platelayers, in fact, came off rather badly under the new rules. It was not yet the requirement that a 'look-out' man should be posted to warn men working on the line of the approach of trains. When working in a tunnel a platelayer needed to have his wits about him, as was revealed in Rule 348:

'Each platelayer working in a tunnel, when trains are approaching in both directions, must, if he be unable to reach any recess in the walls, lie down, either in the space between the two lines of rails, or between the line and the side of the tunnel, with which every man must make himself acquainted, in order that he may select the place which affords the greatest safety.'

It was only under the revision of the Rules in 1889 that the appointment of a look-out man was recommended.

The Rules of 1876 contained detailed instructions for the observance of Greenwich time throughout the railway system. They remind us of the importance of the railways, before the days of BBC time signals, as an agency for achieving common time throughout the kingdom. Where telegraphic communication existed between stations the correct time was to be signalled daily. Rule 25 was to apply in all other cases:

'Each guard must, before starting on his journey, satisfy himself that his watch is correct with the clock at the station from which he starts, and must again compare it and regulate it if necessary by the clock at the station where his journey ends, before commencing the return journey.

'The guard in charge of the first passenger train (starting after 10 a.m.), stopping at all stations on the portion of the Main Line or Branch over which it runs, must, on his arrival at each station, give the station master or other person in charge, the precise time, in order that the station clock may be regulated accordingly; and in the event of the time given by the guard differing from that of the station clock, the latter must be altered to agree.'

The new rules gained more immediate and widespread adoption after 1876 than had their predecessors following 1867. An enquiry conducted by the superintendents early in 1878 revealed that most of the important companies, including the London and North Western Railway, North Eastern Railway, Great Western Railway and Midland, had adopted them. The Great Northern, South Eastern and London, Chatham and Dover followed suit later in 1878. Most of the sixteen companies still witholding their endorsement in July 1878 were small concerns, although the Taff Vale and North British companies were among the dissenters and the directors of the Brighton line had only given qualified acceptance.[1]

As early as 1857 German railway engineers agreed on a rule (No. 197 of their code) for block signalling by the use of the telegraph. A train was not allowed to leave a station until 'all clear' had been received from the next station along the line.[2] Such a system was first introduced in England on the line between Yarmouth and Norwich in 1844, but it was not until forty years later that the adoption of this method by the majority of the companies made possible the acceptance of the first Clearing House code of telegraph signals.

The problem of devising a common code of telegraphic signals was made exceptionally difficult by the uneven progress of the companies; the Midland, for example, pushing ahead with the block system far more rapidly than did the London and North

---

[1] RCH 1/117: Minutes 3455, 3467 and 3753 of the Superintendents Conference, May 24 and July 24, 1878, and April 23, 1879.
[2] Royal Commission on Railways, 1865–7. Report. Appendix C.A. BPP 1867, Vol. XXXVIII, ii, p. 202.

Western Railway. Since each company worked out a code which best suited its own circumstances, 'a great diversity of codes and forms of instrument' came into existence.

The superintendents first gave attention to this problem in 1865 when the representative of the North London Railway tabulated the various codes of telegraph beats in use on the railways, hoping that this would pave the way to the adoption of one agreed code. His idea was rejected as impracticable. Nine years later the best that could be agreed was the adoption of a rule that where running powers were being exercised, the code of the 'home' railway should be used for 'foreign' trains passing over its rails.[1]

As was so often the case with other aspects of railway reform, it required a major catastrophe to shake off the inertia of railway management. In this case the accident which drew attention to the drawbacks of a diversity of telegraphic codes was a triple collision in Canonbury Tunnel on December 10, 1881. On three separate occasions a Great Northern Railway signalman telegraphed to his opposite number on the North London Railway, informing him of the approach of a train. The North London signalman sent back the seven-beat signal which, in his company's code, stood for 'obstruction to the train in rear'. According to the Great Northern code, however, seven beats was the signal for 'caution the train and let it proceed'. As a result of this confusion three trains were sent through the tunnel at barely reduced speeds to collide at the far end. A further collision was prevented only by the timely action of a guard who ran to the entrance of the tunnel just in time to warn the driver of another train on the point of entering it.[2]

At the very next meeting of the superintendents, Mr Neele brought up the question of the adoption of a general code sign to indicate 'danger' or 'obstruction' where lines were worked on the block telegraph system. He argued that, as they had agreed to a common standard of semaphore signals in the Rules and Regulations of 1876, they ought also to work out a uniform code of train telegraphy. The committee agreed.[3] Mr Needham and the six

[1] G. P. Neele: *op. cit.*, pp. 137, 203. RCH 1/116: Minute 2417 of Superintendents Conference of April 24, 1874.

[2] Richard Blythe: *Danger Ahead*, pp. 93–94.

[3] RCH 1/118: Minute 4456 of Superintendents Conference of January 25, 1882.

other men assigned this task had to face formidable difficulties. In the words of Mr Neele:

'In the same way that the constructive engineers cling to their own designs, so the Passenger Superintendents and the Electrical Engineers clung to their own systems and set no store on uniformity.'[1]

A year after the sub-committee had been appointed, its sole achievement was general agreement that six beats signified 'danger' or 'obstruction'. But even here there was not unanimity. The superintendents of the Great Western Railway and the North Eastern Railway registered dissent on the grounds that six beats had a different significance in their codes. However, the opposition was gradually worn down by the persistence and patience of Messrs Neele and Needham, and at a special meeting of the superintendents, held on November 30, 1883, a code of seventeen different signals was recommended for universal adoption from March 1, 1884. It had the blessing of the general managers.[2] Despite this impressive advance, there was a distressingly long list of exceptions. The Great Eastern could not accept the code for beats 1–5; the Rhymney Railway wished to be excused the use of signals 7 to 17 inclusive; the North Staffordshire line could only accept the six-beat signal, and so on. After further revisions it was not until 1904 that the standard Clearing House code was in almost universal use.[3]

When assessing the importance of Clearing House Conferences as vehicles for reform the parallel influence of the Amalgamated Society of Railway Servants and the Board of Trade must not be overlooked. A pamphlet written by Edward Harford, General Secretary of the Amalgamated Society of Railway Servants, and published by the Union in 1886, contained the demand that all railways ought to be worked on the absolute block system; that the

[1] G. P. Neele: *op. cit.* p. 286.
[2] RCH 1/118: Minute 4778 of Superintendents Conference, January 24, 1883. RCH 1/110: Minute 5152 of Superintendents Conference of November 30, 1883.
[3] C. B. Byles: *The First Principles of Railway Signalling*, London, 1910, p. 44. For the 1884 code, see RCH 1/110: Minute 5152 of November 30, 1853.

block and interlocking of signals and points should be electrically combined and controlled and that one code of block signal regulations and one pattern of signal should be adopted throughout the kingdom.[1] From 1873 the Board of Trade demanded annual returns from the companies of the progress made in the block and interlocking systems and under the Regulation of Railways Act, 1889 block signalling and the interlocking of signals and points were made compulsory together with the introduction of continuous brakes on passenger trains. By this time more than 90% of the lines were already being worked under the block system.

Meanwhile, in less spectacular fashion than in earlier years, the work of revising and extending the Clearing House Rules and Regulations continued. There were major revisions in 1883, 1889, 1894, 1897 and 1904. By the end of the nineteenth century the thirty-seven page booklet of 1867 had grown to a weighty volume of 280 foolscap-sized pages. With each revision the subdivisions of the regulations and the number of rules increased. In the 1897 edition there were appendices containing separate regulations for the Westinghouse and the vacuum brake, slip carriages, block working, single-line working and many other subjects. The apologetic submission of tentative proposals in 1867 had become an indispensable and authoritative guide to railway operation throughout the United Kingdom. If at times progress seemed painfully slow this should not blind us to the magnitude of the ultimate achievement.

## II

It cannot be said that the presentation of the accounts of the railway companies was in any way circumscribed or stereotyped before 1868. The directors could not claim that they were being strait-jacketed either by the government or by the Clearing House when they had to draft a financial statement for the meeting of shareholders. On the contrary, the career of George Hudson, the Railway King, revealed that it was by an enterprising and imaginative adjustment of statements of account that an ambitious director could simultaneously make himself a fortune and become

---

[1] E. Harford: *Suggestions for Safe Railway Working*, London, 1886.

the idol of the investing public. By a few strokes of the pen, particularly by charging to capital account items which rightly should have been met from revenue, it was possible overnight to transform a shaky undertaking into a prosperous one. For this reason any meaningful comparison of the financial state of any two companies was out of the question. J. Bagshaw, the chairman of the Eastern Counties Railway, was certainly not exaggerating when he declared in 1849 that it was 'almost impossible' to determine the exact state of affairs of railway companies.[1] In September 1850 *The Times* commented that the financial affairs of the Caledonian Railway were in 'just such a tangle as one might dream of after supping on lobster salad and champagne'.[2] Practices were infinitely varied. Some companies paid dividends while the line was still under construction, others did not; some met the costs of opposition to rival lines out of capital, others debited it to revenue; some had adequate provision for depreciation, others had not. The South Eastern Railway had a depreciation fund between 1849–51, but then abandoned it for some years. These variations in practice can be attributed partly to early inexperience in the financial management of such large concerns. But it was also true that in times of business depression it was sometimes a matter of deliberate policy to stop making payments into a depreciation fund in order to maintain the confidence of shareholders by continuing to pay them a high dividend.[3]

All that Parliament required of the railways in most of the early Railway Acts was that 'proper books of account' should be kept. There was rarely any indication of how the accounts were to be set out. On March 15, 1844 Mr R. Wallace, MP for Greenock, asked Mr Gladstone, president of the Board of Trade,

'Whether for the information of the public generally, and the Railway Department of the Board of Trade especially, it has not become requisite that all railway companies shall periodically in future, furnish to the Board of Trade a debtor and creditor account,

---

[1] Select Committee on the Amending of Railway Acts as to the Audit of Accounts, 1849. BPP 1849, Vol. X, Q. 2903.
[2] *The Times*, September 30, 1850, quoted in H. Pollins: 'Aspects of Railway Accounting Before 1868' in A. C. Littleton and B. S. Yamey (ed.): *Studies in the History of Accounting*, London, 1956, p. 334.
[3] Pollins: *op. cit.* p. 353.

drawn out on a simple and uniform plan, of their half yearly receipts and expenditure?'

Gladstone, replying,

'did not think it had become desirable that any such regulations should be made. Parliament had not yet adopted, nor was it likely to adopt, that any public supervision of the amount of profits which parties who had embarked capital on the faith of Acts of Parliament were realising.'[1]

Gladstone's policy was largely followed under the Companies Clauses Consolidation Act of 1845. Although each company was required to draw up an 'exact' balance sheet which would give 'a true statement of the capital stock, credits and property of every description, the debts due and a distinct view of the profit or loss of the company in the preceding year', there was no requirement that the accounts were to be kept according to any prescribed form.

Captain John Laws, who was a director of the Manchester and Leeds Railway in 1842, told the Select Committee on Audit in 1849 that his company and the London and Birmingham had introduced 'a uniformity of practice in the traffic accounts' through the Clearing House. Although the companies' accounts had, at first, been differently presented, they had found 'very little difficulty in making the one fit into the other'. He found the practice of the Clearing House of sending each company a monthly statement of its debit and credit position in relation to the other member companies, a great advantage. Whereas, formerly, the balances had been 'a little loose', under the Clearing House system, there was not only an absolute protection against misunderstanding between the companies, but also a very considerable protection against any fraudulent practice that any of their own servants might attempt.

'You have a check from the Clearing House as well as in your own office, [he said], and without this system, in the present mode of working railways, it would be almost impracticable to keep accounts without a multiplicity of officers and details in writing which would eat up the profits, almost, in some cases.'

[1] Hansard, Third Series, Vol. 73, March 15, 1844, cols 1070–1.

He considered that the foundation of the Clearing House had made uniformity of accounting practices a matter of great importance. Although the accounts for receipts and traffic were 'almost uniform' in the case of a number of companies, with the capital accounts it was 'altogether otherwise'.[1]

The select committee, in its report, largely endorsed the views which Captain Laws and other railway witnesses had expressed:

'A most serious omission is . . . the want of any prescribed and uniform system of account. Each company is left, at its own will and pleasure, to adopt the form considered by them to be the most convenient, and to vary that form from time to time. The result is that no adequate means are afforded by which to compare the financial affairs of any two railways, or even to compare the accounts of the same railway from time to time; the form of the balance sheet submitted by one railway to its shareholders and auditors has been found to vary in the very same year'.

The committee therefore recommended

'that a form of account should be set forth by authority of law, and enforced in all cases, subject, however; to such modifications from time to time, as in peculiar circumstances may, in the judgement of the Commissioners of the Railways, be deemed expedient'.

The Clearing House committee first considered the possibility of establishing a uniform system of railway accounts in 1850 when Mr W. Pennington of Manchester was interviewed about his scheme for a standard form of railway accounting. The minutes of the committee suggest that he was not given a very sympathetic hearing. His proposal that the Clearing House should audit each company's accounts of through traffic was regarded as being *ultra vires* the Clearing House Act of 1850 as well as being quite unacceptable by the individual companies. The plan he submitted in the same year to take the Clearing House away from London and establish it in the country as a training college for railway clerks was found to be equally unacceptable.[2] There is no evidence that

[1] Select Committee on the Amending of Railway Acts as to the Audit of Accounts, 1849, BPP 1849, Vol. X, Q. 2943–8.

[2] RCH 1/13: Minutes of Clearing House committee, December 11, 1850. W. Pennington: *Proposals for Increasing the Efficiency of the Railway Clearing House*, Manchester, 1850.

the committee, in its collective capacity, considered at all the work of another reformer, George King, who in 1849 published in London an eighty-four page book entitled *Uniformity of Railway Accounts*. The goods managers were the first to be won over to the advantages of reform. In May 1853 they urged the committee to consider 'the expediency of taking steps to secure uniformity in the forms of accounts used by the railway companies'. The committee, at its next meeting, passed on the responsibility to the general managers who, after long deliberation, produced a recommendation in February 1855. They wanted Mr Morison 'to report on the feasibility of introducing the decimal system into the accounts of the Railway Clearing House or railways generally'. The secretary told them, three months later, that he was not prepared, in the absence of an actual trial, to commit himself on so difficult a question. He pointed out a number of difficulties and objections which he said would exist 'until a purely decimal system were adopted by the nation'. However the general managers were not deterred. 'Believing that many were in favour of the use of decimals, they asked Mr Morison to write to the companies explaining his views at length, in order that the subject might have full consideration.'[1] The subject was not considered again until a year later when Mr R. Hodgson of the North British Railway persuaded the committee to appoint five of its members 'to draw up and present for the consideration of the Railway Clearing House a form of half-yearly accounts applicable to railway companies'. After examining the accounts as presented to their shareholders of every railway company in the kingdom, the sub-committee produced a plan which they recommended to the main committee for adoption in December 1856. But this promising development was nipped in the bud by the intervention of George Carr Glyn, the chairman, who claimed that the subject was 'beyond the province of the Railway Clearing House'. This statement influenced the waverers against the proposal which was then dropped.[2]

[1] RCH 1/13: Minute 287 of Committee, June 8, 1853. RCH 1/70: Minutes 58 and 67 of General Managers Conferences, February 8 and May 10, 1855.

[2] RCH 1/13: Minutes 417 and 428 of committees of June 11 and September 10, 1856, and report of meeting of committee held on December 10, 1856.

Ten years later, a full scale government enquiry into the administration of the railways—the Royal Commission of 1866–67 —led to a reconsideration in the Clearing House of the whole subject of railway accounts. Edwin Chadwick reminded the commission, in May 1866, of the uniformity and superiority of the accounting system on the French railways. He was in agreement with other witnesses in stressing the desirability of all the accounts of the British railways being rendered in the same form. In their report the members of the commission gave wholehearted endorsement of these views:

'We are of opinion that with the object of affording a more accurate view of the operations of the railway companies, and of making any undue extravagance apparent, and thus stimulating economy, it is desirable that the several railway companies should render their accounts to the Board of Trade, showing receipts from traffic and the detailed costs of working the line, on a uniform plan; and that after consultation with the railway companies the Board of Trade should not only prescribe the form of such returns and accounts, but lay down the basis on which they are to be computed.'[1]

The editor of *The Times* backed the case for reform when he wrote that nothing had damaged railway property so much 'as the suspicion, notoriously reasonable, that the truth was not put before the public in the reports of the railway directors.'[2]

As soon as they saw that new legislation was inevitable the leading railway managers acted promptly to retain the maximum possible control over their own enterprises. As Carr Glyn was still chairman of the Railway Clearing House and had previously ruled out of order a discussion on the standardisation of railway accounts, it is scarcely surprising that the matter was first dealt with by the recently formed United Railway Companies Committee (in 1869 renamed the Railway Companies Association), rather than at Seymour Street. With the blessing of this new organisation, therefore, the accountants of the Midland, Great Western, Lancashire and Yorkshire, Great Northern, and London and North Western

[1] Royal Commission on Railways, 1867. Minutes of evidence, Q. 17,274, 17,813 and report, p. I, XXVii. BPP 1867, Vol. XXXVIII, I.
[2] *The Times*, November 8, 1867.

railways met at Kings Cross Station early in 1868 and drafted a standard form of railway accounts. At 11.30 a.m. on March 6, 1868, a sub-committee of the United Railway Companies was interviewed at the Board of Trade for a discussion of the Regulation of Railways Bill which was then before Parliament. When it came to a discussion of Clause 3, 'Uniform accounts, etc. to be kept', Mr Thompson, the chairman of the committee, announced that 'a form of accounts would be submitted by the companies to be embodied in the schedule of the Bill'. It is true that, a month later, the Board of Trade produced its own version of a form of accounts for the railways, but following a deputation of railway accountants to Mr Herbert, the President of the Board of Trade, the members of the committee were reassured by Mr Thompson that all was well and that the railway companies' version had been accepted.[1] Under the Regulation of Railways Act which followed later that year, every railway company was obliged to publish, according to the form contained in the first schedule of the Act, a half-yearly statement of accounts and balance sheet for the preceding half year.

These important happenings had taken place outside the Clearing House but not without the blessing of most of its members. Once the Bill had become law, Carr Glyn raised no further obstacles to the discussion of such questions and from then on the Clearing House became the venue of the meetings of the accountants. The United Railway Companies Committee was anxious to follow through its success in Parliament with making uniformity of accounting practices a reality in the railway companies' offices. On November 5, 1868, therefore, it resolved

'. . . that in order to secure uniformity as far as possible in the substance as well as the form of the half yearly accounts, it is desirable that the accountants of the several companies should be called together for the purpose of considering the best appropriation of the various items of expenditure, which do not distinctly belong to any particular department, and the mode of stating in the accounts the mileage run by trains and engine during each half year, as well as any other points which may appear to them

[1] BTHR, RCA/1 IB: Minutes of the United Railway Companies Committee, March 5, 6 and 30, and April 3, 1868.

important in connection with the subject of uniformity of railway accounts.'

It was by virtue of this resolution that the first formal meeting of accountants of companies, parties to the clearing system, was held under Clearing House auspices.[1]

At this first meeting the form of accounts included in the Railway Regulation Act of 1868 was followed through and detailed recommendations made as to the appropriate items to be included under the various headings. Thus, to give but three examples, it was ruled that the cost of cartage should be deducted from traffic receipts whether it was done by the companies themselves or their agents; bad debts were to be deducted from traffic receipts and not shown, and mileage and demurrage due to or by other companies for use of rolling stock was to be shown in revenue statement number nine.[2] It can be seen that although the Clearing House had taken no part in the framing of the Act it was within its walls that very important questions of the interpretation of the Act were resolved.

After this major task was completed the accountants did not meet with the same regularity as did the general managers or goods managers, but their advice was sought from time to time by other committees of the Clearing House concerned with minimising administrative costs. It was for these purposes that they often met in conjunction with sub-committees of the superintendents or goods managers. But it cannot be too much emphasised that the accountants had to rely mainly on recommendation and example, they were not in a position to dragoon the companies into compliance with their findings. There was still plenty of scope for variation in accounting practices. Ten years after the Railway Regulation Act of 1868 had become law the editor of *The Railway Times* commented as follows on the Metropolitan Railway's announcement of an increased dividend:

'Could we divest ourselves of the idea that the dividend that Sir Edward Watkin has each succeeding half year to dispense are

[1] BTHR, RCA/1 1B: Minute 204 of United Railway Companies Committee, November 5, 1868, and RCH 1/359: Report of a meeting of accountants on December 23, 1868, pursuant of a resolution of the United Railway Companies Committee.     [2] RCH 1/359.

prearranged, and depend rather on considerations of financial policy than the result of an actual profit and loss balance, we should hail the announcement of the Metropolitan with unalloyed satisfaction.'[1]

It was also a continuing anomaly that while most other business firms presented their accounts annually the railway companies adhered to the tradition of biannual statements. This need not have been too great an inconvenience but for the fact that there was no agreement among the companies on a date for the ending of the financial year.

In the forty years which followed the Railway Regulation Act of 1868 some railway companies became very different undertakings from the comparatively simple concerns they had been at the start. Hotels, dockyard and steamship services, even motor-bus services, were established. Each Board of Directors made its own decision as to how the finances of these new undertakings were to be shown in the accounts. Thus a new diversity of practice grew up with the passing of the years.

By the end of the nineteenth century British railways were becoming less profitable to the investor. Between 1860 and 1900 the ratio of working expenses to revenue rose from 47 to 62 while the percentage of net receipts to total paid-up capital fell from 4·19 to 3·41. In 1901 a Railway Shareholders Committee was formed to express the investors' disquiet and to ensure that their interests were not overlooked. Renewed doubts were being expressed about the adequacy of the published accounts as guide posts to the financial health and business efficiency of the railways. Investors had suspicions that the capital equipment of the companies was becoming obsolete and was being wastefully employed. But when they examined the leading railways' published statistics they found most of them singularly uninformative. On the other hand, from 1900 onwards the compilation of ton mile and passenger mile statistics on the North Eastern Railway had proved invaluable aids to the more economical operation of the line.

In June 1906, as a first step to meet the demand for more adequate provision of railway statistics and improved methods of accounting, Lloyd George, as President of the Board of Trade, set

---

[1] *The Railway Times*, January 21, 1878, quoted in Pollins's article, 'Aspects of Railway Accounting before 1865', p. 355.

up a departmental committee to find out the facts. Three years before, the Railway Companies Association had nominated a committee of accountants to draft recommendations for uniformity of accounting methods. The findings of this committee, which had met over fifty times by the end of 1906, were fully utilised by the Board of Trade Committee which also listened to twenty-nine witnesses before drafting its report. It left no doubt that it was strongly in favour of eliminating surviving differences in accounting methods:

'It is obviously of the first importance, from the point of view of comparison between different railway companies, that there should be uniformity in practice among all the companies with regard to keeping accounts and statistics, that is to say, that every heading both in the accounts and the statistics, should bear precisely the same meaning in the case of all railways—should in effect be standardised.'[1]

The Railway Companies (Accounts and Returns) Act of 1911, which embodied most of the recommendations of the select committee, substituted annual for biannual statements of account, but did not compel the companies to end their financial year on the same day. It required a more complete separation of the finances of the companies from their returns and statistics. It was far more precise on what was to be included in the different forms of account. The Railway Companies Association played as important a part in helping to draft the detailed provisions of the Act as it had done earlier in influencing the departmental committee. The Report of the Association for 1910 records that 'no opposition was offered in principle to the general scheme of the new forms, but certain suggestions for their practical improvement were made and accepted by the Board of Trade'.[2]

From then on the committees of the Clearing House ensured the smooth working of the Act itself. On 8th November 1910 the general managers appointed a committee of accountants 'to consider questions of securing uniformity in rendering the return'

[1] Report of a Committee appointed by the Board of Trade to make enquiries with reference to the form and scope of the companies and statistical returns rendered by the railway companies, 1909. BPP 1909, Vol. LXXVII, p. 705.  [2] BTHR, RCA 1/5.

under the Act. When it became apparent that the railway department of the Board of Trade was not going to follow the recommendation of the departmental committee to establish its own standing committee of accountants, the general managers, on February 6, 1912, resolved to make the Clearing House committee of Railway Accountants a permanent one.[1] Its subsequent detailed recommendations were of great value.

The author of a book on the financial position of British railways, who was writing while the departmental committee was hearing evidence, considered that the subject of railway statistics was 'a still-born science' in Britain. Most members of the committee would have agreed with him. In their report they stated that the statistical returns, as then furnished by the railway companies under Section 9 of the Regulation of Railways Act 1871, and Section 32 (1) of the Railway and Canal Traffic Act, 1888, were 'very meagre'. The information contained in the returns was 'not framed on any definite system' and was 'very incomplete'.[2] The Act of 1911 brought improvements in both the volume and organisation of railway statistics, but it was still possible for influential business petitioners to complain to the Government in 1919 that railway traffic statistics were so 'jejune' that they were 'useless' either as an index of the trade of the country or for the purpose of international comparison.[3]

A proposal that was considered exhaustively by the committee was that the railway companies should be obliged to include ton mileage and passenger mileage statistics in their returns. Distinguished witnesses such as the veteran Board of Trade statistician, Sir Robert Giffen; Sir Hugh Bell, managing director of the North Eastern Railway; and leading directors of Indian and Canadian Railways, all claimed that the information such statistics provided was indispensable to the more efficient management of the railways. Important working economies (e.g. more goods hauled per train mile) had resulted where the lessons taught by the new figures had

[1] Departmental committee report: 27 and 28. RCH 1/359: Minutes 699 and 784 of general managers, November 8, 1910, and February 6, 1912, A. E. Kirkus: *Railway Statistics*, London, 1927, p. 20.

[2] W. R. Lawson: *British Railways: a Financial and Commercial Survey*, 1913, p. 59. Departmental committee report: 35 and 36.

[3] Kirkus: *op. cit.* p. 17.

been learned. Unfortunately the weight of conservative opinion was against them. Most of the directors of English railways giving evidence were against the innovation on the grounds of its expense, doubtful advantages and the supposed adequacy of train mileage statistics. The influence of the Clearing House was also exerted against change. When Sam Fay, general manager of the Great Central Railway, wrote to the secretary, Mr F. Mansfield, asking for ton mileage statistics for the whole of British railways, he was informed that 'the preparations of the statement would involve an enormous amount of labour, as the mileages and tonnage would have to be extracted from every individual settlement in the accounts, numbering upwards of two millions per annum'. The cost would come to about £4,000 a year. To provide ton mileages for each company separately would double the labour and the cost. When questioned directly by the committee, Mr Mansfield showed no more enthusiasm for extending his responsibilities or the work of the Clearing House clerks:

'Q. With your present information you are not able to help us with what is the amount of traffic dealt with on English railways? A. Quite unable.'[1]

At this stage in the history of British railways the 2,500 Clearing House clerks were fully occupied settling the financial claims of the companies against each other. But the time was not far distant when, owing to the grouping of the railways under the Railways Act of 1921, the chief concern was to avoid redundancy. When that time came a more favourable view was taken of the assumption of new duties. In the meantime the departmental committee hesitated to recommend the compulsory provision of ton mile and passenger mile statistics against the opposition of leading railway directors:

'We are of opinion that however useful they might prove from the point of view of general information . . . the usefulness of these statistics would mainly depend upon their being adopted willingly by the companies. A large part of their usefulness might be lost if their compilation resulted solely from compulsion'.[2]

[1] Departmental committee, minutes of evidence: Qs 7633, 9926, 10,039, 4511–4518, 3002, 1625, 6388.
[2] Departmental committee report: 169.

The gradual learning of the lessons taught by the North Eastern Railway and the experience of unified railway administration during the First World War, hastened change. Under the Ministry of Transport Act, 1919, the new minister was given power to ask for 'such accounts, statistics and returns' as he might require. But the more permanent measure was the Railways Act of 1921 which under Section 77 (2) compelled the companies to supply nineteen different types of statistics. Included were ton mileages and passenger mileages. British railways were at last required to provide something like the standards of statistical information provided by the American and Canadian railways during the previous thirty years. Whatever may have been its modest positive achievement in respect of the standardisation of accounts, it must be admitted that the Clearing House was an influence against modernisation and economy in the discussions on railway statistics before the First World War.

### III

One of the most persistent worries of the superintendents was the extent to which passengers defrauded the companies of revenue from fares. Opportunities for fraud increased as a result of lack of agreement between the companies on procedures for ticket punching, dishonest travellers taking advantage of the many loopholes that existed. In January 1865 Mr Needham drew the attention of the superintendents to the frauds to which the companies were exposed in consequence of the absence of a better system of marking through tickets. He gave instances where passengers had used the same ticket for several journeys without being detected. Mr Neele stressed the disadvantages of punching out parts of tickets with stars or numbers. The consequence of this practice was that by the time some passengers completed their journeys their tickets had become 'fantastic illegible wrecks'.[1] The members of the conference were convinced that it was high time that these irregularities were checked and they appointed a sub-committee of seven to make recommendations. Samples of

[1] RCH 1/114: Minute 24 of Superintendents Conference, January 26, 1865. G.P. Neele, *Railway Reminiscences*, p. 132.

steel ticket nippers were then obtained from all the principal companies. In March 1865 a plan submitted by Mr Harris, superintendent of the London, Chatham and Dover Railway was approved by the sub-committee. Each company was to notify the Clearing House of the stations on its lines at which tickets would be punched. All tickets were to be punched with numbers and each punching station in the kingdom was to have its own number allocated to it by the Clearing House which would also be responsible for providing the standard type punch. With one action this would emboss a number on the back of the ticket and nip out a small triangular piece from the bottom of the cardboard. In November 1865 the main conference of superintendents endorsed the scheme which was put into operation the following year.[1] By this well considered action some order was achieved out of the chaos hitherto prevailing and opportunities for fraud were substantially diminished.

In many other aspects of the passenger traffic the superintendents worked to achieve national uniformity and were largely successful. Before 1865 there were great differences in the conditions under which the companies issued return tickets. A sub-committee of superintendents, meeting in the autumn of 1865, drafted a set of regulations which was eventually approved by the general managers for adoption from May 1, 1866. For distances of up to fifty miles return tickets would be available on the day of issue only; between 51 and 128 miles availability would be for two days; between 126 miles and 200 miles it was three days; between 200 and 300 miles four days and above this distance, five days. Fares were to be at one and a half times the single fare.[2] Among the many other decisions reached by the superintendents were a scale of charges for returned empties sent by passenger train (October 1862); standard fares for dogs on a tapering mileage basis in October 1863; a charge of 1s per mile for the conveyance of corpses (February 1859); and a liberal scale of charges for the conveyance of luggage of commercial travellers agreed in October

[1] RCH 1/114: Report of sub-committee of superintendents, March 17, 1868. Minute 894 of Superintendents Conference, October 26, 1865.
[2] RCH 1/102: Report of sub-committee of superintendents, November 14, 1868. RCH 1/72: Minute 618 of General Managers Conference, February 8, 1866.

1863.[1] The Clearing House made its modest contribution to the spread of the arts in Britain in April 1865 when the superintendents decided that operatic and theatrical parties of not less than ten persons should be given the privilege of travelling first class at second-class fares. Two years earlier a concession had been made to volunteers in training who, from then onwards, were allowed to make a return journey at the single fare.

Since the Clearing House had persuaded the companies to adopt standard sizes for their cattle waggons it was only logical that it should favour the adoption of a uniform scale of charges for the conveyance of livestock. What had already become a widespread practice was given the approval of the Clearing House. In November 1865, when the general managers ruled that, while livestock carried to agricultural shows should be charged the normal rates, those animals which were not sold were to be returned by rail to their owners without further charge. The men in charge of the animals were entitled to a free pass in both directions.[2]

In the last thirty-five years of the nineteenth century the railway milk traffic became increasingly important. With the fall in prices during the period of great depression the standard of living of those fortunate enough to be in steady employment rose substantially. Regular wage earners could afford to spend a larger proportion of their incomes on meat and milk. The Express Dairy Company first began to send milk from country farms to the metropolis in 1864 and the practice rapidly spread. In April 1876 the question of the charges made by some of the metropolitan railways for the conveyance of milk was raised in the Superintendents Conference. The sub-committee that looked into the question was too overwhelmed by the diversity of charges made to consider it possible to recommend a Clearing House scale, but the recommendations they did make for the conduct of the traffic were adopted and helped to pave the way for its rapid growth. Churns were to be distinctly addressed and were to have their capacity and actual content in imperial gallons marked on a durable label of wood or metal. Farmers and retailers were to be responsible for

[1] RCH 1/72: General Managers Conference of November 8, 1866. Appendix.
[2] RCH 1/79: Minute 610 of the General Managers Conference, November 9, 1865.

delivery and collection and were to assist in loading and unloading the churns from the trains. Empty churns were to be returned free of charge.[1] For nearly a quarter of a century committees of the Clearing House helped to spread a practice in the conduct of Parliamentary elections which radicals of the day considered undemocratic and which in 1883 was made illegal. This was the conveyance of an elector to the poll by train at the expense of the candidate or his agent. The spread of the rail network provided ever-growing opportunities for the candidate with the longest purse to bring into his constituency the greatest number of supporters. The practice must already have been widespread when the general managers, in May 1859, appointed a sub-committee to draw up regulations for the conveyance of voters at Parliamentary elections. Owing to poor attendance at the sub-committees, it was not until August 1860 that a set of rules was approved. The arrangement adopted was for candidates or their agents to buy from the railway companies for 1s books of twenty-five 'candidates orders'. These orders were sent to known supporters entitled to vote in the constituency but living outside it. At the railway booking office the voter could then exchange the order for a return ticket to the constituency. The order, with the fare (at full rates) entered on it was posted to the candidate for payment.[2]

For the first five years the scheme did not work very smoothly because some of the candidates were dilatory in returning the order books to the companies after the election. In March 1865, therefore, a special meeting of accountants and superintendents recommended that a deposit be charged for each book of twenty-five orders issued by a railway company. The general managers, however, considered the enforcement of such a regulation impracticable and the suggestion was therefore dropped.[3] However, the continuance of the scheme and the modification of the regulations in other details in 1876 suggest that candidates eventually learned

[1] Express Dairy Company. RCH 1/117; Minute 2944 of Superintendents Conference, April 26, 1876.
[2] RCH 1/79: Minutes 337, 350, 366 and 374 of General Managers Conference at various dates, May 12, 1859, to August 9, 1860, inclusive.
[3] RCH 1/79: Minute 555 of General Managers Conference, March 23, 1865.

to co-operate. For most of the time the regulations were in force they applied to country constituencies only, it being illegal in the boroughs to pay electors' travelling expenses. But in 1880, in the last days of Disraeli's administration, a Parliamentary Elections and Corrupt Practices Bill was rushed through and received the Queen's signature just before the dissolution. By it the payment of travelling expenses to electors was permitted in a number of boroughs. It was a retrogressive step which helps to explain why candidates orders 'cleared' in Seymour Street in the General Election of 1880 were 120% more than in the General Election of 1874 while the receipts were 130% more.[1] Special Parliamentary Commissioners who made enquiry into the conduct of the 1880 election in eight boroughs, found corruption and illegal practices widespread in seven of them. In the case of the borough of Chester the sum of £320 was spent by two candidates in bringing 'outvoters' into the constituency by trains.[2] The scandals revealed in these special enquiries led to the passing of the Corrupt and Illegal Practices Prevention Act in 1883 which declared illegal in both urban and county constituencies the payment of electors' travelling expenses. In October 1883, therefore, the superintendents were simply informed by the secretary of the Clearing House that the 'Regulations for the conveyance of voters at Parliamentary Elections', which had occupied pages 199 to 209 of the Clearing House Book of Regulations, were now obsolete.[3] However, it is doubtful whether the companies' financial loss was of any great significance to them. It was more than made up in subsequent elections as the extension of the franchise in 1884 greatly increased the significance of national issues and intensified electioneering, with an attendant increase in rail travel.

[1] RCH 1/118: Minute 4536 of Superintendents Conference, June 9, 1880.

[2] Report of the Commissioners appointed to enquire into the existence of corrupt practices in the city of Chester. BPP 1881, Vol. XL, p. xvi.

[3] RCH 1/118: Minute 5144 of Superintendents Conference, October 24, 1883.

# CHAPTER XI

# POOLING AGREEMENTS AND RATE CONFERENCES

## I

In the view of most authorities on transport economics, the existence of the Railway Clearing House hastened the process of railway amalgamation in Britain. K. G. Fenelon believed that the Clearing House 'facilitated the process of railway amalgamation since the frequent meetings of officials would tend to show the advantages of combination'. C. E. R. Sherrington expressed a similar view.[1] Few have given much consideration to pooling agreements or rates conferences as alternatives to outright amalgamation and none have considered the role of the Railway Clearing House in their formation and maintenance. Nevertheless it can be shown that, had it not been for services rendered by the Clearing House, these substitutes for amalgamation would have been less viable and durable. In the absence of the impartial tribunal of the Clearing House, distrust between companies participating in pooling agreements would have been far more widespread and railway management would have felt little security from the hazards of cut-throat competition. Amalgamation would have assumed greater importance as the sole safeguard against the depreciation of railway capital.

The outstanding reason for the formation of pooling agreements for the division of traffic receipts between competitive points and the proliferation of rate conferences to reduce competition in freight rates, was the sharp decline in the value of railway capital following the railway mania of 1844–47. Between 1845 and 1853, paid up capital for new railways had been issued to the extent of

[1] K. G. Fenelon: *Railway Economics*, London, 1932, p. 92. C. E. R. Sherrington: *The Economics of Rail Transport in Great Britain*, London, 1928, Vol. 1, p. 233.

£54,000,000, but by 1853 its value had declined to only £18,000,000. In 1851 the stocks of thirty-four out of forty of the leading railway companies stood at a discount.[1] To shareholders and directors alike it was imperative that the ruinous competition of the late 1840s should be curbed.

Although it was by no means the first example of a railway pool, the Octuple Agreement, which came into force on January 1, 1851, was certainly one of the earliest and one of the most important.[2] It may be cited as illustrating the dependence of its promoters on the machinery of the Clearing House for its successful operation. The term 'octuple' arose from the fact that eight companies concerned with the Anglo-Scottish traffic were involved. The lines of three of the eight companies—the London and North Western, Lancaster and Carlisle, and Caledonian Railways— formed a continuous route between London and Edinburgh on the western side of the kingdom; the lines of five other companies—the Great Northern, Midland, York and North Midland, York, Newcastle and Berwick, and the North British, formed an eastern route to the Scottish capital. The agreement provided that the receipts on all through traffic, with the exception of those on minerals and the mails, should be divided equally between the companies of the Western route on the one hand and the Eastern route on the other. The half of the total receipts (less terminals) appropriated to the companies of the Western route was to be divided between them in the proportions 'recognised and acted upon in the Clearing House', i.e. on the basis of mileage as revealed in the distance tables compiled in the Seymour Street premises. The same principle was to be followed in the division of the receipts between the companies of the Eastern route. Arrangements were also made for the division of receipts on traffic between London and places north of York but south of Edinburgh. All rates and fares between the same points were to be the same by whichever route passengers or goods travelled. If, at any time, an

[1] W. A. Robertson: *Combination among Railway Companies*, London, 1912, p. 14.

[2] BTHR, LNW 3/4: Agreement between the London and North Western Railway Co. and the other railway companies carrying between London and Edinburgh dated 17th Day of April, 1851. (The 'Octuple Agreement', signed and sealed on vellum.)

undue proportion of the traffic went by one of the main routes, twenty per cent of the passenger revenues and ¼d per ton mile of the goods revenues, were to be allocated to the companies carrying the excess, before the division of the gross receipts took place. Section ten of the agreement which read: 'All payments shall be made according to the usual course through and by the Clearing House' revealed how important that organisation was to the smooth working of the scheme. In the event of any dispute between the participating companies the Rt Hon. W. E. Gladstone was to be asked to arbitrate. If he declined, the job was to be offered to Samuel Laing. Failing Laing's acceptance, the companies in dispute were to agree on an arbitrator, or to accept one nominated by the attorney general. The agreement was to continue for a period of five years.

The chances of the pooling agreement lasting its full term would have been substantially less had there not existed the Clearing House as a neutral body commanding the respect and confidence of all eight participating companies. At the very first meeting of the Octuple Committee Mr Morison was asked to act as secretary,[1] and we learn from the minutes of the December meeting that 'examples of the mode of dividing the receipts, in accordance with the provisions of the octuple agreement were produced by the secretary and approved by the meeting'.[2] With his scheme adopted, Mr Morison could rest assured that the Boards of the eight companies would trust the Clearing House clerks—'those sweet little cherubs sitting up aloft'[3]—to make an impartial division of the receipts between the members of the pool. The Clearing House was essential for the provision of accurate and unbiased information on traffic flows. Companies suspicious of being cheated of revenue by other partners in the pool, could examine the Clearing House returns, or even request specially prepared statements, to learn the true situation. In March 1853 the Octuple Committee requested

[1] RCH 1/505: Minute 8 of the meeting of the Octuple Committee, September 10, 1851.
[2] RCH 1/505: Minute 46 of the meeting of the Octuple Committee, December 10, 1851.
[3] Superintending Committee on the York, Newcastle and Berwick, York and North Midland and Leeds Northern Amalgamation Bill, 1854. Evidence of Mr S. Wrangham. I am indebted to Mr G. Channon for this quotation.

Mr Morison 'to prepare a statement showing the route by which the respective portions of the traffic were conveyed, and the amount paid over by and received from the several companies for each description of traffic, for the purpose of ascertaining how the agreement has affected the interests of the contracting parties.'[1]

It was a tribute to the impartiality of the Clearing House and its success in carrying out the terms of the Octuple Agreement, that when a new agreement was drafted early in 1856, it was more extensive in scope than its predecessor. Furthermore it was to be valid for a period of fourteen years. The English and Scotch Traffic Agreement, as it became known, was effective from January 1, 1856, until the end of 1869. It provided for a division of receipts on 'all traffic of whatever description, passengers, animals and goods or other articles', except coal and its derivatives, and mail, for the area between London and the North of Scotland. Thus for the first time Glasgow and districts farther north were brought into the scope of the pool. A comparison of the very simple fifty-fifty division of receipts under the Octuple Agreement of 1851 with the considerably more complicated 'Schedule or Tabular Statement of Proportions of Traffic'[2] contained in the agreement of 1856, shows that the proportions listed in the later document were based on information on the actual division of traffic revealed by Clearing House returns. In the absence of the labours of the Clearing House clerks, reaching a fair apportionment of receipts would have been much more a matter of guesswork and disputes would have been more abundant. An unobtrusive statement in Clause XIV revealed the dependence of the signatories on the work of the Railway Clearing House:

'All payments shall be made according to the usual course through and by the railway clearing house.'

The enhanced prestige of the Clearing House was shown in relation to the proposed arbitration of disputes between companies which were to be settled 'by the committee for the time

---

[1] RCH 1/505: Minute 121, meeting of the Octuple Committee, March 9, 1853.

[2] The full text of the English and Scotch Traffic Agreement of January 1, 1856, is contained in RCH 1/508.

being of the Clearing House unless some one or more of the parties in difference object thereto', in which case Mr Gladstone or Mr Laing were to be called in. The rules of procedure for Clearing House committees were to be a model for the General Managers Committee of the Traffic Agreement:

'The proceedings at the meetings of the Committee of Managers shall, so far as may be, be conducted in the manner in which . . . the meetings of delegates to the Railway Clearing House Meetings are conducted.'

As Mr Morison was appointed secretary at the committee's first meeting, the committee was unlikely to deviate far from Clearing House precedent.

It was not long before the scope of the agreement of 1856 was further extended. In a supplemental agreement, signed on January 12, 1859, the Glasgow and South Western, Edinburgh and Glasgow and Leeds, Bradford and Halifax Companies were admitted as parties to the pool.[1]

As a result of negotiations conducted in 1855–56 the Dundee, Perth and London Shipping Company was roped in, an agreement having been signed between this company and the East Coast Route Railways, fixing freight charges and passenger fares between the Scottish ports and London. Although this agreement had to be suspended for a time in 1867 as a result of competition from other steamship concerns, it was resumed later in the year.[2] In April 1868 a further agreement allocated a quarter of the specified types of goods traffic from Dundee and Perth to the railways. The existence of Clearing House traffic returns gave the shipping company confidence that the railways were keeping their part of the bargain. In 1870 the arrangement was revised with smaller proportions of the traffic allocated to the railways but with the promise of stability for at least five years—the period of the new agreement.[3] In

[1] RCH 1/508: English and Scotch Traffic Conference, minute 389 of August 11, 1858, and minute 445 of January 12, 1859.

[2] RCH 1/510: Minutes 1616, 1665, 1713 and 1806 of English and Scotch Traffic Conference, various dates from June 5, 1867, to April 24, 1868.

[3] RCH 1/510: Minute 2154 of English and Scotch Traffic Conferences, July 29, 1870.

February 1867 a similar kind of agreement had been reached between the railway companies and steamship companies formerly competing in services between Liverpool and Glasgow.

With all the uncertainties springing from the emergence of new rail networks and the competition of improved steamboat services it is very unlikely that the English and Scotch Traffic Agreement would have survived for its full term had it not been for the information constantly being provided by the Clearing House. The returns this organisation provided enabled modifications in the agreement to be made in the confidence that the changes introduced would be fair to the participating companies. After complaints made by both the Midland and the London and North Western railways in June 1858 that they were not being given a fair proportion of the receipts, the Clearing House was asked to submit traffic statements as a result of which the agreement was revised to meet the objections of the two companies.[1] In February 1863 Mr Allport, general manager of the Midland, complained to the conference that his company had 'failed to obtain any redress of the numerous complaints they had brought forward' about the working of the agreement. Four months later he moved 'the desirability of revising the agreement without further delay'. At first the conference was in a mood to reject the resolution out of hand, but when Mr Dawson, who was both secretary of the Clearing House and secretary of the conference, drew attention to the large amounts of the receipts held in suspense and showed in what ways the division had been unfair to Mr Allport's company, the resolution was carried, though in a slightly modified form, and a further revision of the agreement was put in hand.[2]

The English and Scotch Traffic Agreement came to an end in 1869 because the development of the Midland Railway network to Carlisle destroyed the comparative simplicity of the situation of the previous two decades.

The role of the Railway Clearing House was no less important for the success of other pooling agreements. The Gladstone

---

[1] RCH 1/508: English and Scotch Traffic Conference. Letters from the Boards of the Midland Railway and the London and North Western Railway and minute 574 of August 28, 1860.

[2] RCH 1/508: English and Scotch Traffic Conferences. Minutes 700 of February 12, 1863, and 719 of August 6, 1863.

Award of February 22, 1851, was a well-known case in point. In August 1850, the Midland and the London and North Western railways reached agreement to end competition in freights and fares between London and the six centres of York, Doncaster, Lincoln, Leeds, Sheffield, and Wakefield.[1] The opening of the Great Northern line from London to Peterborough on August 7, 1880, however, brought a new rival into the field and compelled a redrafting of the agreement. Though all three companies saw the necessity 'to avoid that injurious competition which had frequently arisen between companies occupying the same district', they failed, after several months of negotiation, to reach agreement on a division of traffic. Undoubtedly the chief reason for the breakdown of their efforts was the concern of the more rapidly growing Great Northern to secure as large as possible a share of the traffic before an agreement between the three companies froze the proportion of the receipts each company was entitled to enjoy.[2] Faced with this deadlock, the three Boards of Directors agreed to accept Mr Gladstone as arbitrator.

Although the award was Gladstone's handiwork, it was a viable proposition largely because of services rendered by the Clearing House. In the first place, as was admitted in the memorandum accompanying the award, the Clearing House returns of traffic between London and the six towns were made the basis for the proposed division of traffic receipts.[3] Secondly, as from April 4, 1851, when the award came into force, the settlement of accounts on the basis of the proposed division of receipts was to be made through the Clearing House. In making this stipulation Gladstone realised that the impartiality of the Clearing House was not in question. Thirdly it was possible to appeal to the Clearing House for more detailed information whenever one of the companies felt that it was being unjustly treated. It would be idle to pretend that the arrangements worked without a hitch throughout the five-year term of the award; but disputes, which in the absence of a

[1] BTHR, Mid 1/136: Minutes of the Midland Railway Traffic Committee, August 6, 1850.
[2] BTHR, G. N. 1/15: Minutes of the Great Northern Railway Board of June 25, 1851.
[3] BTHR, G. N. 1/20: Minutes of the Great Northern Railway Board, February 22, 1851, which include the full terms of the Award.

neutral institution like the Clearing House, might well have proved fatal to the continuance of the pool, could be resolved through resort to its impartial services. Thus, early in 1852, acting on information provided in Clearing House returns, the Great Northern accused the other two companies of abstracting an unfair proportion of the traffic receipts by compelling passengers to rebook at Normanton.[1] The dispute was referred to Mr Gladstone who decided, on March 2, 1852, that there had been a violation of the agreement. Mr Morison, secretary of the Clearing House, was asked to meet the accountants of the Midland and Great Northern to assess the sum to be added to total receipts for division between the companies.

In 1856 the pool was renewed and extended by the inclusion of the Manchester, Sheffield and Lincolnshire Railway. The representatives of the four companies which considered the redrafting of the agreement had before them the Clearing House traffic returns which were used as a basis for a new division of receipts. For a brief period the companies, failing to agree, resorted to the fiercest competition, but reason soon prevailed over animosity. Once more an appeal was made to Mr Gladstone to arbitrate. His award, which was to operate from March 1, 1856, to March 28, 1870, was to divide all traffic receipts (except receipts from mails and minerals) between London and fifteen important towns or cities to the north. There was to be no evasion of the pool by rebooking, secret allowances, drawbacks, presents to agents or customers, free passes or undue extension of credit to commercial customers. Section 4 of the award made clear how these prohibitions were to be effectively enforced:

'That all invoices and accounts of each of the companies, and also all the accounts of their agents, shall be placed under the inspection of the Railway Clearing House or the respective accountants of the other companies, to see that proper rates are maintained and accounted for.'[2]

---

[1] BTHR, Mid 1/137: Minutes of the Midland Railway Traffic Committee, March 3, 1852.
[2] BTHR, G. N. 1/280: Reports to the Board of the Great Northern Railway.

It was by such wise precautions as this that disputes about the working of the pool were kept to a minimum and its relative permanence was assured.

II

If Mr Morison's attempt to secure a new Railway Clearing Act in 1859 had been successful, facilities for the interchange of traffic between Britain and the European continent would have been greatly extended. The failure of his attempt and the refusal of the railway companies south of the Thames to join the Clearing House until the 1860s delayed the establishment of a Continental Traffic Pool until 1870. On January 1st of that year the Midland, London and North Western, and Great Northern Railways signed the important Continental Traffic Agreement which remained in being until August 18, 1885.[1] Receipts were divided on all goods and parcels traffic carried from competitive points in England to the Channel Islands, France and those places in Switzerland and Italy served through France, when such traffic passed through London or through any port on the Thames or the Channel coast. The three companies agreed to place in the common pool the mileage proportions (as determined by Clearing House distance tables) of their gross receipts on the continental traffic. The Clearing House classification of goods was used and the traffic returns, prepared by Clearing House clerks, determined the proportion of receipts to be allocated to each company. Thus, from the Scottish traffic, the London and North Western and Great Northern were to receive 35% each and the Midland 30%. The Nottingham traffic was divided in the proportions 10% to the London and North Western and 45% each to the Midland and the Great Northern.

Six months after the agreement was signed it was extended to cover the traffic with Germany,[2] and in February 1871 it was decided to make the rates for the Belgian traffic the same as those

---

[1] RCH 1/372: Continental Traffic Conference, minutes, January 1, 1870.

[2] RCH 1/372: Continental Traffic Conference, minute 95 of June 29, 1870.

for the traffic from France and Germany.[1] In 1875 Holland was brought in.[2]

The reason why the pool ceased to operate after August 1885 was not that the member companies distrusted each other or the Clearing House on which they depended for its successful operation. It was principally the repeated refusal of the Great Western Railway to participate and its determination to quote through rates which undercut those of the pool, which made the continuance of the arrangement impossible. As early as July 1875 the conference was in communication with the Great Western Railway which had 'declined to agree to the London special rates for the continental traffic . . . reserving for themselves liberty of action in the matter'.[3] In consequence the pooling companies were obliged to reduce their own rates. Nearly two years later the London and North Western Railway representative at the conference, citing the lower charges of the Great Western Railway, declared that he could no longer accept the arrangements earlier made for the traffic with Belgium and Holland.[4] Although in 1880 the agreement was extended to include traffic with Spain and Portugal and the Mediterranean and Black Sea areas, both the Great Western Railway and the Great Eastern Railway refused to co-operate.[5] In view of this failure and the increasing difficulties of administering such a wide-ranging pool it was decided, in July 1880, that the division of receipts would be ended and that the conference should, in the future, deal with rates, arrangements and agencies only.[6] Just over five years later, in August 1885, the conference ceased to function.[7] Once the division of receipts was abandoned there was no good reason for its continuance since the Continental Through Rates Conference which began its labours in 1870, only ten months after the Continental Traffic Conference had started to function, was still in being and, in fact, continued to carry out its tasks until the outbreak of the First World War.

[1] RCH 1/372: Continental Traffic Conference, minute 159 of February 13, 1871.
[2] RCH 1/373: Continental Traffic Conference, minute 605 of September 28, 1875. [3] Ibid.
[4] Ibid. minute 704 of February 13, 1877.
[5] Ibid. minute 955 of October 12, 1880.
[6] Ibid. minute 947 of July 23, 1880.
[7] Ibid. minute 1229 of August 18, 1885.

III

In a different category from the pooling agreements were the rates conferences, most of which met on the Clearing House premises. The existence of at least a dozen of these conferences can be traced before the First World War, although records of four of them are not available. Like the pooling agreements, the rates conferences had as their primary objective the elimination of cut-throat competition. But their method of achieving this objective was different. Whereas the pooling agreements sought to reduce competition by a pre-arranged division of receipts, the rates conferences hoped to gain much the same end by the avoidance of rate wars. None of the rate conferences attempted a division of the traffic receipts. In at least two important instances—the English and Scotch Traffic Conference and the Continental Traffic Conference—what began as a pooling arrangement, changed at a later date into a conference for the fixing of traffic rates only.

For many years the most important of the rate conferences was the Normanton Conference, formed in 1865 and functioning until the re-grouping of the railways under the Railways Act of 1921. It dealt with traffic rates affecting the whole of England and Wales. Its work, the fixing of rates, fell into three main areas: between stations competitive at both ends, between stations competitive at one end but not at another, and between stations non-competitive at both ends (provided both the terminal companies gave their consent.) The meetings of this conference were formidable occasions. As many as thirty companies might be represented and the agenda was often very lengthy. At the meeting held in June 1883 there were no less than 144 separate items listed. The decisions of the conference were for all practical purposes binding on the companies. A distinguished railway director, Sir Charles J. Owens, explained the situation when giving evidence before the Departmental Committee on Railway Agreements and Amalgamations in 1910:

'Q. Is it simply a case of honour as between the various companies as to whether they agree and conform to the findings of the Conference?

A. No, it goes a great deal beyond that. For all traffic passing between stations what we call an invoice is issued, and on this invoice the rate is entered, and if one particular dissentient company did not honour the rate which the conference had enforced it would be observed by the other companies who were also engaged in carrying the traffic, because it would be shown on the notice.'[1]

Sir Charles Owens stressed that the 'moral force' of the General Managers Conference and the self interest of the companies prevented any deviation from the scale of charges agreed at the conference. He might have added that it was the settlement of accounts through the Clearing House and the Clearing House returns of traffic carried that provided an invaluable and impartial check that agreements were being honoured. In the absence of the Clearing House, opportunities for evasion would have been much greater and the conference might well have broken down through the distrust of companies of the accuracy of information provided by fellow members.

Making an accurate record of the minutes of the rate conferences was no light undertaking, and once more the companies were indebted to the Clearing House for valuable assistance. In February 1867 the superintending committee received application from the Normanton Conference (as well as from the Metropolitan and Liverpool and Manchester Conferences) 'for the Clearing House to take over the duties of the secretaryship'. The committee agreed.[2] Thenceforward it was the consistent practice to provide Clearing House clerks for all secretarial duties connected with the rate conferences.

The successful formation of the North and South London Conference in June 1863 directly followed the decision of two of the principal southern companies—the South Eastern and London, Chatham and Dover—to join the Clearing House in 1862. It was the purpose of the conference to make through traffic arrangements for places north and south of the river Thames and

[1] Departmental Committee on Railway Agreements and Amalgamations, 1910–11, minutes of evidence. BPP 1911, Vol. xx IX(ii), Qs 11,814–11,817.

[2] RCH 1/25: Minute 994 of superintending committee, February 28, 1867.

the presence of the southern companies was essential for its successful fulfilment. At the very first meeting of the conference a representative of the London, Brighton and South Coast Railway 'did not think it was necessary for them to enter the Clearing House for the division of receipts until the traffic became considerable'. The representatives of the northern companies answered these doubts in no uncertain fashion. They expressed 'their unanimous conviction that no through arrangements for the proper interchange of the traffic could be made by any other method so well as by the Clearing House system'.[1] The delegate from the Brighton line must have been convinced. At the very next meeting of the conference he announced his company's decision to join the Clearing House.[2] In 1864 the conference merged with the Metropolitan Conference which met for the first time on January 1, 1864, and which came to concentrate on the task of controlling charges for station-to-station traffic, the charges for lighterage, wharfage, labour and warehouse rent and all other matters which exclusively applied to the working of the traffic within the metropolis. It was left to other rate conferences to fix charges for the extra-metropolitan area.[3] Nevertheless the Metropolitan Conference could not have operated with anything like the same degree of success had it not been for the decision to utilise Clearing House services to the full. The distance tables, terminal charges, and goods classification of the Clearing House were made the basis of all calculations.[4]

In 1888 a General Rates Conference was established as a measure of rationalisation. Its purpose was to consider the rates then dealt with by no less than nine rates conferences to ensure that they were consistent with each other and that there was no overlapping. The Conferences whose work was supervised included the Birmingham, South Staffordshire and East Worcestershire; the Continental Through Rates; the English and Scotch Traffic Rates; the Humber; the London, Liverpool and Manchester; the Manchester and Liverpool Districts; the Midland

---

[1] RCH 1/641: Minutes of North and South London Conference (afterwards known as the Metropolitan Conference) June 25, 1863.
[2] *Ibid*. minutes for July 3, 1863.
[3] *Ibid*. minute 362 of August 10, 1869.
[4] *Ibid*. minutes 13 and 17 of July 7, 1863.

Association; and the Normanton and the West Riding. The work of each of these conferences had been fully dovetailed into the established Clearing House procedures. As a result of the functioning of all these bodies there were very few areas of the country where there was any competition in freights and fares in the last quarter of the nineteenth century. The findings of a Joint Select Committee of Parliament in 1872 came as no surprise:

'There has on different occasion been effectual competition between railway companies in the matter of charges, and it is probable that the charges now made still bear the traces of that competition. But it may be taken as a general rule that there is now no active competition between different railways in the matter of rates and fares'[1]

In 1909 Mr W. F. Marwood of the railway department of the Board of Trade considered that rate agreements were 'practically universal' and that internal competition was limited to the provision of facilities for the collection and delivery of goods at the railheads. Even this last degree of competition was withering away since, in 1907, some of the principal companies had agreed to put an end to the practice of offering extra cartage rebates from the rates for 'collected and delivered' goods.[2]

IV

The presence of the Clearing House as accountant for the companies' business with each other and as impartial arbiter meant that opposition to pooling agreements and the decisions of rate conferences was very restricted, at least until the effects of the 'Great Depression' began to be felt in the 1880s. Shareholders and railway directors had every reason to be grateful for the work of the pools and the rate conferences in checking the baneful effect on dividends of unrestrained competition. The customers of the railways at least gained the benefit of a greater degree of stability in rates and fares. The absence of much opposition to these methods

[1] Select Committee on Railway and Canal Amalgamations, report. BPP 1872 XIII, p. xxiv.

[2] Departmental Committee on Railway Agreements and Amalgamations, 1910–11. Minutes of evidence, BPP 1911 XXIX, Part 2, Q. 461–71.

of railway management was bound to have its influence on the courts. In the important case of Hare vs the London and North Western Railway in 1861, the plaintiff charged that the English and Scotch Traffic Agreement of January 1, 1856, was illegal on the grounds that the act of incorporation of the London and North Western Railway provided for the division of the company's profits among the holders of it stocks and shares. Hare claimed that, following the terms of the pooling agreement, the London and North Western Railway had paid over £7,329, to the companies of the Eastern route on traffic for the half year ending December 31, 1857. Vice Chancellor Page Wood, giving judgement in favour of the company, gave as one reason for reaching his decision that the pool was not illegal, that during its life of ten years the plaintiff was the only shareholder of the eight companies involved to express any opposition to the agreement in the courts. He noted, also, that there had been no attempt on the part of the public, acting through the attorney general, to challenge the legality of the pool.[1]

The views of Parliament also reflected the concensus of opinion among railway proprietors. Although a rearguard action was fought throughout much of the nineteenth century against the outright amalgamation of railway companies, a more sympathetic attitude was prevalent in respect of pooling agreements. In 1853 a Select Committee of the Board of Trade reported that

'With a view, therefore, of securing to the railway companies and to the public, as far as may be possible, all the advantages of amalgamation and yet of retaining in the hands of Parliament, all the power which it may be necessary to employ in future for better securing from time to time the application of railway facilities to the general good of the community, your committee would advise that working arrangements for a time to be limited, confirming intimate relations between different companies on the subject of the regulation of their traffic and the division of the proceeds, may, with propriety, be sanctioned.'[2]

[1] Hare vs London and North Western Railway Company, *The Law Journal*, 1861, part 1, p. 817.
[2] Select Committee on Railway and Canal Bills, fifth report, p. 8, BPP 1852-3, XXXVIII.

The vital importance of the Clearing House for the success of pooling agreements in Britain can be underlined by means of some comparisons with the economic history of American railroads. Although the situation in the USA was in many respects different from that in Britain, there were also some broad similarities. In both countries the railways passed through a phase of ruinous competition followed by a period dominated by attempts to limit suicidal conflict between the companies. But whereas the competitive mania was at its height in Britain in the 1840s, in the USA the period of fiercest struggle between the lines followed the conclusion of the Civil War in 1865. In the early 1870s, on the railroads of the southern States, rate wars reduced the gross earnings to a level 42% below what regular rates would have yielded.[1]) In the country as a whole freight revenue per ton mile fell from an average of 1.88 cents in 1870 to 1.22 cents in 1880.[2] In the face of the erosion of stock earnings one of the remedies sought was the division of traffic by means of pooling agreements. By 1879 there were at least eight of them in existence.[3] With one important exception, they quickly disappeared, having largely failed to achieve their object. It would be instructive to examine some of the reasons for this failure.

The earliest and best known of the American agreements was the Iowa Pool, founded in 1870. Three railroads, the Rock Island and Pacific, Chicago and North Western and the Chicago, Burlington and Quincy, each of which had terminals both at Chicago and at Omaha, agreed to divide the receipts on traffic between these two cities, each company taking one-third of the total. The three companies entered into no written contract and there was no formal organisation. There was no pool auditor to supervise the accounts and approve the division of receipts. For information on the volume and value of traffic carried on each of the three routes each company had to depend upon the good faith of its neighbour.[4] It is scarcely surprising that the pool was 'a most uneasy alliance with constant infractions and rate cutting'.[5] A year

---

[1] H. Hudson: 'The Southern Railway and Steamship Association,' *Quarterly Journal of Economics*, Vol. 5, 1891, p. 70.
[2] Gabriel Kolko: *Railroads and Regulation, 1877–1916*, Princeton, New Jersey, 1965, p. 7.      [3] *Ibid.* p. 8.
[4] J. Grodinsky: *The Iowa Pool*, 1950, p. 101.
[5] G. Kolko: *op. cit.* p. 8.

after the pooling agreement began it was widely asserted that the Chicago, Burlington and Quincy line was cheating its partners in the pool. However, there was no constructive means of redress for there was no impartial tribunal to whom the parties could turn for a reliable statement of the facts. In consequence of these difficulties and of the encroachments of the Union Pacific Railroad, the pool was virtually destroyed by 1874 although it limped along to its final dissolution in 1885.

This bungling may be contrasted with the efficient and successful management of another pooling agreement, the Southern Railway and Steamship Association, set up in 1875. No doubt the devastation of southern railroads in the Civil War, the damage to railway capital wrought by the freight wars which followed and the limited industrial resources of the south meant that this region was less able to face the hazards of railway competition than were other regions of the USA. These were important reasons for making the pool a more systematic and durable instrument for limiting railway competition than was its predecessor in the north. The agreement covered a territory larger than Britain, its boundaries being the Potomac and Ohio in the north, the Mississippi in the west and the Caribbean and Atlantic in the south and east.[1] Over thirty railway and steamship companies participated. Where it differed so remarkably from the Iowa Pool was in the setting up of a permanent administration which fulfilled much the same role for the association as the Railway Clearing House performed for British pooling agreements. The Annual Convention elected a general commissioner, a secretary, an auditor, a Board of Arbitration and an executive committee. It was the task of the general commissioner to publish monthly returns of the traffic of each line based on the daily reports supplied by the companies. Detailed accounts were submitted to the commissioner at regular intervals. The consequences of following this plan were clearly explained by one historian of the pool:

'By means of these various tables, supplied by the Commissioner, each road was enabled to see at a glance just what business there was to compete for, and what share his road was getting. They

[1] H. Hudson: *op. cit.* p. 70 *et seq.*

showed also the basis on which the percentages of division were calculated.

Having informed the roads, by means of these tables, of the amount of their indebtedness, and of the business from which it arose, the Commissioner and Auditor acted as clearing house agents for the settlement of the accounts.'[1]

As the statements of the commissioner might be challenged, it was provided in Article 18 of the agreement that he had the right to examine the books of any member of the association as a safeguard against fraudulent or irregular reports. From 1886 onwards the commissioner was empowered to appoint two commissioners of weights and classifications to ensure that shippers did not misrepresent their goods as to their quality and class. A sub-committee of the executive, the Rate Committee, undertook the task of drafting a goods classification, and the result of its labours was 'a single uniform classification for the whole southern territory'. Just as the Clearing House classification in Britain simplified the task of those organising the Octuple and other traffic agreements, so the success of the Southern Railway and Steamship Association was partly due to the wisdom of its leaders in working for a satisfactory goods classification in the south. Although the pooling of traffic receipts came to an end when prohibited under the Interstate Commerce Act of 1887, the Association continued as a rate-fixing body into the twentieth century.

It would be safe to conclude, therefore, that but for the work performed by the Clearing House, the fate of the English pooling agreements would have been similar to that of the Iowa Pool, the Colorado Traffic Association (1882), the Transcontinental Association (1883), the Pacific Coast Association (1884) and many others which suffered the severe drawback of an inadequate (or virtually non-existent) administrative machinery. The success of pooling agreements on both sides of the Atlantic depended on some kind of clearing house machinery for checking and settling accounts, publishing returns of traffic and ensuring a uniform classification.

Whereas in Britain the existence of pooling agreements did not arouse any great opposition from the public or the legislature, in

---

[1] H. Hudson: *op cit.*

the USA where most of the pools proved incapable of preventing rebating, undercutting and excessive rate discrimination the public, but especially the farming community, was hostile to the railways attempts to restrain competition.

The contrast between England and the USA in the matter of freight rates is also instructive. In Britain the existence of an universally accepted Railway Clearing House classification of goods helped to make possible the virtual elimination of competition in freight rates over the greater part of the kingdom. The success of the Goods Managers Conference in achieving a common classification had paved the way for the work of the rate conferences. Despite attempts made in 1882 and subsequently, the American railroads failed to achieve a common classification before the First World War. In 1887 there were no less than 138 classification systems in the USA. Ten years later a prominent railroad leader told the Interstate Commerce Commission that the existence of such a numerous variety of goods classifications was 'a great promoter of misunderstandings, dissatisfaction and complaints'.[1] Rate conferences could scarcely expect to exercise much authority in such an environment.

Manifestly, the Railway Clearing House was much more than an organisation for settling the railway companies' accounts with each other. By its existence and the labours of its staff the entire pattern of railway organisation in Britain was affected and assumed different characteristics from those of other countries. In so far as the British railway system in 1914 was unique, its uniqueness owed much to the organisation Kenneth Morison had founded seventy-two years earlier.

[1] G. Kolko: *op cit*. p. 171.

# CHAPTER XII

# THE RAILWAY CLEARING HOUSE IN
# WARTIME AND AFTER

I

Immediately following the declaration of war against Germany on
August 4, 1914, the management of British Railways passed into
the hands of an executive committee (shortly afterwards known
as the Railway Executive Committee) composed of the general
managers of the leading railway companies and a chairman
representing the Board of Trade. Until the Railways Act of 1921
led to the regrouping of most of the railways into four main-line
companies, the Railway Executive Committee was the supreme
policy-making body. With the introduction of this unified control
it was inevitable that the importance of the Clearing House
should decrease as many of its pre-war activities became
superfluous.

The authority of the Railway Executive Committee over railway
management was established with remarkably little resentment or
misunderstanding from the Clearing House. In view of the fact
that there were separate meetings of general managers, goods
managers, superintendents, and carriage and waggon superintendents under both Railway Clearing House and Railway
Executive Committee auspices it is surprising that there was not
much more duplication of effort. It is true that on August 24, 1914,
Gilbert Szlumper, secretary of the Railway Executive Committee,
wrote to Mr Cuff Smart, his opposite number in the Railway
Clearing House, pointing out that nearly all the subjects on the
agenda of a conference of goods managers and superintendents,
due to be held at the Clearing House on the following day, had
already been dealt with by a similar committee of the Railway
Executive Committee a few days previously. To avoid such
overlapping in the future all applications for special freights or
fares were to be submitted to the Railway Executive Committee

before being placed on the agenda of Railway Clearing House conferences. But it is also significant that Mr Cuff Smart replied agreeing to this new ruling without protest or apparent rancour.[1] In December 1916, at the suggestion of the Railway Executive Committee, the number of Clearing House conferences and meetings of general managers, superintendents, etc., held annually was reduced, the general managers, for example, meeting twice a year instead of four times. This change helped to ensure that the Clearing House conferences confined themselves more closely to matters not directly concerned with the war effort.

On the day following the declaration of war a special meeting of goods managers and audit accountants held under the auspices of the Railway Executive Committee recommended that mileage and demurrage records need no longer be kept, but that the Clearing House number takers should continue to send in junction records of the movement of waggons. This recommendation was quickly enforced and more than a hundred Clearing House clerks immediately faced redundancy.[2] Of even greater significance was the decision to stop dividing the traffic receipts of those companies taken over by the government (through the Railway Executive Committee) for the duration. On August 18, 1914, Mr H. Cuff Smart received the following instruction by letter from H. A. Walker on behalf of the Railway Executive Committee.

'I have to inform you that the E.C. have decided that from midnight August 4th no traffic divisions between the railways of Great Britain scheduled hereto will require to be made for traffic originating on and after 5th August, until further notice.'

In order to enable the Clearing House to make necessary comparisons and to have the appropriate information when it came to a question of government compensation payments to the railway companies, the traffic returns had still to be submitted by the companies. But all those clerks whose task it had been to settle the companies' claims against each other had now to be found alternative employment.[3]

---

[1] REC (1914) 1/24.
[2] REC (1914) 1/2: Minutes of a special meeting of goods managers and accountants at the railway Clearing House, August 5, 1914.
[3] REC (1914) 1/2: Minute 155 of REC, August 18, 1914.

As instruction followed instruction from the Railway Executive Committee headquarters at 35 Great George Street, Westminster, the occupations of an ever-growing number of the clerks in Seymour Street were affected. From the beginning of March 1915 the whole of the Clearing House check upon passenger traffic in which controlled companies only were involved, was suspended. It was no longer necessary for returns of the tickets issued to 'two companies' or 'three or more companies', or for the progressive numbers of general series of blank tickets, to be sent in to the Clearing House.[1] All adjustments of receipts made in respect of traffic bonus and pooling agreements came to an end.[2] In July 1915, when the stamp and label prepayment system was introduced for parcels conveyed by passenger train, a great deal of paper work hitherto associated with this kind of traffic was eliminated.[3] The same parcel stamp system was extended to miscellaneous traffic from April 2, 1917, and to the Anglo-Irish traffic on October 1, 1917, thus further reducing the demand for clerical labour.[4] Finally the introduction of the common user system for waggons, sheets and ropes in the course of 1917 provided another opportunity for reducing manpower.[5] The cumulative effect of all these changes was so great that at least one large railway company took the opportunity of selling, at a very advantageous price, a large quantity of paper which had been stored for office use.

Surprisingly enough, in the light of the drastic curtailment of much of the work, there were no dismissals of Clearing House staff during the war, apart from the usual cases of disciplinary action. The clerks themselves greatly eased the problems of the Superintending Committee by volunteering for the armed forces in large numbers. In the month of August 1914 alone 371 men enlisted. Over 200 more had followed their example by the end of that year. The combined effects of conscription and volunteering

[1] REC (1914) 1/24: Instruction no. 231 of REC, March 24, 1915.
[2] REC (1914) 1/24: Instruction no. 184 of REC, January 22, 1915.
[3] RCH 1/12: Report of the superintending committee to the Quarterly Meeting of Delegates, September 13, 1916.
[4] REC (1914) 1/20: REC. Instructions no. 1064 of August 14, 1917, and 1080 of August 23, 1917; F. A. McKenzie: *British Railways and the War*, London, 1917, p. 20.
[5] REC (1914) 1/20: Instruction no. 866 of REC, March 2, 1917, and REC (1914) 1/5: Minute 2646 of REC, February 27, 1917.

were that a peak of 1,136 men had enrolled by September 1917 out of a total Clearing House staff of 3,005 men, women and boys; 144 of the 1,136 were killed in battle or died of wounds. But for the enthusiasm and self-sacrifice of hundreds of clerks and number takers, some dismissals of permanent staff would have been inevitable.[1]

Even apart from the absence of more than a third of the peacetime staff, there would have been redundancies had it not been for the prompt decision of the Railway Executive Committee, on August 5, 1914, to ban all overtime working.[2] It was also fortunate for those clerks whose normal work had suddenly disappeared that some of the large railway companies were seriously short of clerical labour through the enthusiastic enlistment of large numbers of their regular staff. Mr Cuff Smart was therefore able to arrange for hundreds of men to be seconded to the service of the companies, working either at their own desks in the Clearing House or in the railway terminals in London. Some 400 men were thus employed by September 1915, but thereafter the numbers declined to little more than a quarter of this figure by the time of the armistice. In September 1915 the companies declined to take on any additional clerks despite the fact that the threat of redundancy at the Clearing House was increasing. The secretary, therefore, wrote to the treasury to discover whether any government department was in need of clerks. He was again fortunate. The rapidly expanding Ministry of Munitions found places for 100 men by the end of the year, and a further 200 men were found work, partly by the same ministry, but also by the Board of Trade in providing statistics needed for the equitable distribution of household coal, by the end of the war. The number of women on the staff of the Clearing House fluctuated much less violently than did the number of men. At the outbreak of the war 196 were employed. By September 1917 a wartime peak of 275 was reached, but thereafter there was a slow decline to 192 in December 1918.

After deducting from the grand total of about 3,000 employees those who were in the armed forces, working for the companies or

---

[1] Staff figures taken from the quarterly reports of the superintending committee of the Railway Clearing House. Casualty figures quoted in the superintending committee's report of March 10, 1920.

[2] REC (1914) 1/2: Minute 86 of REC, August 5, 1914.

for government departments, a hard core of over 1,400 men, women and boys were left to do the work of the Clearing House. How were they employed? Least changed was the secretarial department where the work in connection with staff arrangements, account keeping and the minuting of hundreds of meetings annually, continued 'practically as in pre-war time'. In the mileage and demurrage sections of the traffic department full records of the exchange of stock were reinstituted from February 1915 (after an earlier decision to curtail this work) largely because waggons were in increasingly short supply and the Railway Executive Committee was particularly anxious to learn of their whereabouts. Thus there were 531 number takers employed in September 1918, as many as had been employed four years earlier. After the beginning of January 1917, when the common user scheme was introduced, daily returns of the exchange of stock were required by the Clearing House. In the merchandise section the volume of work was greatly reduced. Clerks were largely confined to the checking of station abstracts and dealing with discrepancies in the traffic returns. In the passenger department the only operations continued were the apportionment of receipts on traffic in which non-controlled railway companies interests arose. Some of the clerks in this department were employed in preparing, for some of the companies, assessments of the number and value, of naval and military warrants for passenger train travel. In the parcels section, after July 1915 when the prepaid stamp and label scheme came into operation, work was reduced to the checking and clearing of differences in way-bills issued for the small proportion of the traffic not under the stamp system.[1]

II

Undoubtedly one of the most important innovations in railway operation which resulted from the war was the common user system for waggons, sheets and ropes.

The prize for the most optimistic statement about transport in wartime must surely go to the Railway Executive Committee whose minutes for August 5, 1914, read:

[1] RCH 1/39: Report of the superintending committee to the Quarterly Meeting of Delegates, December 12, 1913.

'In view of the probable great decrease in traffic, it is anticipated there will be no difficulty in dealing with rolling stock.'[1]

In the event, traffic volume increased by at least 50% in four years and the members of the committee had more headaches in dealing with bottlenecks in waggon supply than they did over any other railway problem. Less than three months after the gaffe of August 5, Gilbert Szlumper, secretary to the Railway Executive Committee, wrote an anxious letter to the war office calling attention to the growing shortage of railway waggons.[2] In fairness to the Railway Executive Committee it must be conceded that the shortage of waggons would not have been so acute had it not been for the fact that it proved impossible for the companies to maintain their pre-war rate of construction of 31,000 waggons annually to replace worked out vehicles from the total stock of 728,000 owned by the railways. In the course of the two years 1915–16 they were only allocated sufficient material to build 29,000 waggons. Hence by the end of April 1917 there was a shortage of 33,000 waggons, all the more embarrassing because of the greatly increased volume of work the railways were being called upon to perform.[3]

In the light of the unexpected deficiency in rolling stock the Railway Executive Committee reconsidered its earlier decision to abandon mileage and demurrage payments. In February 1915 the Clearing House was instructed to submit periodical records of the detention of waggons so that the causes of delays might be discovered and those responsible for them encouraged to hasten the turn round of waggons to avoid the payment of demurrage charges.[4]

The better informed of the waggon superintendents knew that the railways of the German States had organised a waggon pool with considerable success since 1909.[5] They explored the possibility of introducing a similar scheme in Britain. On May 5, 1915, Sir

[1] REC (1914) 1/2.
[2] REC (1914) 1/2: Minute 467 of the REC, November 3, 1914.
[3] REC (1914) 1/5: Memorandum to the Board of Trade from the REC, May 24, 1917.
[4] REC (1914) 1/3: Minutes 759 of February 2, 1815, 782 of February 10, 1815, and 856 of March 10, 1915.
[5] E. A. Pratt: *British Railways in the Great War*, London, 1921, Vol. 2, p. 680.

George J. Armytage, chairman of the Lancashire and Yorkshire Railway, showed the Railway Executive Committee a copy of a letter he had received from a Mr Barmingham advocating a common user scheme for British railway waggons. The committee took no action on the proposal. When Mr Barmingham wrote again a month later the committee replied that the time was 'not opportune to carry out such a radical change'.[1]

However, at the end of November 1915 the committee relented to the extent of appointing Sir Sam Fay, general manager of the Great Central Railway and W. Bailey accountant of the Midland Railway, as a small committee to report on both the common user of merchandise waggons and the pooling of coal waggons.[2] Within a week of his appointment to the Railway Executive Committee committee, Sir Sam Fay wrote to the general manager of the London and North Western Railway suggesting that representatives of the leading companies in the Clearing House should meet to consider the more economical use of railway rolling stock. The six men who met in the Clearing House on December 7, 1915, as a result of this initiative, formed a common user committee and passed a resolution that the pooling of railway waggons 'would be a distinct advantage and would result in a large saving'.[3] On the last day of November a meeting of the Goods Managers Committee of the Railway Executive Committee came to a similar conclusion. The direct outcome of these deliberations was the publication of a circular by three leading general managers early in December and worded as follows:

'Commencing Monday, December 15th 1915, and until further notice, Great Northern, Great Central and Great Eastern ordinary open goods waggons, having sides of three or more planks, and also the waggon sheets of those companies, must be dealt with and used as common stock, for the purposes of the three companies. All other vehicles must continue to be dealt with under existing instructions.'[4]

[1] REC (1914) 1/3: Minutes 1002 and 1094 of REC, May 5 and June 9, 1915.
[2] REC (1914) 1/3: Minute 1518 of the REC, November 24, 1915.
[3] RCH 1/478: Minutes of common user committee, December 7, 1915.
[4] Pratt: *op. cit.* Vol. 2, p. 679.

Thus by the time Sir Sam Fay and W. Bailey presented their report to the Railway Executive Committee on January 18, 1916, a common user scheme of limited scope and geographical range was already in operation. However, the labours of the two men were by no means wasted. By stating in clear and unequivocal terms the advantages that would accrue from a nationwide common user scheme they helped, in time, to overcome the inertia of the Railway Executive Committee. They listed four outstanding reasons in favour of the proposal:

'1. Avoidance of shunting at station yards, depots and docks, due to the necessity of selecting waggons for particular destinations, when by user in common, any waggon in position for loading might, without shunting, be utilised, irrespective of ownership.
2. The avoidance of shunting empty waggons, and forming them in trains destined for owning companies' exchange points or in that direction which involves, more often than not, shunting at several points.
3. The saving of train mileage and/or waggon mileage incurred by working empty stock (a) in a homeward direction, (b) to points well supplied with foreign waggons which cannot be utilised for loading under existing regulations.
4. The acceleration in the movement of traffic generally resulting from the dimunition of shunting and of train and waggon mileage.'

They did not consider the increased difficulties of conducting repairs and the possibility that poorly equipped companies would take undue advantage of the scheme were big enough obstacles to warrant delay in its introduction.[1]

But before the Railway Executive Committee could be persuaded to issue a directive on the question, five other major companies acted on their own. In March 1916 the general managers of the London and North Western, Midland, Great Western, Lancashire and Yorkshire, and North Eastern railways issued a joint circular stating that thenceforward their waggons—with some specialised exceptions such as coke waggons—would be used in common. The advantages of such a pooling of resources were becoming so

[1] REC (1914) 1/33: Report upon the Pooling of Railway Companies' Waggons and Acquisition or Control of Traders' Waggons, January 18, 1916.

obvious and the shortage of waggons so acute that the Ministry of Munitions intervened to hasten the speedier adoption of a nationwide common user scheme. On November 23, 1916, the director of Munitions and Railway Transport wrote to the secretary of the Railway Executive Committee urging the rapid extension of the scheme. He wanted to know whether a general pooling scheme was likely to materialise 'within a measurably short period' so that its effects could be felt before the winter season was far advanced.[1] Within a fortnight of the dispatch of this urgent letter, the common user committee of the Clearing House had worked out the details of a plan which was put into operation from 4 p.m. on January 2, 1917. Some 300,000 of the waggons of the twelve principal railway companies were brought into the pool, though special purpose vehicles were at first excluded. The Clearing House was to compile periodic statements showing the debit and credit balances of the waggons of each company. The balances due were to be made good within one week. The return of waggons 'owing' to other companies was to be a first charge on the waggon stock of each company.[2] The scheme was so successful that in July 1917 it was extended to include some of the more specialised waggons, such as those with end doors. By May 1918 there were 445,761 waggons in the pool.[3]

As early as the autumn of 1915 the Railway Executive Committee gave consideration to the possibility of pooling the privately owned waggons, principally with the object of effecting economies in the distribution of coal. It informed the Board of Trade that difficulties in carrying out such a plan need not be insurmountable, given one condition, 'that all waggons should be directly and solely under railway control and in fact the private ownership of railway waggons should be abolished'.[4] Sir Sam Fay and Mr Walter Bailey in their report to the Railway Executive Committee on April 26, 1916, also considered that the common working of the privately owned waggons was a feasible proposition and that it

---

[1] Pratt: *op cit.* Vol. 2, pp. 680-2.

[2] RCH 1/478: Minutes of the common user committee, December 6, 1916.

[3] RCH 1/478: Minute 510 of the common user committee, July 20, 1917. Pratt: *op cit.*, Vol. 2, p. 689.

[4] REC (1914) 1/3: Minute 1463 of REC, November 3, 1915.

would result in a considerable improvement in the speed of transit of goods and minerals, provided a satisfactory financial agreement could be reached with the waggon owners.[1] But it proved impossible, despite two years of conferences and discussions in the Railway Clearing House and Railway Executive Committee, to bring into being a national pool of privately owned waggons. The reasons for this failure were many. Interchangeability of parts for repairs was out of the question because of the great variety of waggon types; waggons suited for the coal trade in one area were totally unsuited for use in another part of the country and the opposition of colliery waggon owners to the scheme was formidable. The best that could be achieved was a pooling of some waggons in areas served by the Lancashire and Yorkshire Railway and the hire by the Railway Executive Committee of some 10,000 waggons from private owners. Since the total of privately owned waggons was variously estimated at between 600,000 and 750,000, this could scarcely be counted an outstanding success.[2]

By comparison no great difficulty arose in establishing a pool of railway waggon sheets and ropes. Owing to wartime changes in the flow of traffic some companies soon found their stocks of sheets seriously depleted, with no prospect of an early improvement. When a census of sheets was held in November 1916 one company had but 19% of its sheets in its possession. Another company held less than half of its normal stock. The common user committee of the Clearing House examined this problem in the winter of 1916–17 and recommended that the stock of waggon sheets existing on each controlled railway company in Great Britain should be pooled and that periodic balances should be struck between the companies on the same principles as applied to the waggon pool. The scheme was approved by the Railway Executive Committee and put into operation at the beginning of March 1917.[3] A similar arrangement for the pooling of ropes was introduced at the end of July 1917.[4]

[1] REC (1914) 1/3: Report on the Control of Traders' Waggons During the Period of Government Control of the Railways, April 26, 1916.

[2] REC (1914) 1/20: Circular 746 of the REC, November 27, 1916.

[3] RCH 1/478: Minutes of common user committee, January 16, 1917, and REC (1914) 1/20: Circular 866 of March 2, 1917.

[4] RCH 1/478: Minute 552 of the common user committee, 21–24 July, 1917.

The benefits of the common user scheme were undeniable. Whereas in October 1913, before pooling was introduced, nearly 61% of waggons in transit were running empty, the comparable figure for the same month of 1919 was only 20%. It was estimated that the six largest railway companies alone saved some £470,000 a year through this more economical use of rolling stock. A million shunting hours per year were saved on British railways. The advantage to traders through the quicker turn round of goods waggons was also significant. It is scarcely surprising that after the freeing of the railways from Government control the companies chose to maintain the common use of their waggons.[1]

Second only in importance to the pooling of waggons as a lasting reform originating in the wartime emergency was the parcel stamp scheme. Long before the outbreak of war no less than ten of the leading companies used the adhesive stamp prepayment system for the conveyance of parcels on their own networks. But for through carriage of parcels a waybill had to be made out for each separate consignment and detailed accounts and book records kept. Since this arrangement was very wasteful of manpower, a special meeting of the superintendents of the English and Welsh companies under government control recommended that, from July 1, 1915, the railways should adopt the 'paid' stamp and 'to pay' label system for through parcels traffic carried by passenger train.[2] All prepaid parcels were to be stamped and all parcels whose carriage was to be paid at their destination station were to have a 'to pay' label for the appropriate account affixed. Although the recommendation was endorsed by the Railway Executive Committee, the saving in clerical labour was not as great as it would have been if all parcels had been prepaid. On the recommendation of the superintendents, therefore, the Railway Executive Committee eventually decided that all parcels sent by passenger train on and after March 1, 1917, with the exception of traffic from the continent, should be prepaid.[3]

[1] RCH 1/498: Minute 46 of a meeting of goods and mineral managers, December 9, 1921. *The Railway Gazette*, February 3, 1922, p. 169.

[2] RCH 1/149: Minutes of special meetings of representatives of English and Welsh companies under government control held at the Railway Clearing House, June 18 and 21, 1915.

[3] RCH 1/150: Minutes of a meeting of superintendents, January 5 and 10, 1917.

From April 2, 1917, the same ruling applied to all miscellaneous traffic carried by passenger train.[1] As a result of these changes the volume of clerical work at the stations and at the Clearing House was greatly reduced and the companies showed wisdom in retaining these reforms when the period of government control came to an end in 1921.

### III

After the armistice the coalition government acted more speedily in releasing men from the armed forces than it did in coming to a decision about the future of the railways. The superintending committee had promised to keep open the jobs of those who enlisted during the war and in 1919 and 1920 had to find these men employment before knowing what tasks the Clearing House would be called upon to perform under peacetime conditions. In the course of 1919 more than a thousand officers and men who were on the books of the Clearing House, were demobilised, leaving only just over a hundred more to return to civil employment early in the following year.[2]

As a result of Mr Cuff Smart's representations to the Railway Executive Committee and to the Treasury work for some of the demobilised staff was found in various government departments. In September 1919, for example, over three hundred members of the staff were working for the Ministry of Pensions.

After the establishment of the Ministry of Transport by Act of Parliament in 1919, the Clearing House was required to compile statistics of ton mile goods traffic; the division of railway expenses between passenger and goods services; the age of the locomotive stocks classified into five year groups; the number of miles of line under absolute block and electric signalling; and many other detailed returns. The new requirements of the government were considered by a special committee of accountants in October 1919 and a large proportion of the demobilised clerks—almost seven

[1] RCH 1/150: Minutes of a meeting of headquarters representatives of companies in the REC, February 15, 22 and 28, 1917.
[2] RCH 1/12: Quarterly reports of superintending committee for 1919 and 1920.

hundred men—was employed in carrying out the detailed recommendations made by the committee in fulfilment of government orders.[1]

The concern of the railway companies after the war was to
return to 'normal' peace time conditions as quickly as possible.
In particular they were anxious to re-establish the division of
traffic receipts and passenger receipts on the basis of mileage.
It was appreciated that the full resumption of peacetime practices
would involve the employment of most of the recently demobilised
clerks. In two interviews with Sir George Beharrell at the Ministry
of Transport in April and May 1921 the chairman and secretary
of the Clearing House pleaded that the ministry should waive its
demand for ton mile and other statistics, at least for the time
being, so that the companies could employ the clerks on the
division of traffic receipts. As the government was pre-occupied
with its Railways Bill and its plan for the regrouping of the companies, Sir George Beharrell expressed the opinion that 'the action
contemplated by the railway companies in re-establishing the
division of traffic receipts was premature', and he further intimated
that the Ministry of Transport could not agree to forgo the
statistical information being rendered by the companies. Eventually a compromise was reached. Commencing with the accounts
for April 1921, an approximate division of traffic receipts, but
without actual cash clearances, was instituted as a first step to
full resumption of peactime practice at a later date. For its part
the ministry modified its requirements for statistical information
without abandoning its demand for the essential ton mile statistics.[2]
Division of receipts on traffic with Irish companies had been
resumed in September 1920.[3]

## IV

The uncertainty about the future role of the Clearing House
was to a large extent removed with the passing of the Railways

[1] RCH 1/529: Deliberations of the committee of accountants. RCH
1/40: Report of the superintending committee, March 10, 1920.

[2] RCH 1/78: Minutes 3477 and 3488 of General Managers Conference
of February 15 and May 10, 1921.

[3] RCH 1/78: Minute 3453 of General Managers Conference, November
9, 1920.

Act in 1921. Under Part I and the First Schedule of the Act the principal railways of the country were grouped into four main line companies, though details of the grouping were not all settled until the Railway Amalgamation Tribunal completed its work in the following year. Section 14 of the Act specifically concerned the constitution and powers of the Railway Clearing House. As an outcome of the Act it was eventually decided that each of the main line companies was entitled to send four representatives to the quarterly meeting of delegates of the Railway Clearing House. Twenty-nine other bodies including the Cheshire Lines Committee, the various London tube railways and the Irish railways were each entitled to send one representative.[1] On the passing of the London Passenger Transport Act in 1933 the representative of the London Passenger Transport Board replaced the metropolitan and tube railway delegates to the Clearing House committee. The Act of 1921 left undisturbed the earlier Acts such as the Railway Clearing Act of 1850 and the Railway Clearing Committee Incorporation Act of 1897.

At the beginning of March 1922 a record number of 3,431 persons were employed by the Clearing House. By the terms of the Railways Act of 1921 an extensive range of railway statistics had to be supplied to the Minister of Transport and many clerks were fully occupied in the preparation of these returns. The increase in the number of meetings held in the Clearing House from 500 each year in 1913 to 1,800 in 1939 provided additional secretarial work for the staff.[2] But the long run tendency of employment was bound to be in a downwards direction because of the effects of the amalgamation of railway companies and the adoption of simpler methods of dividing traffic receipts. In 1925 the number employed fell to under three thousand for the first time since the summer of 1921. With the onset of trade recession the staff was reduced to below the two thousand mark at the beginning of 1932. By the outbreak of the Second World War there had been a further fall to 1,800. The falling demand for clerical labour was met by the dismissal of some of the staff

[1] RCH 1/18: Minute 3250 of the Clearing House committee, November 22, 1922. Appendix B: 'Railways in the Clearing House.'

[2] 'The Work of the Railway Clearing House 1842–1942', first appeared in *Railway Gazette*, London, 1943, p. 23.

casually employed, the curtailment of recruiting and the retirement of many clerks at sixty (or even earlier) instead of sixty five. In 1939 an unusually large proportion of the staff was included in the age groups of the forties and fifties. Inevitably promotion prospects were bleak and this was an aspect of the conditions of employment in the Clearing House always stressed by the Railway Clerks Association when negotiating over wages and hours. The Railway Clerks Association was able to secure from the superintending committee a satisfactory scheme of compensation for redundant staff under which a man was entitled to one-sixtieth of his last annual salary for each year of service with additional increments for those who had served over five years.[1]

When the grouping of the companies came into effect in June 1923 it looked for a time as if the future of the number men would be even bleaker than that of the clerks. Early in 1923 the goods managers seriously considered a proposal that the Clearing House should cease to employ number takers but that this work should be transferred to the staff of the main line companies. It was suggested that the Clearing House men might find employment as guards in the service of the companies. However, a subcommittee of the goods managers reported decisively against this proposal, incidentally giving an unsolicited testimonial to this important section of the Clearing House staff:

'Numbertakers who are employed by an impartial body like the Clearing House, are able to specialise in the class of work required, and give it their full attention; these men obtain more accurate results than are secured from numbertakers employed by the railway companies, who frequently have other duties to perform, which interfere both with the correctness of their records and the importance they attach to the work. Moreover the companies generally place far more confidence in the records taken by a neutral body like the R.C.H., than they do in the records made by one of the companies themselves. Inasmuch as payments for the use of waggons between companies will be made in future as in pre-war days on the numbertakers records, the sub committee

[1] A. G. Walkden: *The Reorganisation of British Railways*, London, 1922, p. 30.

283

regard the retention of the Clearing House numbertakers as essential.'[1]

It is not surprising that after such an unequivocal report nothing further was heard about the abolition of this grade of employee of the Clearing House. With the introduction of more economical methods of using waggons, particularly the journey payment scheme (to be described hereafter), the number employed gradually declined from a peak of 763 in March 1921 to 388 in June 1939. The employment of Clearing House number takers ceased entirely at the end of 1948.

In the course of an address given in January 1939 the secretary of the Railway Clearing House, Mr E. E. Painter, described the role of the organisation as 'the maid of all work of British railways'. In the sense that, compared with the pre-war years, the Railway Clearing House had a much diminished importance in the formulation of railway policies but retained a great deal of the responsibility for their detailed implementation, he was undoubtedly right. For example, before 1914 the Goods Managers Conference of the Clearing House drafted the classification of goods for the railways: after 1921 this work was done by the Railway Rates Tribunal and its subsidiaries. In pre-war days the Superintendents Conference was responsible for major decisions on passenger fares and many other kindred subjects: after 1923 the general managers and passenger superintendents of the four main line companies made their own decisions and left it to the conferences at the Clearing House to work out the details. We have seen that the Superintendents Conference in 1865 worked out a national plan for numbers of ticket nippers, but in 1925 the London Midland and Scottish Railway replaced the Clearing House ticket nippers with its own set with a different series of numbers for the different ticket inspection stations.[2]

[1] RCH 1/189: Goods Managers Conferences, April 26, 1923, Appendix A.

[2] BTHR, RB 2/144/5: The LMS. Instructions to ticket inspectors, 'ticket collectors, train attendants and other staff' of April 1923, paragraph 57, read: 'The staff must make themselves acquainted with the various ticket nippers described in the pamphlet issued by the RCH.' The similar publication for 1925 made no reference to ticket nippers but included a new set of LMS numbers and designs for nippers.

It would be quite erroneous to suggest that Clearing House conferences in the inter-war years were not responsible for any important innovations. One of the most important reforms introduced after the war, the journey payments scheme, originated from joint meetings of goods and mineral managers held in the Seymour Street premises between February and July 1922. The question to be settled was what should be the method of charging the companies for the use of other railways' goods waggons when the four main line companies took over in the summer of 1923? At an early stage of their deliberations they decided that they must devise an uncomplicated scheme:

'The financial scheme to be applied after amalgamations are completed should be on a broad basis to avoid, as far as possible, detailed calculations, and thus secure the benefit of a reduction in cost incurred by the railway companies and the R.C.H. under the pre war method of ascertaining the payments to be made between companies for the use and detention of stock.' [1]

Under the pre-war system a company that sent one of its waggons on to the lines of another company was liable to pay a mileage charge proportional to the distance it was hauled on 'foreign' rails and a demurrage charge when it was detained for more than a stipulated number of days at its 'foreign' destination. Such an arrangement meant that clerks in the traffic department of the Clearing House had to calculate detailed charges for the movement of each waggon as soon as it had left its 'home' lines. Under the journey payment scheme devised by the goods and mineral managers and put into effect from July 1, 1923, such detailed calculations were no longer needed. Instead, fixed payments were to be made in respect of every loaded waggon (excluding waggons carrying coal and other minerals) exchanged between the four main line groups. The rate per journey was to be based on the *average* journey payment made in 1913 in respect of the traffic between each of the companies individually, though payments were increased by agreed percentages to make allowance for the rise in prices and costs. Thus every waggon moved from

[1] RCH 1/330: Minutes of a joint meeting of goods and mineral managers. February 15, 1922, and report of sub-committee dated March 3–July 5, 1922.

the Southern Railway to the Great Western Railway was charged 4s 4.86d irrespective of the length of the particular journey actually undertaken, and every waggon moved from the North Eastern group to the Southern was charged 2s 11.43d. A scale of demurrage charges for waggons detained on 'foreign' lines for more than six days was also agreed. One of the great advantages of this plan was that it was consistent with the common user of waggons and sheets which the Clearing House companies, at first for very limited periods, and then for much more extended periods, decided to continue throughout the inter-war period; (the common user of ropes was ended from the beginning of August 1921).[1] Censuses of waggon movements were, of course, needed from time to time to take account of changes in the flow of traffic and these led to modifications in the scale of charges. But the principle of the scheme remained unimpaired throughout subsequent years.

Though the Clearing House could claim some credit for the more rational use of the railway companies' own waggons, the wasteful employment of privately owned waggons continued largely unabated throughout the inter-war years, the Clearing House being powerless to effect any substantial improvement. The Samuel Commission in 1925 found excessive waste in the movement of coal waggons.[2] On its recommendation a standing joint committee of the Ministry of Transport and the Mines Department (the Duckham Committee) was set up to make proposals for the more economic use of this important part of railway rolling stock. In its report it emphasised that one of the principal reasons why the coal waggons of France, Germany and Belgium were used roughly twice as effectively as the British waggons (over four round trips a month compared with two in the UK, despite longer average journeys) was that demurrage charges were higher and more promptly applied on the continent.[3] This

[1] RCH 1/330: Report (as above) and RCH 1/78: Minute 3573 of the General Managers Conference of February 6, 1923. For common user decisions see minute 2212 of general managers' meeting, March 6, 1923, and 3732 of general managers, January 1, 1927.

[2] Report of the Royal Commission on the Coal Industry, 1925, BPP 1926, Vol. XIV, pp. 118–19.

[3] Standing Committee on Mineral Transport, first report, 1929. BPP 1929–30, Vol. XVI, p. 353 and Appendix XIV.

was a clear pointer to the need to replace the very light siding rents the railway companies charged the coal merchants by demurrage charges of such severity as would have prompted the quicker turn round of waggons. However, the interests of the colliery owners and coal merchants were too powerful for the carrying out of this much-needed reform and the best that could be achieved before 1939 was formation of a number of regional pools of coal waggons.

In respect of passenger traffic an important innovation of the late 1930s was the Bulk Travel Plan for businessmen. (Lest the name of the plan should mislead, it must be made clear that it contained no suggestion that the average British businessman was more portly than his contemporaries.) Books of ticket vouchers were made available to traders who had occasion to travel frequently between any two stations and who were willing to deposit a sum with the railway in advance of travel and on the understanding that this sum would be expended in fares within the ensuing twelve months. The voucher entitled the holder to reduced rate fares. The successful functioning of this scheme was dependent upon the co-operation of the Clearing House which kept the voucher accounts of the many firms which seized the opportunities if offered.[1] The inroads which road haulage firms made into the parcels traffic of the railways would have been much greater in the 1920s and 1930s but for the successful functioning of the Prepaid Stamp Plan introduced during the war. In 1926 this method of financing the transport of parcels by passenger train was described by the secretary of the Clearing House as 'a very short and simple method when compared with the labour involved in the way-billing and abstracting necessary under the old system'.[2]

Prompted by the knowledge that in 1923 the expenses of running the Clearing House were not far short of double what they had been in 1913, the committee asked the accountants to suggest economies in administration and in the division of the traffic receipts. Reforms which were the outcome of the accountants' report included the division of receipts from mineral and livestock traffic held yearly instead of quarterly; the elimination of separate

[1] *The Railway Gazette*, June 19, 1942, p. 676.
[2] P. H. Price: 'The Railway Clearing House', *Journal of the Institute of Transport*, May 1926, p. 334.

'light traffic' statements, station grand summaries being utilised instead; the division of traffic receipts for sums of £3 or less pro rata the traffic for sums of over £3 and the simplification of the accounts for traffic carted across London.[1]

The consequence of the adoption of these reforms, the increased mechanisation of much of the routine work,[2] and the reduction in the size of the staff, was a rapid reduction in the costs of running the Clearing House from 1924 onwards.

If the peace of Europe could have been prolonged a further two years in the face of the growing menace of Nazi Germany, some at least of the staff of the Clearing House would have been provided with more modern accommodation in which to carry out their duties. In March 1938 the committee approved plans for the erection of new premises in Barnby Street to replace the leased building to the south in Seymour Street. But in October 1939 the London Midland and Scottish Railway notified the Clearing House that the work on the erection of the new building had had to be suspended because of the outbreak of war. By 1945 there were different reasons for not proceeding with the project.

V

Following the declaration of war against Germany on September 3, 1939 there was no repetition of the wholesale depletion of staff which had occurred in the early months of the First World War. The very limited scale of staff recruitment in the 1930s resulted in a large proportion of the staff being over the age limit for recruitment to the armed forces. Furthermore the Railway Clearing House was scheduled under the Essential Work (Railway Undertakings) Order of 1941 by which many of the staff were not free to leave the service. In consequence no more than 157 men out of a total staff of 1,800 at the outbreak of war were absent in the services at any one time.[3] Apart from the employment of some

[1] P. H. Price: 'The Railway Clearing House', *Journal of the Institute of Transport*, May 1926, p. 239.

[2] See RCH 1/574: Interim report of a committee appointed to consider the use of mechanical appliances in the Railway Clearing House, December 30, 1920, and subsequent reports of the superintending committee.

[3] Information for this section has been taken from *The Origins, Constitution, Organisation and Work of the Railway Clearing House*, a pamphlet published by the clearing house in 1947.

250 members of the staff on clerical work for the railway companies, there was no need for large scale redeployment of the labour force despite the assumption of full control over the railways by the Railway Executive Committee and the cessation of the division of traffic receipts between the companies from September 1, 1939. There was ample work for the clerks who remained in the direct employment of the Clearing House. Records of railway staff and of the movement of rolling stock had to be kept; the general and dangerous goods classification needed revision; the commutation of siding rent charges employed a large number. The work of the secretarial department increased rather than diminished. Meetings of the superintending committee, the Premises Trust, and the Superannuation Fund Corporation continued as in peacetime; but there were many additional meetings for which agendas had to be drafted, the memoranda prepared and minutes recorded. Over 2,000 meetings were held in the Clearing House in 1945 compared with some 1,800 in 1939.

During the First World War requisitioning of private owners' waggons was considered but rejected as presenting too many complications. No such hesitation was shown in 1939. A Ministry of Transport order dated September 3, 1939, requisitioned approximately 600,000 privately owned waggons. The Railway Executive Committee gave instructions to the Clearing House to arrange for payments to be made to the owners for the hire and repair of their vehicles. A staff of seventy-five clerks was at once made responsible for this work. It was a move which paved the way to the public ownership of rolling stock under the Transport Act of 1947 and was one of the most important changes wrought by the war.

For nearly a hundred years railway reformers had pleaded in vain, the advantages to be gained by re-siting the Clearing House 'somewhere in the country'. After September 1939 the Reichwehr and the Luftwaffe proved more effective agencies for such a change. Following the outbreak of war, the headquarters of the four main line companies were moved out of London and the general managers advised the superintending committee of the Clearing House to follow this example. Within a few weeks alternative accommodation for most of the Clearing House staff was found on three separate sites. Most of the secretarial department was rehoused at Coleshill Lodge, Amersham, Bucks, where many of the meetings for railway officers were subsequently held. The Railway Clearing House Athletics Ground at Whetstone, Middlesex, provided another site where staff of the goods section of the traffic department were accommodated in four large huts. The third site at Horley, Surrey, was rented from the Southern Railway for the use of the clerks in the coaching section of the traffic department. The movement to these emergency sites was completed by March 1940, but while the change was in progress, clerks were encouraged to do as much of their work as possible in their own homes, reporting from time to time at the Seymour Street (by then renamed Eversholt Street) premises to deposit or collect the necessary papers. As it happened very little damage was sustained by the old premises and the Whetstone premises suffered as much as did those at Euston from enemy air attacks.

## VI

After Labour's electoral landslide in July 1945 it was confidently asserted that the days of the Clearing House were strictly numbered. It was a confidence which was reinforced with the passage of the Transport Act on August 6, 1947, under which ownership of the railways passed to the British Transport Commission. But after vesting date, January 1, 1948, the Clearing House was a long time in dying. A number of 'farewell' lunches and dinners were held, without apparent effect on the vitality of the organisation. One of the most splendid occasions was the farewell luncheon held at the Great Western Royal Hotel at Paddington on January 26, 1955, when, appropriately enough, the grandson of George Carr Glyn was present.[1] But eight years later the superintending committee of the Clearing House was still meeting regularly. The explanation of this anomaly lies not in any tendency to gluttony on the part of railway officials, but in the fact that in January 1955 by an order (the Railway Clearing House Scheme Order) made under Section 38 of the Transport Act of 1947, all Acts of Parliament in which the Railway Clearing House had been incorporated were repealed. All property rights, powers and liabilities of the Clearing House were transferred to the British Transport Commission from May 24, 1954. The Railway Clearing

[1] *The Railway Gazette*, January 28, 1955, p. 115.

House Corporation had held its last meeting on November 24, 1954, a few weeks before the Paddington luncheon. But although, by these decisions of the government, the railway Clearing House lost its separate identity and independence, it was at the same time announced by the Minister of Transport that much of the work of the Clearing House, in the preparation of maps, handbooks of stations, the provision of secretarial services, etc., would be carried out as before in the Eversholt Street premises and that the organisation would continue to be known as the Railway Clearing House.

During the Beeching era of the early 1960s however it was considered uneconomical to maintain the establishment of the Clearing House in a separate building more than a mile away from the headquarters of British Railways in Marylebone Road. Thus as soon as outstanding legal problems connected with dissolution could be settled, the Clearing House was dissolved. The institution which had served British railways for more than 120 years was disbanded on March 31, 1963.[1]

While architects and town planners were engaging in a keen controversy as to whether Philip Hardwick's famous Euston portico should be preserved or demolished, some two hundred yards to the north another act of demolition aroused no opposition and passed almost unnoticed by the public. The bulldozers of a building contractor were busy demolishing that part of the Clearing House premises, south of Barnby Street, which included the famous 'long office'. Although this large room could lay no claim to architectural distinction, it can be stated without exaggeration that for many decades it was the nerve centre of transport services in Britain. If its physical preservation is now impossible, it is worth while to recall its vital importance in the great railway age.

The practice of passengers personally thanking the driver of a train for carrying them safely over a long journey has, fortunately, not entirely died out. But men of this grade are more frequently in a position to attract the praise (or blame) of the public than were the large numbers of clerks and number takers who for three generations toiled largely unnoticed by the millions who used the railways of Britain. And yet their work in the dingy offices near Euston and at windswept junctions all over the country was every bit as vital to the progressive enrichment of the British people.

[1] *Modern Transport*, March 16, 1963, p. 1.

# APPENDIX 1

# THE CHAIRMEN AND SECRETARIES OF THE CLEARING HOUSE COMMITTEE, 1842–1955

## Chairmen

| | |
|---|---|
| 1842–73 | George Carr Glyn (elevated to Peerage, Dec. 1869, thereafter Lord Wolverton). Company: London and North Western.[1] |
| 10.9.1873–75 | Robert Benson. Company: London and North Western. |
| 16.3.1875–86 | Rt Hon. George Grenfell Lord Wolverton. Company: London and North Western. |
| 10.3.1886–96 | Oscar Leslie Stephen. Company: London and North Western. |
| 11.3.1896–1908 | Lord Claud John Hamilton. Company: Great Eastern. |
| 11.3.1908–15 | Charles Mortimer. Company: Great Western. |
| 10.3.1915–18 | Hugh Wyndham Luttrell Harford. Company: Midland. |
| 13.3.1918–29 | Sir Edmund Russborough Turton. Company: North Eastern. |
| 9.3.1929–48 | Sir Francis Henry Dent, C.V.O. Company: Southern. |
| 9.1.1948–54 | Sir Michael Barrington-Ward, C.B.E., D.S.O., Delegate of the Railway Executive. |
| 17.3.1954–55 | K. W. C. Grand, Delegate of British Transport Commission. |

(1) Acting chairman, 1842–50. Elected on annual basis on June 26, 1850.

(2) 'Company'—which individual represents as a delegate to the Clearing House.

## Sources

[1] Minute books of the Railway Clearing House committee.
[2] Bradshaw's shareholders guides.

## Secretaries

| | |
|---|---|
| 1842–61 | Kenneth Morison |
| 11.12.1861–90 | Philip William Dawson |
| 10.12.1890–1907 | Harry Smart |
| 11.3.1908–12 | Frank Mansfield |
| 9.3.1912–19 | H. Cuff Smart |
| 10.12.1919–35 | P. H. Price |
| 9.10.1935–39 | Ernest Edward Painter |
| 8.3.1939–47 | Joseph Edmund Thomas Stanbra |
| 10.10.1947–55 | Thomas John Lynch |

# APPENDIX 2

## MEMBERSHIP OF THE CLEARING HOUSE

| DATE[1] | COMPANY[2] | |
|---|---|---|
| January 2, 1842 | Birmingham and Derby Junction | London and Birmingham |
| | Great North of England | Manchester and Leeds |
| | Hull and Selby | Midland Counties |
| | Leeds and Selby | North Midland |
| | | York and North Midland |
| December 31, 1845 | Birmingham and Gloucester | Liverpool and Manchester |
| | Chester and Birmingham | Manchester and Birmingham |
| | Grand Junction | Newcastle and Carlisle |
| | Lancaster and Preston | North Union |
| December 31, 1850 | Ardrossan | Glasgow, Dumfries and Carlisle |
| | Caledonian | Great Northern |
| | Cockermouth and Workington | Huddersfield and Manchester |
| | Eastern Counties | Manchester, Sheffield and Lincolnshire |
| | East Lincolnshire | Maryport and Carlisle |
| | Fleetwood, Preston and West Riding Junction | |

[1] Under the heading 'Date' the companies admitted during the five years previously.

[2] Under the heading 'Company', the name given is the title of the railway at the time of admission to the Clearing House. Many of these names disappear in time as railways were absorbed into larger companies bearing different names.

Outstanding mergers include the growth of the Midland Company. In the first instance, during 1844, the Midland Company was formed from the amalgamation of three companies which were members of the clearing house from its inception in 1842. These companies were Midland Counties, the North Midland and the Birmingham and Derby Junction.

Another development of this kind was a feature of the formation of the North Eastern in 1854. Early members of the Clearing House, the Leeds and Selby, the Hull and Selby, the York and North Midland and the Great North of England, made up the new corporate identity, the North Eastern.

This kind of story was repeated throughout the period considered in the Table, viz. the Great Eastern, the Great Western, the London and North Western etc.

By December 1862, some thirty-six companies were struck off the Clearing House List as separate identities—they were vested in other companies through some form of combination.

**December 31, 1850—*continued***

| | |
|---|---|
| North British | St Helens |
| Preston and Wyre | Stirling and Dunfermline |
| Shrewsbury and Chester | Whitehaven Junction |
| South Staffordshire | York, Newcastle and |
| Stockton and Darlington | Berwick |
| Stockton and Hartlepools | |

**December 31, 1855**

| | |
|---|---|
| Cork and Bandon | Monmouthshire Railway |
| Dublin and Belfast Junc- | and Canal |
| tion | Newport, Abergavenny |
| Dublin and Drogheda | and Hereford |
| Forth and Clyde Junction | Norfolk |
| Furness | North and South West |
| Great Southern and | Junction |
| Western | Oxford, Worcester and |
| Irish South Eastern | Wolverhampton |
| Killarney Junction | Peebles |
| Leeds, Bradford and | Perth and Dunkeld |
| Halifax | Shrewsbury and Here- |
| Leven Crieff Junction | ford |
| London and South | St Andrews |
| Western | Ulster and Dundalk |
| London Tilbury and | Waterford and Kilkenny |
| Southend | Waterford and Limerick |
| Monklands | |

**December 31, 1860**

| | |
|---|---|
| Bradfield, Wakefield and | Hertford and Welwyn |
| Leeds | Junction |
| Carlisle, Silloth Bay Rail- | Inverness and Aberdeen |
| way and Dock | Junction |
| Coleford, Monmouth, | North Yorkshire and |
| Usk and Pontypool | Cleveland |
| Darlington and Barnard | Port Carlisle Dock |
| Castle | Rhymney |
| Dunstable Welwyn | South Wales Railway |
| Glasgow, Dumbarton and | Stamford and Essendine |
| Helensburgh | Taff Vale |
| Great North of Scotland | Vale of Clwyd |
| Great Western | Warrington and Stock- |
| | port |

**December 31, 1865**

| | |
|---|---|
| Cambrian | London, Brighton and |
| Highland | South Coast |
| South Eastern | London, Chatham and |
| | Dover |

**December 31, 1870**

| | |
|---|---|
| Cheshire Lines Committee | Metropolitan Railway |

# APPENDIX 3

## ROUTE MILES OF THE COMPANIES WHICH WERE MEMBERS OF THE CLEARING HOUSE

| DATE | (A)<br>Route mileage of companies parties to Clearing House | (B)<br>Total route mileage open in the U.K. | %(A)/(B) |
|---|---|---|---|
| June 30, 1842 | 464 miles | 1,938 miles[1] | 23·9 |
| Dec. 31, 1850 | 3,496 | 6,621[2] | 55·8 |
| 1855 | 4,949 | 8,280 | 59·6 |
| 1860 | 7,225 | 10,433 | 69·4 |
| 1865 | 11,790 | 13,289 | 88·7 |
| 1870 | 14,683 | 15,537 | 94·5 |
| 1875 | 15,267 | 16,658 | 91·5 |
| 1880 | 15,543 | 17,933 | 86·6 |
| 1885 | 17,380 | 19,169 | 90·7 |
| 1890 | 18,939 | 20,073 | 94·3 |
| 1895 | 20,166 | 21,174 | 90·5 |
| 1900 | 20,642 | 21,855 | 94·5 |
| 1905 | 21,045 | 22,847 | 92·1 |
| 1910 | 21,233 | 23,387 | 90·8 |

[1] Taken from Lewin's book *Early British Railways*. Unfortunately, the author does not reveal his source of information. In spite of an extensive search among contemporary journals and Parliamentary sources, no alternative *complete* breakdown of route mileage in operation, has been found.

[2] Railway Returns from 1843 onward.

[3] It was not until 1865 that the Railway Clearing House Regulations Book contained a complete list of the member companies. For the years 1842–65, new admissions were nearly always mentioned in the minute books of the Clearing House committee. It is possible, however, that some were not mentioned. The route mileage stated in (A) for the years before 1865, probably is an underestimate of the real total.

[4] Some companies, not *parties* to the clearing system but whose accounts were dealt with by the Clearing House, have not been included. Not until 1910 were these listed in the Railway Clearing House Regulations Book.

[5] For the sake of comparability with other tables it is desirable that the 1913 figures be included. Unfortunately, this has not proved possible; the railway returns for this year do not include a breakdown of the route mileage of individual companies.

[6] For the years after the First World War there are only a very few Railway Clearing House Regulations Books lodged at the Archives.

## APPENDIX 4

## COMPARATIVE STATEMENT OF THE TRAFFIC ON ALL THE RAILWAYS OF THE UNITED KINGDOM FOR THE YEARS 1845–1854

| Year ending | Route miles open: 30th June | 1st Class | 2nd Class | 3rd Class | 'Parliamentary' | Total passengers | 3rd Class of parliamentary as percentage of total |
|---|---|---|---|---|---|---|---|
| June 30, 1845 | 2,343 | 5,474,163 | 14,325,825 | 13,135,820 | — | 33,791,253 | 35·9 |
| June 30, 1846 | 2,765 | 6,160,354 | 16,931,066 | 14,559,515 | 3,946,922 | 43,790,983 | 42·0 |
| June 30, 1847 | 3,603 | 6,572,714 | 18,599,288 | 15,865,311 | 6,985,493 | 51,352,163 | 44·5 |
| June 30, 1848 | 4,478 | 7,190,779 | 21,690,509 | 15,241,529 | 13,092,489 | 57,965,070 | 48·8 |
| June 30, 1849 | 5,447 | 7,078,690 | 23,392,450 | 14,378,377 | 15,432,457 | 60,398,159 | 49·3 |
| June 30, 1850 | 6,308 | 7,734,728 | 24,226,668 | 15,547,748 | 19,249,974 | 66,840,175 | 52·1 |
| June 30, 1851 | 6,698 | 9,175,781 | 28,883,044 | 16,980,973 | 23,820,723 | 78,969,622 | 51·7 |
| June 30, 1852 | 7,076 | 10,143,442 | 30,967,913 | 15,642,137 | 29,973,552 | 86,758,997 | 52·6 |
| June 30, 1853 | 7,509 | 11,463,073 | 33,492,212 | 49,983,140 | | 94,966,439 | 52·6 |
| June 30, 1854 | 7,640 | 13,647,485 | 38,214,833 | 55,687,227 | | 107,573,748 | 51·8 |

## APPENDIX 4 contd.

| Year ending | Route miles open 30th June | Receipts from passengers | | | | | | Receipts from goods (including cattle, parcels and mail) £s | Total receipts £ | Receipts from goods as a percentage of total receipts |
| --- | --- | --- | --- | --- | --- | --- | --- | --- | --- | --- |
| | | 1st Class £s | 2nd Class £s | 3rd Class £s | Parliamentary £s | Total £s | 3rd Class and Parliamentary as percentage of total | | | |
| June 30, 1845 | 2,343 | 1,516,805 | 1,598,115 | 651,903 | — | 3,976,341 | 16·4 | 2,233,373 | 6,209,714 | 36·0 |
| June 30, 1846 | 2,765 | 1,661,898 | 1,937,947 | 738,474 | 293,732 | 4,725,216 | 21·8 | 2,840,354 | 7,565,569 | 37·5 |
| June 30, 1847 | 3,603 | 2,048,080 | 2,048,080 | 737,452 | 539,977 | 5,148,003 | 24·8 | 3,362,884 | 8,510,886 | 39·5 |
| June 30, 1848 | 4,478 | 1,792,533 | 2,352,153 | 661,038 | 902,851 | 5,720,382 | 28·0 | 4,213,170 | 9,933,552 | 42·4 |
| June 30, 1849 | 5,447 | 1,880,646 | 2,502,588 | 651,366 | 1,059,786 | 6,105,975 | 28·0 | 5,094,926 | 11,200,901 | 45·5 |
| June 30, 1850 | 6,308 | 1,960,246 | 2,594,818 | 688,407 | 1,211,634 | 6,465,575 | 29·0 | 5,943,277 | 12,407,853 | 47·9 |
| June 30, 1851 | 6,598 | 2,212,778 | 2,847,469 | 624,480 | 1,402,593 | 7,177,341 | 28·2 | 6,719,558 | 13,997,900 | 48·7 |
| June 30, 1852 | 7,076 | 2,389,972 | 3,010,922 | 652,230 | 1,809,164 | 7,984,652 | 30·9 | 7,458,836 | 15,443,489 | 48·8 |
| June 30, 1853 | 7,509 | 2,454,770 | 2,980,789 | 2,527,995 | | 8,099,559 | 31·2 | 8,941,904 | 17,034,330 | 52·4 |
| June 30, 1854 | 7,640 | 2,709,398 | 3,210,095 | 2,829,760 | | 8,913,347 | 31·8 | 10,355,846 | 19,279,293 | 53·7 |

Source: Railway Returns

# APPENDIX 5

## THROUGH TRAFFIC OF COMPANIES IN THE RAILWAY CLEARING HOUSE FOR THE YEAR ENDING DECEMBER 31, 1845

| Company | Route miles | Number of passengers booked through | | | Total passengers booked through | Total passengers | Passengers booked through as a percentage of total passengers | Number of miles travelled by passengers booked through 000's | Carriages booked through | Trucks (privately owned) booked through | Horse boxes booked through | P.O. waggons booked through | Goods waggons booked through |
|---|---|---|---|---|---|---|---|---|---|---|---|---|---|
| | | 1st Class | 2nd Class | 3rd Class | | | | | | | | | |
| London and Birmingham | 326 | 83,199 | 61,728 | 19,992 | 164,919 | 1,505,323 | 11.0 | 31,009 | 7,087 | 2,080 | 2,058 | 650 | 17,699 |
| Midland | 271 | 36,143 | 45,154 | 5,590 | 86,887 | 1,795,620 | 4.8 | 19,610 | 10,960 | 1,076 | 1,525 | 525 | 38,723 |
| Manchester and Leeds | 56 | 8,898 | 15,781 | 4,501 | 29,180 | 1,921,351 | 1.4 | 2,250 | 2,492 | 101 | 293 | | 34,943 |
| York and North Midland | 169 | 19,671 | 28,116 | 9,790 | 57,577 | 640,678 | 8.9 | 5,961 | 14,543 | 359 | 610 | 8 | 24,896 |
| Great North of England | 45 | 7,350 | 9,370 | 8,223 | 24,943 | 228,634 | 10.9 | 2,508 | 5,431 | 453 | 494 | 594 | 9,605 |
| Newcastle and Darlington | 56 | 14,269 | 21,250 | 7,728 | 43,247 | 965,463 | 4.5 | 5,567 | 3,168 | 231 | 752 | 1 | 8,098 |
| Stockton and Darlington | 23 | 753 | 1,264 | 167 | 2,184 | 342,919 | 0.6 | 150 | | 11 | 27 | | 869 |
| Stockton and Hartlepool | 8¼ | 2,863 | 7,467 | 2,080 | 12,410 | 95,543 | 13.0 | 449 | 12 | 4 | 2 | | 578 |
| Newcastle and Carlisle | 60½ | 493 | 304 | | 797 | 283,996 | 0.2 | 142 | 6 | 24 | 2 | | 338 |
| Birmingham and Gloucester | 37½ | 3,931 | 3,290 | | 7,221 | 622,660 | 1.2 | 921 | 557 | 159 | 239 | | 4,026 |
| Manchester and Birmingham | 85 | 10,698 | 1,876 | 450 | 13,024 | 1,264,782 | 1.0 | 2,999 | 5,605 | 199 | 291 | | 14,629 |
| Grand Junction | 119 | 34,799 | 12,708 | 9,452 | 56,959 | 2,108,509 | 2.7 | 10,426 | 8,574 | 909 | 1,079 | 655 | 22,707 |
| Chester and Birkenhead | 15 | 2,440 | 1,010 | 608 | 3,450 | 309,250 | 1.1 | 553 | 8 | 1 | 6 | 173 | — |
| North Union | 37 | 2,595 | 3,001 | 608 | 6,204 | 628,981 | 1.0 | 629 | 533 | 67 | 70 | | — |
| Lancaster and Preston | 20½ | 4,387 | 1,636 | | 6,023 | 151,703 | 3.8 | 1,030 | 781 | 111 | 107 | | — |
| Preston and Wyre | 19½ | 1,521 | 1,342 | | 2,863 | 207,779 | 1.4 | 576 | 2 | 28 | 19 | | 495 |
| Total | 1,128¼ | 234,010 | 215,297 | 68,581 | 517,888 | 13,073,191 | 4.0 | 75,783 | 59,765 | 5,813 | 7,573 | 2,607 | 180,606 |

*Sources:*
K. Morison: *The Origin and Results of the Clearing System which is in Operation on the Narrow gauge Railways*, London, 1846.
Statistical Returns made to the Lords Committee of Privy Council for Trade for year 1845 Appendix 2, BPP 1846.

# APPENDIX 6

# THE RECEIPTS CLEARED THROUGH THE
# RAILWAY CLEARING HOUSE, 1842-1913

## Sources

The minute books of the Railway Clearing House committee.

## Compilation

(1) The data in Table 1 are to be found in the reports presented twice each year to the Railway Clearing House committee. During the period 1842–85, these reports were presented by the secretary to the Clearing House committee. After 1885, though, this duty was performed by the superintending committee. The superintending committee, as the name implies, was set up in 1862 to superintend the internal management of the Railway Clearing House.

(2) From a brief glance at the Table, it is evident that that there are considerable gaps in the information available for the period 1842 to 1864. The main reason for this deficiency, is the failure of the secretary and the committee to include the information in the recorded minutes. These gaps in available data cannot be bridged. For one thing, none of the original accounts of the Clearing House has survived. The accounts were in fact deliberately destroyed after a few years. A resolution passed by the Clearing House committee in 1862 states this explicitly, 'The Clearing House is authorised to destroy all accounts after seven years.' A further line of approach is equally unrewarding. This is the examination of the records of railway companies which were members of the Clearing House, to see if their records contain any references to the content of the accounts.

(3) The receipts cleared in any particular year by the Clearing House were not of the same value as the amount of traffic carried in that year, by the companies party to the system. That is, there was usually a backlog of past transactions to be settled. For example, in the report for the half year ending June 30, 1905, it is stated that receipts were up 'due to a large amount of traffic carried between April 1902 and December 1904, not previously dealt with by the Clearing House, the terms of division for which have but recently been decided'. Between 1842 and 1895, for the main part, there are few references to the value of the suspense account. The accounts themselves are concerned with all the receipts cleared in a particular year, irrespective of the date at which the traffic was actually moved. From 1895 onwards, the accounts do differentiate between the value of current traffics cleared and the value of past traffics cleared. For the sake of providing a continuous and comparable statement of the receipts cleared by the Clearing House during the entire period 1842 to 1913, it has been decided to ignore this additional data which is available only after 1895. Therefore, the table shows the value of work settled by the Clearing House in any particular year. It does not show the value of traffic moved in that year; traffic receipts for which might be settled in a following year.

## RAILWAY CLEARING HOUSE—RECEIPTS CLEARED

| Year ended June 30th | Annual goods and livestock receipts | Annual passenger receipts £ | Annual parcels receipts £ | Total annual receipts £ | Five-year annual average of total £ |
|---|---|---|---|---|---|
| 1842 | | | | 193,246 | |
| 1843 | | | | 225,231 | |
| 1844 | | | | 322,280 | |
| 1845 | | | | 462,390 | |
| 1846 | | | | 502,535 | |
| 1847 | | | | 583,282 | |
| 1848 | | | | 1,151,961 | |
| 31/12 1849 | | | | 1,693,104 | |
| 1850 | | | | 2,410,452 | |
| 1851 | | | Gap in half-year | | |
| 1852 | | | | 3,391,958 | |
| 1853 | | | | | |
| 1854 | | | | | |
| 1855 | | | | | |
| 1856 | | | | 5,116,311 | |
| 1857 | | 1,475,578 | | 5,744,762 | |
| 1858 | | 1,243,717 | | 5,316,626 | |
| 1859 | | 1,179,369 | | 5,716,903 | |
| 1860 | | 1,708,184 | | 6,434,008 | |
| 1861 | | 1,574,209 | | 6,970,352 | |
| 1862 | | 1,809,171 | | 7,705,206 | |
| 1863 | | 1,488,662 | | 8,044,791 | |
| 1864 | 6,634,720 | 1,949,985 | 324,951 | 8,909,656 | 7,612,798 |
| 1865 | 7,081,757 | 2,010,084 | 375,019 | 9,466,860 | |
| 1866 | 7,784,107 | 2,544,565 | 516,604 | 1,084,276 | |
| 1867 | 7,830,750 | 2,697,212 | 550,322 | 11,078,284 | |
| 1868 | 8,035,484 | 2,639,143 | 573,671 | 11,248,298 | |
| 1869 | 8,340,200 | 2,600,263 | 579,716 | 11,520,179 | 10,831,779 |
| 1870 | 8,883,048 | 2,538,410 | 630,358 | 12,051,816 | |
| 1871 | 9,789,911 | 2,813,006 | 679,140 | 13,282,057 | |
| 1872 | 10,040,484 | 2,907,204 | 674,337 | 13,622,025 | |
| 1873 | 11,352,513 | 3,269,356 | 786,944 | 15,408,813 | |
| 1874 | 11,993,814 | 3,252,957 | 840,507 | 16,087,278 | 14,090,198 |

## RAILWAY CLEARING HOUSE—RECEIPTS CLEARED

| Year ended Dec. 31st | Annual goods and livestock receipts | Annual passenger receipts £ | Annual parcels receipts £ | Total annual receipts £ | Five-year annual average of total. £ |
|---|---|---|---|---|---|
| 1875 | 12,122,514 | 2,969,515 | 847,495 | 15,939,524 | |
| 1876 | 12,087,736 | 2,999,375 | 820,978 | 15,908,089 | |
| 1877 | 12,110,245 | 3,017,250 | 870,598 | 15,998,093 | |
| 1878 | 11,595,831 | 2,981,329 | 906,245 | 15,483,405 | |
| 1879 | 11,158,238 | 2,866,750 | 927,216 | 14,952,204 | 15,656,223 |
| 1880 | 12,267,945 | 3,133,265 | 960,011 | 16,361,221 | |
| 1881 | 12,564,799 | 3,223,434 | 997,087 | 16,785,330 | |
| 1882 | 13,138,161 | 3,380,284 | 1,048,059 | 17,566,504 | |
| 1883 | 13,237,760 | 3,516,808 | 1,063,637 | 17,814,205 | |
| 1884 | 12,998,181 | 3,413,826 | 1,144,086 | 17,556,092 | 17,216,670 |
| 1885 | 12,388,918 | 3,285,992 | 1,163,090 | 16,838,000 | |
| 1886 | 12,143,869 | 3,692,983 | 1,156,251 | 16,993,103 | |
| 1887 | 12,288,203 | 3,328,645 | 1,193,444 | 16,810,292 | |
| 1888 | 12,820,323 | 3,363,477 | 1,200,485 | 17,384,285 | |
| 1889 | 14,105,353 | 3,538,074 | 1,286,308 | 18,929,735 | 17,391,083 |
| 1890 | 14,310,791 | 3,776,059 | 1,408,609 | 19,495,459 | |
| 1891 | 14,539,702 | 3,809,256 | 1,461,074 | 19,910,032 | |
| 1892 | 14,559,273 | 3,966,203 | 1,515,996 | 20,041,472 | |
| 1893 | 14,166,607 | 3,775,231 | 1,545,808 | 19,487,646 | |
| 1894 | 14,247,518 | 3,777,165 | 1,544,898 | 19,569,581 | 19,700,838 |
| 1895 | 16,744,151 | 5,325,363 | 1,750,001 | 23,819,515 | |
| 1896 | 16,374,082 | 4,578,581 | 1,800,460 | 22,743,123 | |
| 1897 | 16,767,133 | 4,786,127 | 1,865,629 | 23,418,889 | |
| 1898 | 17,518,313 | 5,037,297 | 1,929,945 | 24,485,555 | |
| 1899 | 18,386,165 | 5,315,202 | 1,994,548 | 25,695,915 | 24,032,599 |
| 1900 | 18,750,556 | 5,541,474 | 2,113,621 | 26,405,651 | |
| 1901 | 18,634,332 | 5,552,796 | 2,204,975 | 26,392,103 | |
| 1902 | 19,353,926 | 5,670,387 | 2,314,518 | 27,338,831 | |
| 1903 | 19,230,750 | 5,732,194 | 2,377,399 | 27,340,343 | |
| 1904 | 19,146,522 | 4,773,570 | 2,418,534 | 26,338,626 | 26,763,110 |
| 1905 | 19,849,485 | 4,885,507 | 2,439,321 | 27,174,313 | |
| 1906 | 19,771,825 | 5,011,417 | 2,566,033 | 27,349,275 | |
| 1907 | 20,551,595 | 5,213,739 | 2,696,418 | 28,461,752 | |
| 1908 | 19,547,218 | 5,502,382 | 2,712,946 | 27,762,546 | |
| 1909 | 19,940,915 | 5,353,060 | 2,778,718 | 28,072,693 | 27,764,116 |

RAILWAY CLEARING HOUSE—RECEIPTS CLEARED

| Year ended Dec. 31st | Annual goods and livestock receipts | Annual passenger receipts £ | Annual parcels receipts £ | Total Annual receipts £ | Five-year annual average of total. £ |
|---|---|---|---|---|---|
| 1910 | 21,166,331 | 5,659,742 | 2,855,937 | 29,682,010 | |
| 1911 | 21,935,842 | 5,770,474 | 2,932,769 | 30,639,085 | |
| 1912 | 22,245,024 | 5,866,337 | 2,968,549 | 31,079,910 | |
| 1913 | 23,693,868 | 6,398,726 | 3,123,507 | 33,216,101 | |
| 1914 | | | | | 31,154,277 (4 yr. av.) |

---

## APPENDIX 7

# THE PROPORTION OF UNITED KINGDOM GOODS AND TOTAL TRAFFIC RECEIPTS PASSING THROUGH THE RAILWAY CLEARING HOUSE, 1842–1913

*Sources*

(1) The minute books of the Railway Clearing House committee.

(2) The railway returns and abstracts for England, Scotland and Wales, reprinted in the *Abstract of British Historical Statistics* compiled by Mitchell and Deane.

*Compilation*

(1) For details of the problems involved in the use of the returns and abstracts see the footnotes in Mitchell and Deane.

(2) For the present purpose of indicating the proportion of goods and total traffics that were cleared through the Clearing House, several comments on the returns and abstracts are necessary.

(a) The Board of Trade compilers of the published returns were not responsible for the accuracy or quality of the information submitted to them by the railway companies. And before the Railways Regulation Act of 1868, when the companies were given fairly detailed guidance to the form and content of published accounts, some companies never even bothered to submit any statistics at all. Almost complete accuracy and uniformity in the company returns was achieved after the Act of 1868.

(b) A writer who has stressed the difficulties in using the company accounts is H. Pollins in his chapter, 'Aspects of Railway Accounting before 1868'. This chapter appears in *Studies in the History of Accounting*, edited by Littelton and Yamey. Of particular interest is the quote from the remarks made by W. Bailey, the accountant to the Midland Railway, in the Jubilee of *The Railway News*, published in 1914. Bailey had this to say about company accounting methods in the years before 1868.

'The accountants of those days must have been giants indeed if they were able to make useful comparisons with each others' accounts from the published material at their disposal. There is scarcely an account, abstract or statement, in either of these half-yearly reports which is paralleled by a corresponding account abstract or statement in the report of another company.'

For these reasons, care should be exercised in making long-run comparisons between the information that appeared in the railway returns and abstracts, in the years before 1868, and the information published after 1868.

(3) Between the years 1843 and 1848 the Board of Trade returns were compiled with the year ending June 30th. For the sake of correct comparison, the same time interval has been adopted for setting down the total of receipts cleared by the Clearing House, during those years. After 1848, the Board of Trade returns were compiled with the year ending December 31st. The same time interval has been adopted for the setting down of the receipts passing through the Clearing House.

## THE PROPORTION OF UNITED KINGDOM GOODS AND TOTAL TRAFFIC RECEIPTS PASSING THROUGH THE RAILWAY CLEARING HOUSE

| Year end June 30th | % Goods cleared per annum | % Goods cleared per five-year annual average | % Passenger Train receipts cleared per annum (includes parcels) | % Passenger Train receipts cleared per five-year annual average | % Total per annum receipts | % Total receipts, five year annual average |
|---|---|---|---|---|---|---|
| 1842 | | | | | 5% | |
| 1843 | | | | | 6·5 | |
| 1844 | | | | | 7·5 | |
| 1845 | | | | | 6·8 | |
| 1846 | | | | | 6·9 | |
| 1847 | | | | | 11·7 | |
| 1848 | | | | | | |
| **Dec. 31st** | | | | | | |
| 1849 | | | | | 14·8 | |
| 1850 | | | | | 19·1 | |
| 1851 | | | | | | |
| 1852 | | | | | 22·6 | |
| 1853 | | | | | | |
| 1854 | | | | | | |
| 1855 | | | | | | |
| 1856 | | | | | 23·25 | |
| 1857 | | | | | 24·9 | |
| 1858 | | | | | 22·8 | |
| 1859 | | | | | 23·3 | |
| 1860 | | | | | 24·4 | |
| 1861 | | | | | 25·7 | |
| 1862 | | | | | 27·8 | |
| 1863 | | | | | 27·1 | |
| 1864 | 37·6 | | 14·5 | | 27·6 | 26·5 |
| 1865 | 37·9 | | 14·5 | | 27·7 | |
| 1866 | 38·8 | | 17·6 | | 29·7 | |
| 1867 | 37·6 | | 18·1 | | 29·4 | |
| 1868 | | (4 yr. av.) | | (4 yr. av.) | | (4 yr. av.) |
| 1869 | 38·9 | 38·3 | 16·8 | 16·8 | 29·7 | 29·1 |
| 1870 | 38·6 | | 16·4 | | 29·2 | |
| 1871 | 38·4 | | 16·9 | | 29·3 | |
| 1872 | 35·1 | | 15·9 | | 29·9 | |
| 1873 | 36·8 | | 17·0 | | 29·0 | |
| 1874 | 38·6 | 37·5 | 16·4 | 16·5 | 29·6 | 29·4 |
| 1875 | 37·7 | | 14·8 | | 28·2 | |
| 1876 | 36·9 | | 14·6 | | 28·0 | |
| 1877 | 36·9 | | 14·6 | | 27·5 | |
| 1878 | 35·9 | | 14·5 | | 26·7 | |
| 1879 | 34·7 | 36·4 | 14·6 | 14·6 | 26·2 | 27·3 |
| 1880 | 35·3 | | 15·0 | | 27·1 | |
| 1881 | 35·4 | | 15·4 | | 27·4 | |
| 1882 | 35·9 | | 15·3 | | 27·9 | |
| 1883 | 35·3 | | 15·5 | | 27·2 | |
| 1884 | 35·5 | 35·5 | 15·2 | 15·3 | 26·0 | 27·1 |
| 1885 | 34·6 | | 14·9 | | 26·3 | |
| 1886 | 34·5 | | 16·0 | | 26·4 | |
| 1887 | 34·0 | | 14·8 | | 25·8 | |
| 1888 | 34·1 | | 14·7 | | 26·0 | |
| 1889 | 35·5 | 34·5 | 14·8 | 15·0 | 26·7 | 26·2 |
| 1890 | 35·1 | | 15·1 | | 26·4 | |
| 1891 | 34·7 | | 15·0 | | 26·5 | |
| 1892 | 34·9 | | 15·3 | | 26·6 | |
| 1893 | 35·7 | | 15·3 | | 26·5 | |
| 1894 | 34·4 | 35·0 | 14·6 | 15·0 | 25·6 | 26·3 |
| 1895 | 39·4 | | 18·9 | | 30·5 | |
| 1896 | 36·7 | | 16·2 | | 27·8 | |
| 1897 | 36·2 | | 15·7 | | 27·6 | |
| 1898 | 36·8 | | 14·7 | | 28·0 | |
| 1899 | 36·5 | 37·1 | 16·7 | 16·5 | 27·8 | 28·3 |
| 1900 | 36·2 | | 17·0 | | 27·7 | |

## THE PROPORTION OF UNITED KINGDOM GOODS AND TOTAL TRAFFIC RECEIPTS PASSING THROUGH THE RAILWAY CLEARING HOUSE

| Year end June 30th | % Goods cleared per annum | % Goods cleared per five-year annual average | % Passenger Train receipts cleared per annum (includes parcels) | % Passenger Train receipts cleared per five-year annual average | % Total per annum receipts | % Total receipts, five year annual average |
|---|---|---|---|---|---|---|
| 1901 | 36·3 | | 16·6 | | 27·5 | |
| 1902 | 36·5 | | 16·8 | | 27·8 | |
| 1903 | 36·1 | | 16·7 | | 27·6 | |
| 1904 | 35·8 | 36·2 | 14·9 | 16·4 | 26·4 | 27·4 |
| 1905 | 36·3 | | 15·0 | | 26·8 | |
| 1906 | 35·0 | | 15·2 | | 26·2 | |
| 1907 | 34·6 | | 15·6 | | 26·4 | |
| 1908 | 34·3 | | 15·9 | | 26·1 | |
| 1909 | 34·7 | 35·0 | 15·9 | 15·5 | 26·4 | 26·4 |
| 1910 | 35·6 | | 14·6 | | 27·0 | |
| 1911 | 35·4 | | 16·1 | (4 yr. av.) | 27·1 | |
| 1912 | 35·9 | | 16·2 | 15·5 | 27·3 | |
| 1913 | 36·7 | | 14·9 | | 27·1 | |

# APPENDIX 8

## TO SHOW THE VOLUME OF WORK UNDER-TAKEN BY THE RAILWAY CLEARING HOUSE ESTABLISHMENT

| Year ending Dec. 30th | No of goods settlements between pairs of stations | No. of passenger settlements |
|---|---|---|
| 1864 | 848,938 | 779,920 |
| 1867 | | 1,457,071 |
| 1869 | 1,220,970 | |
| 1874 | 1,792,933 | 3,092,407 |
| 1879 | 2,159,815 | 3,757,567 |
| 1884 | 2,914,655 | 5,235,187 |
| 1889 | 3,883,840 | 5,000,035 |
| 1894 | 4,723,851 | 5,963,688 |
| 1899 | 5,802,227 | 8,113,068 |
| 1904 | 7,244,123 | 8,639,029 |
| 1909 | 8,070,208 | 8,231,947 |
| 1913 | 9,586,360 | 7,984,311 |

---

# APPENDIX 9

## A TABLE TO SHOW THE COSTS OF MAINTAINING THE RAILWAY CLEARING HOUSE ESTABLISHMENT

| Year ending Dec. 30th | Five year average costs £ | Costs as a % of receipts cleared |
|---|---|---|
| 1860–64 | 65,851 | 0·86 |
| 1865–69 | 94,766 | 0·87 |
| 1870–74 | 136,844 | 0·98 |
| 1875–79 | 195,591 | 1·25 |
| 1880–84 | 224,280 | 1·32 |
| 1885–89 | 223,919 | 1·29 |
| 1890–94 | 231,676 | 1·18 |
| 1895–99 | 258,056 | 1·07 |
| 1900–04 | 294,720 | 1·09 |
| 1905–09 | 322,857 | 1·25 |
| 1910–13 | 335,737 | 1·07 |

*Source*

Reports of the Secretary to the Committee of Delegates presented twice yearly.

# BIBLIOGRAPHY

## I. PRIMARY SOURCES

### (a) *The Records of the Railway Clearing House*

The manuscript and printed records of the Railway Clearing House, housed in British Rail's Archives Department at 66 Porchester Road, Paddington, and comprising over a thousand separate items, are grouped into ten different categories.

The 688 volumes of minutes of Clearing House conferences, meetings, and committees, classified under RCH/1, are by far the most useful items in the collection. As there were as many as 104 separate committees (not including sub-committees) functioning at one time or other during the lifetime of the organisation, the range of competence of only the more important of them will be indicated.

The minutes of the committee of delegates are an indispensable source of reference for the years before 1847. After that date conferences of goods managers and others began to assume many of the responsibilities hitherto shouldered exclusively by the committee of delegates. Nevertheless, the committee continued to have the final word on all matters until a reorganisation of the work of the Clearing House took place at the beginning of 1884. Its regular meetings continued until the dissolution of the Clearing House in 1955, but for the period after 1914 the minutes contain little of value to the historian. The minutes of the superintending committee, which extend from June 1862 to May 1954, are a principal source of reference for the organisation of the Clearing House itself, though details of staff recruitment, promotion, pay and discipline can be discovered in the minutes of the office committee (May 1857–April 1941). The General Managers Conference, first meeting in January 1851 and continuing until 1927, rapidly grew in importance until, by the 1880s it outshone the Clearing House committee itself. Its records are of great value for decisions on the broad issues of railway policy. The time span of the conference of passenger superintendents was the same as that of the general managers. The minutes of these proceedings are important for all aspects of passenger traffic, including excursion arrangements, ticket issuing regulations and the establishment of a uniform telegraphic code. Throughout the life of the Clearing House the most remunerative side of the railways business was the goods traffic and for all aspects of its organisation the records of the Goods Managers Conference, continuous from January 1, 1847, are of outstanding value.

Until 1884 the Clearing House committee of delegates was the supreme authority. The decisions of all other committees and conferences had to be submitted to it for final approval. But by this date the work of the organisation had grown to such an extent that it was considered advisable to divide the agenda. The Clearing House committee still retained full responsibility for all matters directly arising from the Clearing Act of 1850. All other decisions, from whichever conference or committee originating, required the approval of the general managers. From 1884 onwards matters arising from the Act of 1850 were dealt with, as before, at the *conferences* of general managers, superintendents, etc., and decisions were printed on blue paper. All other matters were considered at the general managers, superintendents and other *meetings* whose minutes were printed on white paper.

Information on the standardisation of rolling stock is to be found in the minutes of the conferences of locomotive engineers and carriage and waggon superintendents which are continuous from 1894 until the Second World War. The records of the Accountants Committee, 1870–1912, the Accountants Standing Committee, 1912, and the Accountants Permanent Committee (1912–15, the shortest lived of the three) throw valuable light on the standardisation of railway companies' accounting practices.

In addition there are complete sets of minutes for the more important of the pooling arrangements and rate conferences. Examples include the Octuple (1851–55), the English and Scotch Traffic Committee (1856–65), the Continental Traffic Conference (1870–85), the Metropolitan Conference (1864–1942), the Normanton (formed in 1865, but records surviving only for the period 1883–1923), and the General Rates Conference (1888–1948).

An insight into the relations between the railways and the Post Office can be gained from the minutes of the Parcel Post Conference (1883–1932).

The thirty-three volumes included in class RCH/2 consist of various junction diagrams. Deeds, agreements, contracts and plans of the Clearing House premises are grouped together in RCH/3. Under the heading 'Miscellaneous, Books and Records' in RCH/4 are included details of the pay of Clearing House staff and of petitions for improved conditions of service, as well as reports on law cases and a disappointingly small and relatively uninformative collection of letters. Eighteen volumes of station handbooks, giving the names of all railway stations, at different dates, are included under RCH/5. RCH/6 comprises ninety-two volumes of authorised distance tables covering the years 1852–1924. The regulations of the Clearing House (particularly valuable from the 1860s onwards, as they cite the conference decision on which each regulation is based) and the various classifications of goods from 1850 to 1936 occupy ninety-two volumes in the class RCH/7. Twenty-eight volumes of coaching arrangement books are classified under RCH/8. RCH/10 includes order registers for the period of 1848–1885 and a final class, RCH/15, contains records of the numbers and grades of staff and their distribution among the different departments of the Clearing House over the years 1862–1901.

(b) *Railway Company Records*

The Board minutes, locomotive and other committee minutes of the railway companies provide essential additional information on the

formation of the Clearing House and on the extent to which its decisions
were followed. Particularly valuable in this context were the minutes of the
Coaching and Police Committee of the London and Birmingham Railway
between 1840 and 1842 inclusive (LBM 1/22). The London, Midland
and Scottish Railway's collection of historical documents, classed under
H.L. 2/9, provided some very welcome early letters to supplement the
meagre supply in the Clearing House records.

(c) *Parliamentary Papers*

Although the railway returns and the minutes of evidence and reports
of all select committees and royal commissions concerned with railway
questions are of some value to a study of the Railway Clearing House, the
following items were particularly helpful:

*Select Committee on Cummunication by Railway, 1839 (reappointed in
1840).* BPP 1839 X and 1840 XIII. Invaluable for the role of the
private carriers in the early days of railways and for Thomas Edmondson's description of his ticket issuing system. (Edmondson is here
called Edmondstone).

*Select Committee on Railway and Canal Bills, 1852-3,* (Cardwell's Committee). BPP 1852-3 XXXVIII. Evidence of Captain Mark Huish
on the Railway Clearing House and arbitration of disputes.

*Royal Commission on Railways, 1867.* BPP 1867 XXXVIII, Vols I and II.
Appendix CP contains the Clearing House classification of goods.
The minutes of evidence contain many references to Clearing House
regulations especially relating to terminal charges. The evidence of
Mark Huish, J. Allport, and A. C. Sheriff is particularly informative.

*Joint Select Committee on Railway Companies Amalgamation, 1872.* BPP
1872 XIII, Vols I and II. The minutes of evidence include a first-
hand account of the working of the Clearing House by the secretary,
William Dawson. (Qs 5545-5579) Appendix O (106 pages) contains
the regulations of the Clearing House, the general classification of
goods and the Clearing Act, 1850.

*Report of the Board of Trade Railway Conference, 1909.* BPP 1909 LXX,
Vol. VII. For memoranda by railway directors and traders on the
question of amalgamation.

*Departmental Committee on Railway Agreements and Amalgamations, 1911.*
BPP 1911 XXIX, Vol. II. The evidence of A. G. Walkden and H.
Romeril concerns the threat of redundancy of Clearing House clerks.
The evidence of Sir Charles Owens, F. H. Dent, and W. F. Marwood
is of value in relation to rate conferences and pooling agreements.

*Report of the Advisory Council of the Ministry of Reconstruction on the Standardisation of Railway Equipment, 1918.* BPP 1918 XIII, p. 15. Important for assessing the achievements of the Conference of Locomotive Engineers and Carriage and Works Superintendents 1894–1914.

*House of Lords Record Office.* House of Lords Papers 1859, Box 6. 'Act for Extending and Improving the Railway Clearing System and minutes of evidence of the Lords' Select Committee on the Bill.

## 2. SECONDARY WORKS—GENERAL

No full-length study of the Railway Clearing House was written during its existence of over 110 years.

### (a) *Principal Shorter Accounts*

Morison, K.: *The Origins and Results of the Clearing System Which is in Operation on the Narrow-gauge Railways, With Tables of Through Traffic in the Year 1845,* London, 1846, 26 pp. The founder of the clearing system giving reasons for its establishment.

*The Railway Clearing House, its Object, Work and Results,* London, 1876, 32 pp. Reprinted from the *Railway Fly Sheet and Official Gazette.*

McDermott, E.: *The Railway Clearing House: Its Place in Relation to the Working and Management of English Railways,* London, 1890, 64 pp. Reprinted from *The Railway News and Joint Stock Journal.* A fairly detailed account of the day-to-day working of the Clearing House.

Dowden, T. F.: *The Railway Clearing System as Practised in the English Clearing House in 1876,* London, 1877, 164 pp., Preface IV. The most detailed description of the working of the clearing system.

*The Railway Clearing House: Its Origin, Object, Work and Results,* London, 1892, 37 pp. Printed together with articles and correspondence from *The Times* of January 1869 and January 1892, articles in *The Railway Official Gazette* and Morison's Account of 1846.

Sekon, G. A.: *The Railway Clearing House: Illustrated Interview With Mr Harry Smart,* London, 1898, 15 pp. with illus. Reprinted from *The Railway Magazine,* November 1898.

Smart, H. C.: *The R.C.H. What It Is and What It Does,* London, 1912, 15 pp. with illus. Reprinted from *The Railway and Travel Monthly,* May 1912.

Smart, H. C.: 'The Railway Clearing House,' in *Jubilee of the Railway News, 1846–1914,* London, *The Railway News,* 1914, 53–59 pp.

Carlile, H.: *Allgemeine Darstellung der Centralen Eisenbahn—Abrechnung —Systems in England und Betrachtungen über die Vortheile der Einführung dieses Systems in Russland,* Riga, 1880, 56 pp. A description of the clearing system.

*The Railway Gazette:* 'The Work of the Railway Clearing House, 1842–1942,' London, 1943, 24 pp. with illus. A reprint from *The Railway*

*Gazette*, January 2 and June 19 and 26, 1942. One of the best short accounts; includes a reproduction of the common seal of the Railway Clearing House.

British Railways Board: *The Railway Clearing House*, London, 1960, 12 pp. with illus. Mainly describes the work of the Railway Clearing House after 1948.

(b) *Specialised Aspects of the Work of the Railway Clearing House*

The following are a selection of the works found most useful. For additional references the reader is referred to George Ottley's *Bibliography of British Railway History*, London, 1965, 683 pp.

(i) *Early Impact of the Clearing House*

Lewin, H. G.: Early British Railways, London and New York, 1925. 202 pp., Preface XII.

Cole, H.: *A Few of the Miseries of the Break of Gauge at Gloucester, Which Occasions the Shifting of Passengers' Luggage and Goods From One Carriage to Another*, 1846.

Sidney, S.: *The Commercial Consequences of a Mixed Gauge on Our Railway System Examined*, London, 1848, 47 pp.

Lardner, D.: *Railway Economy*, London, 1850, 528 pp., Preface XXIII.

Head, Sir F.: *Stokers and Pokers*, London, 1849, 208 pp. Chapter XIV describes the working of the Railway Clearing House in its earliest days.

(ii) *Passenger services*

Wiener, L., *Passenger Tickets*, London, 1939, 357 pp., Preface XXIX, with illus. (Abstracted from *The Bulletin of the International Railway Congress Association*.) Chapter 3 includes illustrations of early Edmondson printed tickets and the Edmondson patent ticket-stamping machine.

Neele, G. P.: *Railway Reminiscences*, London, 1904, 544 pp. Preface VI. Neele was for many years a leading member of the Superintendents Conference.

Railway Clearing House: *The Railway Companies' Book of Regulations Regarding Traffic by Passenger Train or Other Similar Service*, London, 1927, 77 pp., Preface VIII.

(iii) *The Goods Traffic*

Poole, B.: *Twenty Short Reasons for the Railway Companies Being Themselves the Carriers of Goods Without any Intervening Parties Existing Between Them and the Public on the Same Principle as They are Carriers of Passengers*, Liverpool, 1844. Poole was chairman of the Goods Managers Conference in the early years.

Paish, G.: *The British Railway Position*, London, 1902, 322 pp. Preface XIV.

Stevenson, D.: *Fifty Years on the London and North Western Railway and Other Memoranda in the Life of David Stevenson*, London, 1891, 153 pp. Recalls the early days of goods traffic on the London and North Western Railway.

Bureau of Railway Economics: *Comparison of Railway Freight Rates in the US With the Principal Countries of Europe*, Washington, 1915.

Paish, G.: *The British Railway Position*, London, 1902, 322 pp., Preface XIV.

Waghorn, T.: *Carriers and Railway Companies*, London, 1907, 24 pp. Growth of the monopoly of cartage by railway companies.

(iv) *Organisation of the Clearing House*

Fulford, R: *Glyns, 1873–1953*, London, 1953, 266 pp., Preface XVI. Glyns were bankers for The Railway Clearing House.

(v) *The Clearing House Staff*

Railway Clerks Association: *The Life of the Railway Clerk*, London, 1911, 30 pp. Railway Clerks Association: *Permanency or Dismissal? A Question for You*, edition 2, Wolverhampton, 1913, 35 pp.

Railway Clerks Association: *Progress, Combination and Agreement Amongst Clerks.* (The address of H. Romeril, President of the Railway Clerks Association and an employee of the Railway Clearing House, at the 17th Annual Conference, 1914), London, 1914, 15 pp.

(vi) *Standardisation: Rolling Stock and Locomotives*

Clarke, D. K.: *Railway Machinery*, London, 1855, 2 vols, 328 pp. Reveals the diversity of types of goods waggons.

*The Railway News:* 'Railway Rolling Stock', In *Jubilee of The Railway News 1864–1914*, London, 1914, 95–98 pp. with 7 illus.

Stone, S.: *Railway Carriages and Waggons: Their Design and Construction*, London, 1911, 178 pp., Preface VIII, with illus.

Allen, C. J.: *The Locomotive Exchanges, 1870–1948*, London, 1949, 176 pp. with illus.

Allen, C. J.: *Locomotive Practice and Performance in the Twentieth Century*, Cambridge, 1949, 302 pp., Preface XV, with illus.

vii) *Standardisation: Railway Operation*

Nock, O. S.: *Fifty Years of Railway Signalling*, London, 1962, 22 pp. with illus.

Blythe, R.: *Danger Ahead*, London, 1951, 132 pp. with illus.

Lewis, L. P.: *Railway Signal Engineering, Mechanical*, London, 1912, 358 pp. Preface XVIII, with illus.

Wilson, H. R.: *The Safety of British Railways*, London, 1909, 240 pp., Preface VIII.

Wilson, H. R.: *Railway Accidents: Legislation and Statistics, 1825–1942*, London, 1925, 39 pp.

Pollins, H.: 'Aspects of Railway Accounting Before 1868,' in *Studies in the History of Accounting*, ed. Littleton, A. G., and Yamey, B. S., London, 1956, pp. 332–55.

Browne, G. A. R.: *Report on the System of Accounts in Force on English Railways and in the English Railway Clearing House*, Calcutta, Government of India Printing Office, 1896, 107 pp., Preface VII.

Wang, Ching-Ch'an: *Legislative Regulation of Railway Finance in England*, Urbana, Illinois, 1918, 196 pp.

(viii) *The Parcels Traffic: The Railway Clearing House and the General Post Office*

HMSO: *The Post Office: An Historical Summary*, London, 1911, 139 pp.

Hill, Sir R., and Hill, G. B.: *The Life of Sir Rowland Hill and the History of the Penny Postage*, London, 1880, 2 vols.

(ix) *Pooling Agreements and Rate Conferences*

Robertson, W. A., *Combination Among Railway Companies*, London, 1912, 105 pp.

Stevens, E. C.: *English Railways: Their Development and Their Relation to the State*, London, 1915, 332 pp., Preface XVI.

Simnett, W. E.: *Railway Amalgamation in Great Britain*, London, 1923, 276 pp.

(x) *The Railway Clearing House in Wartime and After*

Pratt, E. A.: *British Railways and the Great War*, London, 1921, 2 vols, 119 pp., Preface XX, with illus. Indispensable for the work of the Railway Executive Committee.

Bell, R.: *History of British Railways During the War*, 1939–1945, London, 1946, 291 pp.

Savage, C. I.: *Inland Transport*, London, 1957, 678 pp., Preface XVII.

# INDEX

Printed in the United States
by Baker & Taylor Publisher Services